MILITARY GENERALS OF INDIA

Military Generals of India

Col. (Retd.) S. C. Narang

Prashant Publishing House
DELHI - 110094 (INDIA)

PRASHANT PUBLISHING HOUSE
C-34, 28 Foota Road, Gali No. 3
West Karawal Nagar, Delhi-110094
Phone : 9810396373, 22963970

Military Generals of India

First Published : 2009

ISBN : 978-81-908282-9-1

PRINTED IN INDIA

Published by Mr. R. K. Jha M/s. Prashant Publishing House, Delhi and Printed at H.S. Offset Press, Delhi.

PREFACE

The Indian Army is the world's second largest army in terms of military personnel (after China). It is a completely voluntary service, the military draft having never been imposed in India. The army has rich combat experience in diverse terrains, due to India's diverse geography, and also has a distinguished history of serving in United Nations peacekeeping operations.

The force is headed by the Chief of Army Staff, currently General Deepak Kapoor. The highest rank in the Indian Army is Field Marshal, but it is a largely ceremonial rank and appointments are made by the President of India, on the advice of the Union Cabinet of Ministers, only in exceptional circumstances. General S.H.F.J. Manekshaw and the late General K.M. Cariappa are the only two officers who have attained this rank.

This book is all about the military Generals from the Independence till date with their works in their respective service periods. I hope that it will be liked among the readers.

— *Author*

CONTENTS

1

INTRODUCTION

The Indian Armed Forces is the primary military organization responsible for the territorial security and defence of India. The President of India serves as the supreme commander of the armed forces, which are subordinate and responsible to the Government of India headed by the Prime Minister of India. The armed forces are administered by the Ministry of Defence and are composed of the Indian Army, the Indian Navy and the Indian Air Force. Auxiliary services include the Indian Coast Guard, the Paramilitary forces of India and the Strategic Forces Command.

All service personnel are volunteers although the government is empowered to undertake conscription if considered necessary for India's defence. However, India has never had conscription, even during the Indo-Pakistani Wars and the Sino-Indian War. The armed forces retain much of the organizational structure established by the British. However, the armed forces are an essential character of India's strategic importance, power and capabilities, which have increased after India became a declared nuclear weapons state.

ORGANIZATION AND COMMAND STRUCTURE

The headquarters of the Indian Armed Forces is in New Delhi, the capital city of India. The Indian armed force are split into different groups based on their region of operation. The Indian Army is administratively divided into 7 tactical commands, each under the control of different Lieutenant Generals.

STRUCTURE OF THE INDIAN ARMY

The Indian Army fields 34 divisions. Its headquarters is located in the Indian capital New Delhi and it is under the overall command of the Chief of Army Staff (COAS), currently General Deepak Kapoor.

The army has 6 commands and one training command known as ARTRAC. Each command is headed by General Officer Commanding-in-Chief with the rank of Lieutenant General. Each command is directly affiliated to the Army HQ in New Delhi.

There are 3 types of Corps in the Indian Army: Strike, Holding & Mixed. The Corps HQ is the largest field formation in the army. Other field formations include: Divisions, Brigades, Battalions, Companies, Platoons, and Sections.

These are several Battalions or Units under the same formation in a Regiment. The Gurkha Regiment, for instance, has several battalions. All formations under a Regiment are battalions of the same arms or Corps (i.e. Infantry, or Engineers). Regiments are not exactly field formations in the sense they mostly do not make a formation. For instance, all Regiments of the Gurkha's would not fight together as one formation, but can be dispersed over various Brigades or Corps or even Commands.

In addition, the Indian Army has 63 Armoured Regiments, see List of Armoured Regiments in the Indian Army.

The Regiment of Artillery constitutes a formidable operational arm of Indian Army. Historically, it takes its lineage from Moghul Emperor Babur, who is popularly credited with introduction of artillery to India in the Battle of Panipat in 1526. However, evidence of earlier use of guns by Bahmani Kings in the Battle of Adoni in 1368 and King Mohammed Shah of Gujrat in fifteenth century have been recorded.

RANK STRUCTURE

The highest ranking Commissioned Officer is the Field Marshal and only two have been awarded this rank so far. The rank of General is held by the Chief of Army Staff, followed by Lieutenant-General, Major-General, Brigadier, Colonel, Lieutenant-Colonel, Major, Captain, and finally the Lieutenant.

Among the Junior Commissioned Officers (JCOs), the ranks are organized from Honorary Captain (given to Outstanding JCO's Rank and pay of a Captain), Honorary Lieutenant (given to Outstanding JCO's Rank and pay of a Lieutenant), Subedar Major, Subedar to Naib Subedar.

Finally, among the Non-commissioned Officers (NCOs), the ranks are organized from Company Havildar Major, Company Quarter Master Havildar, Havildar, Naik, Lance Naik to the Sepoy.

Structure of the Indian Navy

The Indian Navy is organized into three main commands and one joint command.

- Eastern Naval Command at Visakhapatnam
- Western Naval Command at Mumbai
- Southern Naval Command at Kochi
- Far Eastern Naval Command (Joint command) at Port Blair in the Andaman & Nicobar Island chain

STRUCTURE OF THE INDIAN AIR-FORCE

Recruitment and Training

Recruitment is through three military related academies. These include the National Defence Academy, Indian Military Academy and Officers Training Academy. For entrance, one must display that they are both physically and mentally fit to be in the military by sitting examinations and undergoing medical checkups. The complete list of institutions training Indian army were listed in Military academies in India section.

Indian Army

Strength: During a conflict, the air-arm of the Indian army plays a crucial role in providing essential supplies and air cover to the ground forces. Shown here is the Indian Army's HAL Dhruv.

Indian Army Statistics

Active Troops	1,325,000 (2nd)
Artillery	7100
Battle Tanks	5010
Aircraft	52 squadrons of helicopters
Surface-to-air missiles	90,000+

The Indian Army is the world's second largest army in terms of military personnel (after China). It is a completely voluntary service, the military draft having never been imposed in India. The army has rich combat experience in diverse terrains, due to India's diverse geography, and also has a distinguished history of serving in United Nations peacekeeping operations.

The force is headed by the Chief of Army Staff, currently General Deepak Kapoor. The highest rank in the Indian Army is Field Marshal, but it is a largely ceremonial rank and appointments are made by the President of India, on the advice of the Union Cabinet of Ministers, only in exceptional circumstances. (See Field Marshal (India)). General S.H.F.J. Manekshaw and the late General K.M. Cariappa are the only two officers who have attained this rank.

The Indian Army has seen military action in the Indo-Pakistani War of 1947, the Indo-Pakistani War of 1965,the Indo-Pakistani War of 1971, and others such as Operation Polo in 1948, the Sino-Indian War in 1962 over the McMahon Line, and the Kargil War against Kashmiri insurgents and the Pakistan military personnel

Currently, the Indian army has dedicated one brigade of troops to the UN's standby arrangements. Through its large, sustained troop commitments India has come in for much praise for taking part in difficult operations for prolonged periods.

The Indian Army has participated in several UN peace-keeping operations, including the ones in Cyprus, Lebanon,

Congo, Angola, Cambodia, Vietnam, Namibia, El Salvador, Liberia, Mozambique and Somalia. The army also provided a paramedical unit to facilitate the withdrawal of the sick and wounded in Korea.

War Heroes

Major Som Nath Sharma	4th Battalion, Kumaon Regiment	November 3, 1947	Badgam, Kashmir, India
Lance Naik Karam Singh	1st Battalion, Sikh Regiment	October 13, 1948	Tithwal, Kashmir, India
Second Lieutenant Rama Raghoba Rane	Corps of Engineers	April 8, 1948	Naushera, Kashmir, India
Naik Jadu Nath Singh	1st Battalion, Rajput Regiment, now 4th Battalion, Brigade of the Guards (1st Rajput)	February 1948	Naushera, Kashmir, India
Company Havildar Major Piru Singh	6th Battalion, Rajputana Rifles	July 17/18, 1948	Tithwal, Kashmir, India
Captain Gurbachan Singh Salaria	3rd Battalion, 1st Gorkha Rifles (The Malaun Regiment)	December 5, 1961	Elizabethville, Katanga, Congo
Major Dhan Singh Thapa	1st Battalion, 8th Gorkha Rifles	October 20, 1962	Ladakh, India
Subedar Joginder Singh	1st Battalion, Sikh Regiment	October 23, 1962	Tongpen La, Northeast Frontier Agency, India
Major Shaitan Singh	13th Battalion, Kumaon Regiment	November 18, 1962	Rezang La
Company Quarter Master Havildar Abdul Hamid	4th Battalion, The Grenadiers	September 10, 1965	Chima, Khem Karan Sector
Lieutenant-Colonel Ardeshir Burzorji Tarapore	17th Poona Horse	October 15, 1965	Phillora, Sialkot Sector, Pakistan
Lance Naik Albert Ekka	14th Battalion, Brigade of the Guards	December 3, 1971	Gangasagar

2/Lieutenant Arun Khetarpal	17th Poona Horse	December 16, 1971	Jarpal, Shakargarh Sector
Major Hoshiar Singh	3rd Battalion, The Grenadiers	December 17, 1971	Basantar River, Shakargarh Sector
Naib Subedar Bana Singh	8th Battalion, Jammu and Kashmir Light Infantry	June 23, 1987	Siachen Glacier, Jammu and Kashmir
Major Ramaswamy Parmeshwaran	8th Battalion, Mahar Regiment	November 25, 1987	Sri Lanka
Captain Vikram Batra	13th Battalion, Jammu and Kashmir Rifles	July 6, 1999	Point 5140, Point 4875, Kargil Area
Captain Manoj Kumar Pandey	1st Battalion, 11th Gorkha Rifles	July 3, 1999	Khaluber/Juber Top, Batalik sector, Kargil area, Jammu and Kashmir
Grenadier Yogendra Singh Yadav	18th Battalion, The Grenadiers	July 4, 1999	Tiger Hill, Kargil area
Lance Naik Ghulam Mohammed Khan	12 Jammu and Kashmir Light Infantry	July 1999	Kargil area
Rifleman Sanjay Kumar	13th Battalion, Jammu and Kashmir Rifles	July 5, 1999	Area Flat Top, Kargil Area
Captain Haneef uddin	11 Rajputana Rifles	July 1999	Turtuk, Kargil area

- Lt. Nawang Kapadia
- Major Navneet Vats
- Major Rajesh Singh Adhikari, MVC
- Lance Naik Ahmed Ali
- Lieutenant Kieshing Clifford Nongrum

INDIAN NAVY

The Indian Navy is the naval branch of the armed forces of India. With 55,000 men and women, including 5,000 naval aviation personnel and 2,000 Marine Commandos (MARCOS), it is the world's fifth largest navy. The Indian Navy currently operates more than 155 vessels, including the aircraft carrier INS Viraat.

The navy is considered to have blue-water capabilities. It is fairly advanced in terms of technology and is in control of one of two Asian aircraft carriers. Two more aircraft carriers are on order and will be joining the Indian Navy. The ships of the Indian Navy are of Indian and foreign origin.

In its maritime doctrine, the Indian Navy establishes its role in providing support to maritime neighbours during natural disasters. This was demonstrated during the Asian tsunami crisis during which the Indian Navy sent 35 ships to support relief efforts in neighbouring countries.

The Indian navy has taken part in UN missions in the coast of Somalia and has provided security to an African Union summit held in Mozambique. India uses its navy to enhance its international relations through joint exercises, port visits, and humanitarian missions, including disaster relief. The Indian Navy is increasing its capabilities as a true blue-water navy; the Indian Navy's doctrine states that this is for the collective good of nations.

INDIAN AIR FORCE

The Indian Air Force is the fourth largest air force in the world. In its history, it has generally relied on Soviet technology to support its growth. However, in recent times, India has begun building its own original aircraft, including the HAL Tejas, which is a 4.5 generation fighter.

Also India and Russia are currently building a 5th generation stealth aircraft jointly. India has also developed UAV called Nishant and HAL Dhruv, an advanced light helicopter. Recently it has completed a test of long range BVR air to air missile named Astra and also conducted a successful test of Anti ballistic missile defense system and hence became the 4th country after US,Russia and Israel to do so.

PARAMILITARY FORCES OF INDIA

Indian Nuclear Power

It is estimated that India possesses around 200-250 nuclear warheads which could be deployed at short notice.

Nuclear Doctrine

The Indian military possesses nuclear weapons and sufficient means — by means of missiles and aircraft — to deliver anything over long distances. However, India has a *nuclear no-first-use* and no use against non-nuclear weapons state policy. It also maintains a non-nuclear doctrine based on *credible minimum deterrence.*

India is not a signatory to the Nuclear Non-proliferation Treaty (NPT), arguing that it unfairly favours the established nuclear powers: While the treaty places restrictions on the non-nuclear weapons states, it does little to curb the modernization and expansion of the nuclear arsenals of the nuclear weapons states; it provides no provision for complete nuclear disarmament.

Gallantry Awards

The highest wartime gallantry award given by the Military of India is the Param Vir Chakra (PVC), followed by the Maha Vir Chakra (MVC) and the Vir Chakra (VrC). Its peacetime equivalent is the Ashoka Chakra. The highest decoration for meritorious service is the Param Vishisht Seva Medal.

Future

Several reports have mentioned that the Indian military will be an even greater force to reckon with in the future given the twin advantage of economic growth and an increasing population.

Analyses of the Central Intelligence Agency indicates that India is projected to possess the fourth most capable concentration of power by 2015. According to a report published by the US Congress, India is the developing world's leading arms purchaser.

ARMY

The army numbers about one million personnel and fields 34 divisions. Designed primarily to defend the country's frontiers, the army has become heavily committed to internal security duties in Kashmir and the Northeast.

In 2002 the Indian Army had 980,000 active troops, along with an Army Reserve consisting of: 300,000 first line troops (those within five years of full time service), and another 500,000 second line troops (subject to recall to service until 50 years of age). The Territorial Army numbered 40,000 first line troops (and 160,000 second line troops). In 1994 the army had approximately 940,000 men and women on active duty, and another 36,000 in the Territorial Army. As of 1998 the Army had a sanctioned troop strength of 1,045,000, but there was a shortage of about 59,000 troops.

At the beginning of World War II there were 170,000 soldiers in the Indian Army all regulars, but by June of 1948 there were 2,000,000. This was the reason British Officers were needed to help train and form new units. Each Battalion needed eight British Officers to take command, as all the lower ranks were manned by Indian Viceroy Commissioned Officers, and NCOs.

The army is headquartered in New Delhi and is under the direction of the chief of the army staff, always a full general. The chief of the army staff is assisted by a vice chief, two deputy chiefs, a military secretary, and the heads of four main staff divisions: the adjutant general, the quartermaster general, the master general of ordnance, and the engineer in chief.

The Army consists of a number of arms and services. These are: Armoured Corps, Regiment of Artillery, Corps of Engineers, Corps of Signals, Mechanised Infantry, Infantry, Army Service Corps, Military Nursing Service, Army Medical Corps, Army Dental Corps, Army Ordnance Corps, Corps of Electrical and Mechanical Engineers, Remount and Veterinary Corps, Military Farms Service, Army Education Corps, Intelligence Corps, Corps of Military Police, Judge Advocate General Department, Army Physical Training Corps, Pioneer Corps, Army Postal Service Corps and Defence Security Corps. In addition, the Army has its own Recruiting Organisation, Record Offices, Depots, Boys Establishments and Selection Centers and training institutions. These units are organized in twelve corps-level formations.

The army has five tactical area commands: the Northern Command headquartered at Udhampur in Jammu and Kashmir, the Western Command headquartered at Chandimandir in Chandigarh, the Central Command headquartered at Lucknow in Uttar Pradesh, the Eastern Command headquartered at Calcutta, and the Southern Command headquartered at Pune in Maharashtra. Each command is headed by a lieutenant general.

In the Indian context, Command Headquarter can be likened to a Field Army or even an Army Group Headquarter with a General Officer Commanding-in-Chief presiding over matters in the rank of a (three-star) Lieutenant General. Next the line are the Corps Headquarters, which are Field Army Headquarters elsewhere. The Indian Army's combat formations are now grouped and tailored under many such Corps Headquarters (with some forces being retained under static Area Commands). As with the American Army, all Corps have numerical designations. They also have names, by which they are more commonly known. These names may derive from the city in which they are headquartered [XVI Corps / Nagrota Corps], or they may be evocative [IV Corps is Gajraj Corps, meaning "King Elephant."

The field force is grouped into Corps. Some of these are defensively oriented and have, over the years, acquired an unofficial-'Holding'. The others are called reserve or, unofficially again, 'Strike' Corps. The former is really a misnomer since these contain ample offensive potential. Corps Headquarters are designed to. handle an all-arms field army-of three to five divisions or their equivalents. Army Headquarters reserves could be mammoth-size or small, but powerful in either case. Heavy-tracked-Corps are an instance of the former, and the three parachute commandos (battalion-size units), which perform special forces duties, of the latter. Airborne, Air Assault or Parachute troops are usually held centralized. The mounts', in all cases, are provided by the Indian Air Force.

The Division and Independent Brigade Group are the lowest (or the highest, depending on the view-point) individual formations. They integrate in themselves all arms and services for sustained independent operations. There is great flexibility in their force mix, and in 'grouping for tasks'. Brigade (regiment in some armies) size combined-arms groups can be shed or added on at will. Standard Tables of Organization and Equipment do exist, but these are taken lightly for accounting purposes only. Divisions and independent brigade groups are designated by function, terrain of operation, or by their equipment mix.

The Army has in its Order of Battle, mountain divisions, infantry divisions, armoured divisions (in which tank units predominate) and mechanized divisions (in which mechanized infantry units predominate). An Infantry Division typically has about 15,500 combat troops, with 8,000 support elements (artillery, engineers, etc).

It consists of 3 to 5 Infantry Brigades, an Armoured Regiment and an Artillery Brigade. A Brigade is commanded by a Brigadier, and an Infantary Brigade consists of three Infantry Battalions. A regiment can be a type of battalion (eg. in the Artillery/Engineers) or a grouping of a number of battalions of the same type (eg. The Rajput Regiment). The approximate strength of an infantry battalion, commanded by a Colonel, may be taken as 900-1,000 personnel. A battalion may consist of three to four companies, and may be commanded by a Lieutenant Colonel or a Colonel. A company normally consists of 100-120 men and is commanded by a Major.

Independent brigade groups, as the name suggests, are vested with limited capability to carry out an independent mission. Independent brigade groups or independent brigade-sized formations may be armoured, mechanized, air defence (missile or gun), parachute, engineer, field artillery, electronic warfare or even standard infantry and mountain. These form 'Corps/Army troops', that is, they are held at Corps and Army levels for balancing out missions and task forces. At these levels, one would find heavy logistic support units in terms of supply, transport, field ordnance depots, and medical facilities.

An extensive body of schools and centers supports army operations. The officer corps is largely drawn from the National Defence Academy at Khadakvasla, Maharashtra, a joint services training institution that provides educational equivalents to the bachelor of arts or bachelor of science degrees to cadets for all three service arms.

Cadets spend their first three years at the National Defence Academy and then are sent to their respective service academies for further training before being commissioned in the armed forces. A preparatory school, the Rashtriya Indian Military College, at Dehra Dun, Uttar Pradesh, provides education to candidates for the National Defence Academy.

After completing their studies at the National Defence Academy, army cadets are sent to the Indian Military Academy at Dehra Dun. Other Indian Military Academy cadets are graduates of the Army Cadet College or are direct-entry students who have qualified by passing the Union Public Service Commission Examination. They spend between twelve and twenty-four months at the Indian Military Academy before being commissioned in the army as second lieutenants. Still other officer training occurs at the Officers' Training Academy in Madras, Tamil Nadu, where a forty-four-week session is offered to university graduates seeking a short-service commission.

In addition to the Indian Military Academy, the army runs a number of military education establishments. The more prominent ones include the College of Combat at Mhow, Madhya Pradesh; the High Altitude Warfare School at Gulmarg, Jammu and Kashmir; and the Counter-Insurgency and Jungle Warfare School at Vairengte, Mizoram.

The army also operates the Defence Services Staff College at Wellington in the Nilgiri Hills in Tamil Nadu, which provides master of science-level joint-service training for mid-level staff appointments and promotes interservice cooperation.

In 1994 it was reported that there were 200 women in the armed forces. In the army, which employs women as physicians and nurses, the participation of women is small but growing.

The Indian Military Nursing Service was formed in 1926 and has eight nursing schools (five army, two navy, and one air force) and one nursing college in Pune. Bachelor of science graduates are commissioned as lieutenants in the Medical Nursing Service and attached to the various components of the armed forces.

Ranks as high as colonel can be attained by career officers. In the mid-1990s, a small but increasing number of women officers were being assigned to nonmedical services. In 1994, there were fifty women nonmedical army officers and another twenty-five in training. They are university graduates who have been put through rigorous training and are reported to be eager for combat unit assignments.

2

A HISTORICAL OVERVIEW OF THE ARMY

INTRODUCTION

The origin of the Indian Army goes back to the beginning of the British rule over India. During the last 250 years, it has undergone many changes, accomplished many feats and fought countless battles at home and abroad on different continents. It has been a unique organisation, vastly different in its ethos and traditions from the other armies of the world. Winston Churchill referred to the over two million strong Indian Army during the World War-II, as the largest volunteer army known to history. Even today at around 1.2 million personnel, the Indian Army it is one of the largest volunteer armies in the world. Like the caste system, which permeates our society, the theory of martial races has influenced the composition of the Indian Army. Though this theory has long been officially discarded it continues to survive, albeit on a gradually reducing scale. The regimental ethos based on regional and class affinity often reinforced by heredity, has always been a strong motivating factor for the soldiers of this army. This was an important ingredient of their high morale at a time when they did not have a nationalistic cause to serve.

This Army, while greatly influencing the course of political developments in its own country, has never participated in politics. It is one of the few apolitical armies in the world to not have a Cromwell or a Napoleon trying to acquire political power. Raised by a foreign power to serve its commercial and imperial interests, the Indian Army did not have a nationalistic cause to serve for the first 200 years, but it was never a mercenary army. Its soldiers did not enlist for money to sell their loyalty to the highest bidder. They joined the Army, because they considered fighting an honourable profession and they fought for their honour which included that of the family, community, region and regiment.

The concept of nationhood was non-existent in 18th Century India. Thus many Indians enlisted in the Army of a foreign power and had no hesitation in fighting under their flag against their own countrymen and contributing to the establishment of British Imperial rule over India. However this duty got compensated by the action of many of them in the Great Revolution of 1857. The first spark of nationalism in the country in the modern period under British rule was lit by the Indian soldier. The revolution was thus essentially an affair of the Army. Even though the revolution failed, it became a source of inspiration for the subsequent generations in the freedom struggle. It is noteworthy that notwithstanding the Jallianwala Bagh incident, the Army was sparingly used against the freedom fighters. Terrorism or the non-violent struggle for freedom were mostly contained by the civil administration, using police for the purpose.

When the Army had to be called out, it was more like the British Army in India than the Indian Army. In 1930, the Garhwalis refused to open fire on the Red Shirts during the non-cooperation movement. They were court-martialled for mutiny but their action was applauded by the nation. Indian soldiers served all over the world during the British regime. They fought from China in the East to France and Africa in the West. They fought bravely during during the First and Second World Wars. The tales of their valour have been spread worldwide. The secret of success of the Indian Army has been its unflinching sense of duty, discipline and traditions of valour. During the Second World War, the emergence of the Indian National Army (INA) from the ranks of Indian Army prisoners with the Japanese, under the leadership of Netaji Subhash Chandra Bose, to fight for Indian independence became a major development. In military terms, the contribution of the Indian National Army was limited but its political and psychological impact was tremendous.

After the war, the mutinies of the Army, Navy and Air Force at Bombay, Jabalpur and Karachi respectively, convinced a militarily and economically exhausted Britain that she could not rely on the Indian Army to uphold her imperial rule on India. This became an important factor in influencing her decision to quit. Thus the Indian Army, made a silent but significant contribution to the independence of India. Lord Wavell, the Viceroy of India, in his farewell speech on 21 March 1947, five months before Independence, said, "I believe that the stability of the Indian Army may perhaps be a deciding factor in the future of India." Later events more than justified this belief. At the time of Independence, the Indian Army had to undergo a major surgical operation with many Muslim Officers leaving for the newly created state of Pakistan. The senior ranks in the Army were all held by the British Officers and they left for home.

They were replaced by Indian Army Officers with much less experience. Besides there were other problems too. Most of the Army personnel were from North-India and the families of many had been uprooted from their homes a result of partition and were living in refugee camps. Their pay was slashed considerably just before independence and they accepted these cuts in a most disciplined manner. There were no representations nor any case was filed in any court of law. It was against this background that the Army was called upon to tackle the unprecedented carnage and the movement of millions of refugees in Punjab. The civil administration had collapsed. The Army was the only credible instrument available with the State to restore order. Within a couple of months after independence, normalcy was restored in riot-ravaged Punjab.

No sooner has this been done, the Army was called upon to defend J&K against an armed invasion first from Phatan rebels in October 1947 and then in 1948 from the Pakistan Army. Military operations in Jammu & Kashmir, in the most difficult terrain and at forbidding heights raged from October 1947 to January 1949, ended in a proud victory for the Indian Army and Pakistan failed to achieve its objectives. However, a cease-fire was accepted by India which enabled Pakistan to hold portions of Jammu & Kashmir state. These areas under Pakistan's occupation are called Pak-occupied Kashmir (PoK). In the wake of independence the question of integrating over 500 Indian States into the Union of India posed a major problem. The Army constituted the final sanction behind Sardar Vallabhai Patel's moves for integration. Where, this could not be achieved through diplomatic negotiations, the Indian Army had to be employed to enforce the nation's will, as happened in Junagarh, Hyderabad and Goa.

On 15 January 1948, General K.M. Cariappa became the first Indian Commander-in-Chief of the Indian Army. January 15, is now celebrated every year in India, as Army Day. On this occasion the Chief of the Army Staff (COAS) takes the salute at the Army Day Parade in the Delhi cantonment. The first decade or more after independence was an era in which India's moral authority stood very high in all chanceries of the world. The Indian Army was employed on tasks to promote international peace in Korea, Gaza, Lebanon and Congo on behalf of the United Nations and earned great honour for the country. China's belligerence in 1962 shook the nation. This was defeat, pure and simple, born of short-sightedness and bad decision. India was outclassed and outsmarted by masters of real geopolitik. This rude awakening in the Himalayas, caused the failure of the political & military leadership and brought about a great national humiliation.

The Army however soon recovered from this trauma. The glorified battles of the war with Pakistan three years later in 1965, helped partly to heal wounds. But honour was not really restored till the resounding victory in the 1971 Indo-Pak war, with tales of impossible victories won in places like Longewala with scores of Pakistani tanks destroyed. A decisive victory like this, had not taken place in centuries. Today India is at the cross-roads. In some spheres, we have creditable progress, but in many others there has been alarming deterioration and are facing mounting crisis. Divisive and secessionist forces have been increasingly asserting themselves. Various contradictions in our society not only persist but have accentuated. The Army cannot remain totally isolated from these developments. The Sikh problem had its repercussions in the mutiny of some Sikh soldiers. The Gorkhaland problem may have ramifications amongst the Gorkha soldiers, if proper care is not taken. The Sikhs and the Gorkhas have been our finest soldiers and their record of loyalty and gallantry should not be allowed to get tarnished.

The Army also has certain organisational and functional problems which must be suitably resolved. Notwithstanding all the difficulties we face as a nation and problems faced by the Army, we can rely on the Indian Army to continue to serve the nation loyally and with a high standard of professionalism and gallantry. This may help the nation in proceeding along the desired path from the present cross-roads. A code of honour has come down to the Jawans from the great commanders and soldiers of the past eras. It is a matter of great pride that whenever India has been attacked, the Army stood by this code of valour, fidelity and honour. The tradition never to surrender has remained ingrained in our fighting men and the Army always has resolute soldiers who are ever ready to do their duty unto death without hesitation.

ETHOS OF THE INDIAN ARMY

- The safety, honour and welfare of your country comes first, always and every time.
- The honour, welfare and comfort of the men you command come next.
- Your own ease, comfort and safety come last, always and every time.

Characteristics of the Indian Army

- *Valour*. Fearlessness in combat, in the face of the enemy even when fighting at a great disadvantage or facing sure death.

- *Non-discrimination.* On account of caste, creed or religion. Total impartiality in performance of duty.
- *Comradeship and brotherhood of the brave.* Within the Army regardless of caste, creed or religion.
- *Discipline and integrity.* Patriotism, honesty and courage under all circumstances.
- *Spirit of selfless sacrifice.* The tradition never to question but to do or die.
- *Fairness and honesty.* Even towards the enemy, prisoners or wounded.
- *Fidelity, honour and courage.* Stand out as an example to others.
- *Dogged determination.* Even in defeat or adverse situations.

DEFENDING SARAGARHI, 12 SEPTEMBER 1897

Saragarhi is the incredible story of 21 men of the 36th Sikh Regiment (currently the 4th Sikh Regiment) who gave up their lives in devotion to their duty. In keeping with the tradition of the Indian Army, they fought to the death rather than surrender. The Battle at Saragarhi is one of eight stories of collective bravery published by UNESCO (United Nations Educational, Scientific and Cultural Organization). It has been mentioned as one of the five most significant events of its kind in the world which includes the Saga of Thermoplyae associated with the heroic stand of a small Greek force against the mighty Persian Army of Xerxes in 480 B.C.

THE BATTLE

The British colonial rulers had constructed a series of forts to control the NWFP (North West Frontier Province-today a state in Pakistan) and to provide security to troops against marauding tribesmen and their *lashkars* (large body of troops). Most of these forts had initially been built by Maharaja Ranjit Singh as part of the consolidation of the Sikh empire in Punjab and the British added some more. The British had only partially succeeded in gaining control over this region, consequently, skirmishes and sometimes serious fights with the tribals were a frequent occurrence. However, the NWFP was a good training ground for the Indian Army to hone its skills and techniques.

Two such forts on the Samana ridge of the Hindukush & Sulaiman ranges that is Fort Lockhart and Fort Gulistan were a few miles apart. Since these forts were not inter-visible, a signalling relay post called Saragarhi was located mid-way on a bluff to provide heliographic communications between them. This post or picket had been fortified to provide safety and protection to the signalling detachment.

In 1897 there was a general uprising in the NWFP engineered by Afghans as part of their policy, which came to be known as the 'prickly heat policy' to direct the wrath of the tribals against the British. In this uprising, *Mullahs* (Muslim religious leaders) played a prominent role. It was the duty of the 36th Sikh to occupy Gulistan and Lockhart forts. On 3rd and 9th September 1897, Orakazai and Afridi *lashkars* attacked Fort Gulistan. On both occasion the attacks were beaten back. A relief column was sent from the fort to assist in beating back these attacks.

The relief column from Lockhart on the return trip reinforced the signalling detachment at Saragarhi making its strength to 1 NCO (Non-Commissioned Officer) and 20 ORs (Other Ranks). In a renewed effort, on 12 September 1897, hordes of tribesmen laid siege to Fort Lockhart and Saragarhi, with the aim of overrunning the latter and at the same time preventing any help from the former.

The Commanding Officer of 36th Sikh, Lt. Col. Haughton, was at Fort Lockhart and was in communication with the Saragarhi post through helicograph. The defenders of Saragarhi under the indomitable and inspiring leadership of their detachment commander, Havildar Ishar Singh, resolved to defend their post in the best tradition of their race and regiment. They were not there to hand over the post to the enemy and seek safety elsewhere. Havildar Singh and his men knew well that the post would fall, because a handful of men in that makeshift fort of stones & mud walls with a wooden door could not stand the onslaught of thousands of tribesmen. These plucky men knew that they will go down but they had resolved to do so fighting to the last.

From Fort Lockhart, troops and the Commanding Officer could count at least 14 standards and that gave an idea of the number of tribes and their massed strength against the Saragarhi relay post (estimated at between 10,000 to 12,000 tribals). From early morning the tribals started battering the fort. The Sikhs fought back valiantly. Charge after charge was repulsed by the men of the 36th Sikh. The tribal leaders started to make tempting promises so that the Sikhs would surrender. But Havildar Singh and his men ignored them. For quite some time, the troops held their own against the determined and repeated attacks by the wild and ferocious hordes. A few attempts were made to send a relief column from Fort Lockhart but these were foiled by the tribals.

At Saragarhi, the enemy made two determined attempts to rush the gate of the post and on both occasions the defenders repulsed the assault. While the enemy suffered heavy casualties, the ranks of the defenders too kept dwindling as the fire from the attackers took its toll and their ammunition stocks were depleting. Unmindful of his safety, Sepoy Gurmukh Singh kept signalling a minute-to-minute account of the battle from the signal tower in the post to Battalion HQs. The battle lasted the better part of the day. When repeated attacks failed, the enemy set fire to the surrounding bushes & shrubs and two of the tribesmen under cover of smoke, managed to close in with the post's boundary wall in an area blind to the defender's observation and rifle fire from the post holes. They succeeded in making a breach in the wall. This development could be seen from Fort Lockhart and was flashed to the post.

A few men from those defending the approaches to the gate were dispatched to deal with the breach in the wall. This diversion by the enemy and the defenders' reaction resulted in weakening of the fire covering the gate. The enemy now rushed the gate as well as the breach. Thereafter, one of the fiercest hand-to-hand fights followed. One of the Havildar Singh's men, who was seriously wounded and was profusely bleeding, had taken charge of the guardroom. He shot four of the enemy as they tried to approach his charge. All this time, Sepoy Gurmukh Singh continued flashing the details of the action at the post. Beside this the Commanding Officer of 36th Sikh and others at Lockhart Fort also saw his unique saga of heroism and valour unfold at Saragarhi. The battle had come too close for Sepoy Gurmukh Singh's comfort, so he asked Battalion HQs for permission to shut down the heliograph and take up his rifle. Permission was flashed back. He dismounted his heliograph equipment, packed it in a leather bag, fixed bayonet on his rifle and joined the fight. From this vantage point in the tower he wrought havoc on the intruders in the post. He died fighting, but took 20 of the enemy with him.

The tribals set fire to the post, while the brave garrison lay dead or dying with their ammunition exhausted. Next morning the relief column reached the post and the tell tale marks of the epic fight were there for all to see. The tribals later admitted to figure of 180 dead and many more wounded. This episode when narrated in the British Parliament, drew from the members a standing ovation in the memory of the defenders of Saragarhi. The story of the heroic deeds of these men was also placed before Queen Victoria. The account was received all over the world with awe and admiration. All the 21 valiant men of this epic battle were awarded the Indian Order of Merit Class III (posthumously) which at the time was one of the highest gallantry awards given to Indian troops and is considered equivalent to the present-day Vir Chakra. All dependants of the Saragarhi heroes were awarded 50 acres of land and 500 Rupees. Never before or since has a body of troops-that is, all of them won gallantry awards in a single action. It is indeed a singularly unique action in the annals of Indian military history.

A tablet erected in the memory of these brave men. The tablet reads;

"The Government of India have caused this tablet to be erected to the memory of the twenty one non-commissioned officers and men of the 36 Sikh Regiment of the

Bengal Infantry whose names are engraved below as a perpetual record of the heroism shown by these gallant soldiers who died at their posts in the defence of the fort of Saragarhi, on the 12 September 1897, fighting against overwhelming numbers, thus proving their loyalty and devotion to their sovereign, the Queen Empress of India, and gloriously maintaining the reputation of the Sikhs for unflinching courage on the field of battle."

165 Havildar Ishar Singh

332 Naik Lal Singh	834 Sepoy Narayan Singh
546 Lance Naik Chanda Singh	814 Sepoy Gurmukh Singh
1321 Sepoy Sundar Singh	871 Sepoy Jivan Singh
287 Sepoy Ram Singh	1733 Sepoy Gurmukh Singh
492 Sepoy Uttar Singh	163 Sepoy Ram Singh
182 Sepoy Sahib Singh	1257 Sepoy Bhagwan Singh
359 Sepoy Hira Singh	1265 Sepoy Bhagwan Singh
687 Sepoy Daya Singh	1556 Sepoy Buta Singh
760 Sepoy Jivan Singh	1651 Sepoy Jivan Singh
791 Sepoy Bhola Singh	1221 Sepoy Nand Singh

HARI SINGH NALWA AND THE BATTLE OF NAUSHERA

India has had to face foreign invaders many more times than most other nations. The majority of these came through the Khyber pass in the North West of India. These invaders were lured either by riches of India, zeal to convert people to their beliefs or world domination through force. Th Afghans were among the last to come across the Khyber. By the late 1700s Afghans has set up small city states all over Punjab and North West. Rohillas of Awadh (UP), Tipu Sultan of Mysore, Nawab of Malerkotla, Multan, Kashmir all were ultimately descended from the invaders. The Afghans wrecked havoc on local population in their territories. Rapes and forced conversions were commonplace in the Afghan ruled territories. Children born out of forceful marriages and rapes were given a special caste of "Ranghars". And Ranghars were specially targeted by

Maulavis to fill them a zeal of Islam, in order to make them fighters of Islam.

The Sikhs opposed these Afghan landlords and were able eventually to wrest control of the biggest city in Punjab, named Lahore, under the leadership of Maharaja Ranjit Singh Sandhu. In an attempt to bring the North West under their rule the Sikhs sought to sweep away isolated pockets of Afghan power. In his enterprise Maharaja Ranjit Singh Sandhu was helped by his many generals. Hari Singh Nalwa was the most illustrious of them all.

Hari Singh Nalwa

Sardar Hari Singh Nalwa was born to Gurdial Singh Uppal and Dharam Kaur at Gujranwala (now in Pakistan) in the year 1791. Gurdial Singh was an officer in Ranjit Singh 's army. He died during a campaign fighting Afghans in 1798, when Hari Singh was only seven years of age.

Hari Singh eventually assumed the responsibility of supervising the affairs of his father's lands. Hari Singh presented himself before Maharaja Ranjit Singh in his open Durbar. The Maharaja was so impressed by the feats of chivalry shown by him that he was taken in the royal service as a personal *khidmatgar* or an attendant.

Maharaja commissioned him into the army in 1804 by granted him a command of a cavalry of 700 men and horses with the honor of Sardar. Hari Singh Nalwa named his regiment 'Sher-Dil-Rajman'. Hari Singh earned a reputation for bravery quite early on. During the course of hunting expedition he happened to be a victim of a sudden attack of a tiger. The attack was so subtle and unexpected that he did not gain time to pull out his sword.

Sardar Hari Singh Nalwa faced the crucial situation with such boldness that he managed to catch hold of the jaw of the beast forcefully with his hands and pushed it away with the prowess of arms arranging thus to kill it with his sword. Baron Charles Hugel says he was called Nalwa for 'having cloven the head of a tiger who had already seized him as its prey'.

The Sikhs passing established themselves as the pre-eminent power in Punjab following their defeat of Ahmad Shah Abdali's governor at Lahore in 1765. But their mode of fighting then was hardly suited to the requirements of a well organized state. Maharaja Ranjit Singh out of these Sikhs became leader of whole Khalsa (Sarbat Khalsa). He built up a strong, centralized and efficient military system by drawing the best elements in foreign with the best elements found in the indigenous fighting systems.

After some major campaigns of Multan and Kasur where Hari Singh Nalwa's regiment fought with distinction, Maharaja turned towards Kashmir. Hari Singh Nalwa's regiment "Sher-Dil-Rajman' was in forefront in campaign to get back Shah Shuja from the Governor of Kashmir, Shah Shuja's wife Wafa Begum had promised Kohinoor Diamond for Maharaja if her husband was to be freed from prison of Kashmir. In 1814 A.D., Hari Singh routed the Kashmiri forces. Shah Shuja gave Ranjit Singh kohinoor Diamond, from that day on till his death Maharaja Ranjit Singh wore that Diamond on his right shoulder. Meanwhile, through political means, Ranjit Singh installed his own governor (Jahan Dad Khan) in Peshawar.

In 1821, Dost Mohammed Khan and Yar Mohammed Khan, two Afghans were able to expel the Maharaja's nominee Jahan Dad Khan from Peshawar and thus an expedition was undertaken by Ranjit Singh's Army. A large army under illustrious commanders was dispatched to rectify the situation in Peshawar (Cavalry commanded by Sardar Hari Singh Nalwa, Infantry by Dhanna Singh Malwai, and Jagat Singh Attariwala, Artillery by Mian Ghaus Khan). Dost Mohammed Khan managed to reconcile by paying a handsome nazarana to Maharaja and by accepting the submission to Khalsa kingdom rather than to kingdom of Kabul.

Battle of Naushera

Ranjit Singh's forces at this time were divided into regular and irregular infantry, regular and irregular cavalry and artillery. Regular forces were directly under Lahore Sultanate of Ranjit Singh, irregular forces were supplied by allies or by those kingdoms that were bound by treaties. Artillery was completely under state control and was led by Mian Ghaus Khan and General Allard. Ranjit Singh employed several foreigners in his military services. Famous ones were General Allard leading an artillery regiment and General Ventura leading a regiment made up of Poorbia (Bihar, Bengali, and UP) soldiers. Both Allard and Ventura had earlier fought in the armies of Napoleon Bonaparte of France. Ranjit Singh's motive to include foreigners in his army was to modernize his forces.

In 1822 Fakir Azizudeen, Maharaja Ranjit Singh's "foreign officer" was sent to Peshawar to collect annual tribute. He was well received by Yar Mohammed, who ordered the city to be illuminated in the Fakir's honor. Yar Mohammed paid the tribute in cash and horses. Then Fakir Azizuddin returned to Lahore well satisfied with his mission. This incident lowered the prestige of Yar Mohammed Khan among his people.

Mohammed Azim Khan who then ruled Kabul taunted Yar Mohammed for paying tribute to Sikh infidels. Azim Khan marched out of Kabul and the cry of jihad echoed at Khyber. Over forty-five thousand Khattaks and Yusufzai tribesmen under the leadership of Syed Akbar Shah of Balmer volunteered to fight. Yar Mohammed abandoned Peshawar and went into hiding. And once more Maharaja Ranjit Singh ordered his army to move north towards Peshawar.

Prince Sher Singh, Misr Dewan Chand and General Ventura were led the battalions of infantry. Hari Singh Nalwa, Phula Singh, Fateh Singh Ahluwalia, Desa Singh Majithia and Attar Singh Sandhawalia led the cavalry, while artillery was commanded by Mian Ghaus Khan and General Allard. Recently trained and incorporated battalions of Purbia (Bihari soldiers) and Gurkha Soldiers were also sent. These were led by General Ventura and General Balbhadra (Gurkha General). A grand total of about 25,000 men moved to defend the Sikh kingdom.

In December 1822 orders were given to march out of Lahore and Prince Sher Singh, younger son of Maharaja Ranjit Singh led the march with his battalions of Cavalry and Infantry. Hari Singh Nalwa whose Sher-e-Dil Rajaman battalion was replenished by additional soldiers making it the largest Cavalry regiment of about 5000 men and horses in the Lahore Darbar's army closely followed Prince Sher Singh. These advance columns of Lahore Durbar reached Attock river a month ahead of other forces.

They crossed the Attock river using a pontoon bridge and occupied the Sikh fort of Jehangiria. Mohammed Azim Khan and his Afghani Jihadis soon surrounded the fort of Jehangiria. Other men helping Mohammed Azim to lead their 45,000 forces of Mujahdeen were his brothers, Dost Mohammed (who had more than once paid tribute to Lahore), Sayyid Akbar Shah and Jabbar Khan, the ex-governor of Kashmir. They destroyed the pontoon bridge over river Attock so that Sikh forces could not cross and started pounding the fort with their guns. Hari Singh Nalwa and Prince Sher Singh with much grit and determination held the fort with their total of less then 10,000 men. Since this fort was right on the banks of a river, there was no shortage of water or other supplies. Hari Singh Nalwa led his cavalry in numerous sorties outside fort destroying two of the invaluable guns of Afghanis.

Meanwhile, Maharaja Ranjit Singh and rest of the Khalsa force which was following his advance columns leisurely arrived in January to find the only pontoon bridge across the river destroyed. To make matter worse next day there was a heavy snowfall. The Maharaja was being informed through his network of intelligence of the rapidly rising force of the enemy but decided to wait for his heavy guns to arrive which were due by mid-day (March 14, 1823) But, that morning Sikh a Gurmata (Resolution) was passed that the Afghans would be attacked before their forces could gather greater strength and irrespective of whether the heavy guns arrived or not. Fortunately, the artillery also arrived in time for the attack.

Hari Singh Nalwa and Prince Sher Singh had already taken on the enemy earlier crossing the river before the bridge was destroyed and capturing the fort of Jehangiria. They were exerting powerful pressure on the enemy but badly needed reinforcements which had arrived on the other side of that river, but could not wait for the bridge to be constructed under the threat of enemy fire. Ranjit Singh one early morning leading himself riding on his white horse he dipped in the freezing water to cross the river. Whole force followed but in this exercise much of the equipment was lost, that included much needed guns. Akali Phoola Singh's suicide squad who was following Ranjit Singh, now took the lead, and, without a moment's thought, plunged their horses in the swollen and turbulent river. How could the others stay behind ? Every one followed suit, but before they crossed over, the enemy had taken flight from Jehangiria leaving even their dead or dying in the battle-field and saying in despair:—" Toba, Toba,Khuda Khud Khalsa shud." (God forbid, but it appears, God himself has turned a Khalsa !)." It was believed that no one could cross the river at its full fury.

Thus catching the enemy by surprise Ranjit Singh and his forces broke open the cordon massacring more than 1,000 Afghans. The Afghanas who were from the Khattak and Yusufzai tribes, fled and entrenched themselves nearby a city then called Pir Sabak (this later became the British cantonment of Naushera, which is currently one of the major bases of Pakistan Army). This put a gap between the main Afghan force under Azim Khan's brothers and the column of tribal Jihadis. A small but swift stream called Landai put a further obstacle between the two Afghan armies. And he Sikhs were determined to maintain the initiative.

Consequently, whatever was left of Sikh artillery was sent to the bank of the Landai to forestall any attempts by the two Afghan columns to link up. Meanwhile when news of the disaster reached Azim Khan he made a dash from Peshawar to join his brothers on the bank of the Landai river. They could not cross the stream because of constant firing by Durbar guns. Azim Khan and his brothers then decided to launch an attack early morning when Punjabi guns were being rested. However, the Sikh Army decided to wipe out the tribal column before Azim Kahn could strike. As a result, the Gurkha and Purbia battalions were dispatched to deal with Pir Sabak Hill where tribal mujahids were resting. And though the Tribal column fought desperately they were overwhelmed by the Gurkhas and Purbias. General Balbhadra of Gurkha Infantry lost his life during this action in the midst of some of the fiercest to hand-to-hand fighting.

Meanwhile, seeing their comrades getting killed all Afghanis came together in a desperate effort to hold the attack by Darbar's army. Darbar's forces surrounded them from all sides. Both Hari Singh Nalwa and Akali Phula Singh from one end lead the cavalry charge while Gurkhas who were leaderless after martyrdom of General Balbhadra and Purbias under General Ventura and Punjabi soldiers under General Dewan Misr Chand holding their positions. Hari Singh Nalwa pressed on his cavalry deploying with precision and raising war cries of *Bole So Nihal Sat Sri Akal* from time to time, Hari Singh Nalwa and his disciplined soldiers emptied their muskets on Jihadis. A wave of about 50 soldiers on their horses would charge at Jihadis, firing their muskets and then sending more to meet their creator through their bayonets as they gallop across the battlefield.

Hari Singh Nalwa and Akali Phula Singh with their cavalry regiment of Sher-Dil-Rajman and Nihangs as Khushwant Singh succinctly puts it gave them "coup de grace." They drove the Khattaks and Yusufzais from Pir Sabak Hill. Heavy artillery on the land surrounded the Jihadis and opened up a barrage to complete the slaughter.

While Hari Singh was leading his Sher-Dil-Rajman attacking Jihadis from one end, from other side Akali Phula Singh and his Cavalry of Nihangs, or the "Crocodile Sikhs who fight till death" were performing similar feat. Jihadis were surrounded by Gurkha Infantry at one end, General Ventura soldiers at other end, while waves of Cavalry charges were attacking from the one side. Jihadis changed their tactics and decided to go for the leaders in order to demoralize the Khalsa forces.

General Bhalbhadra was shot, General Ventura was injured and Akali Phula Singh's horse was shot. This angered Akali Phula Singh and he made a grave mistake by getting on an elephant. Now Akali Phula Singh's towering torso was seen from all over the battlefield. Ghazi Jihadis saw the Khalsa

General on top of an elephant and immediately trained their muskets on him. Akali Phula Singh's body was riddled with bullets, he collapsed in his howdah exhorting the Nihang Sikhs to not to give way. Akali Phula Singh through his dashing feats had inspired other Sikh commanders his martyrdom renewed the vigor to fight.

Mohammed Azim Khan watched the massacre from the other side of the stream without being able to help his tribesmen brother. He did not had the will to fight till death. By the day's end, Four thousand tribesmen were left dead on the field. Probably two times that number were injured and left dying at the battlefield. It was a crushing defeat for Afghanis. Hari Singh Nalwa whose ideal was Akali Phula Singh, chased the remaining Afghans deep into their territory killing hundreds more.

Mohammed Azim was too ashamed to face the people of Peshawar and he returned to Afghanistan, where he died in couple of months. This battle proved the effectiveness of organized military. Death of a General Akali Phula Singh at this battle was the biggest loss of the campaign for Maharaja Ranjit Singh. Azim Khan's Jihadis had lost heart and abandoned their zeal for Jihad in complete disorder. 14 large and 18 small guns were captured by the Sikhs.

It showed them the effectiveness of organized artillery and cavalry regiments as well as old tactics of Guerilla warfare. In this battle not all of Ranjit Singh's forces took part, some regiments just waited for their turn which never came. General Allard and Ventura's participation in this battle with their divisions and trained army of Lahore kingdom with Akali division of the army had absolutely no match for untrained militia who although surpassed in sheer numbers, Afghans after a great massacre submitted and Naushera was captured. Albeit, the Lahore troops lost an indispensable commander. Hari Singh Nalwa played a conspicuous role first by inflicting a crushing defeat upon the enemy and secondly by pursuing the enemy after the defeat in order to be sure about the victory of the Lahore troops. The battle of Naushera made it evident to the frontier tribesmen that the Afghan militia was weaker than those of Lahore troops. This battle sealed the further prospects of Muhammad Azim of Kabul and established the Sikh supremacy over Peshawar.

"Akali Phula Singh's memorial still stands intact there. For Ranjit Singh as much as for others, the joy of a superb victory was marred by this sad and heart-rending event. This monument (now situated in the Frontier Province of Pakistan) on the bank of the river Kabul was endowed wish a Jagir by Ranjit Singh and a Gurdwara was also built on the site. Sardar Gurbaksh Singh. well-known Punjabi writer and editor of Preet Lari", settled there in early thirties of this century. and tilled the farm attached to this monument. The place is still called Samadh Akali Phoola Singh."

"Three days later the Maharaja entered Peshawar the head of his victorious troops. The citizens welcomed him and paid him homage with nazarana (gifts). The Maharajah's sojourn was, however, not a peaceful one. what the tribesmen could not achieve in open combat, they tried to gain by the cold-blooded murder of Punjabi soldiers under cover of darkness."

Ranjit Singh knew about the tactics of these tribesmen. A few days later both Yar Mohammed and Dost Mohammed presented themselves at court and sought the Maharajah's pardon. He forgave them readily and accepted their tribute of presents and horses. Yar Mohammed was reinvested governor of Peshawar on promising an increased annual revenue of Rs.1,000,000 to the Lahore Durbar.

This was first time that Afghanis were totally beaten and humiliated in their own country by their former subjects. Ranjit Singh made this possible through his able generals and brilliant military tactics. So huge was this victory that it caused apprehensions in British circles. British realized that sooner or later showdown with Ranjit Singh was inevitable. In particular, they realized that the Durbar's conquests had reached the furthest geographical limits of the Punjab in the north and north-west. Beyond were impassable mountains and inhospitable, unprofitable regions.

In order to pacify his new conquests Ranjit Singh ordered Hari Singh Nalwa and Prince Sher Singh to remain in North West Frontier province at the end his campaign. He also ordered them to construct series of small forts all along the highway leading to Khyber pass. He correctly had assessed the importance of Khyber pass, and thus organized the defenses of his frontier around Kabul.

DEFENDING KASHMIR

Why did Pakistan invade Kashmir in the first place? First, Kashmir being a Muslim-dominant state was considered a natural part of Pakistan, which had made Islam the basis of its modern nationality. Second, Khan Abdul Gaffar Khan's Pathanistan Movement was gaining momentum and Kashmir was held out as a bait for luring the poor tribals away. The internal conditions of Jammu & Kashmir with religious passions aflame, lawlessness rampant and authority paralysed offered the right mix for the raiders to strike.

Operation Gulmarg

The Army Headquarters of Pakistan planned the main invasion plan, code-named Operation Gulmarg. Conclusive proof of this came through two different sources-Major Onkar Singh Kalkat, then serving as the Brigade Major at HQ Bannu Frontier Brigade Group, and GK Reddy, a journalist. Both happened to stumble upon the plan by chance. The invasion was planned meticulously with considerable strategic and tactical insight. According to Operation Gulmarg, as described by Major Kalkat, every Pathan tribe was required to enlist at least one Lashkar of 1,000 tribesmen.

These Lashkars were to be concentrated at Baftnu, Wana, Peshawar, Kohat, Thal and Nowshera by the first week of September 1947. The Brigade Commanders at these places were to issue them arms, ammunition and some essential clothing items. Each Lashkar was also to be provided with a Major, a Captain and ten JCOs of the regular Pakistan Army. The entire force was to be commanded by Major General Akbar Khan, who was given the code name Tariq.

All Lashkars were to meet at Abbottabad by October 18th. According to the plan, six Lashkars were to advance along the main road from Muzaffarabad to Srinagar via Domel, Uri and Baramula, with the specific task of capturing the aerodrome and subsequently advancing to the Banihal Pass. Two Lashkars were to advance from the Haji Pir Pass direct on to Gulmarg, thereby securing the right flank of the main force advancing from Muzaffarabad. Another two Lashkars were to advance from Tithwal through the Nastachhun Pass for capturing Sopore, Handwara and Bandipur. And 10 other Lashkars were to operate in the Poonch, Bhimbar and Rawalkot area with the intention of capturing Poonch and Rajauri before advancing to Jammu. Arrangements were also made for detailing of guides/informers from the so-called Azad Army, to all these tribal Lashkars.

Major General Khan was also given the task of organising the Azad Army, the major portion of which was to come from the Muslim element of the J&K State forces. Dumps of arms, ammunition, supplies and clothing were to be established forward of Abbottabad by October 15th. These were to be subsequently moved to Muzaffarabad and Domel after the D-day. Pakistan's 7 Infantry Division was to concentrate the Murree-Abbottabad area by October 21st and was ordered to be ready to move immediately into J&K territory to back up the tribal Lashkars and consolidate their hold on the Valley. One infantry brigade was also held in readiness at Sialkot to move on to Jammu. The D-day for Operation Gulmarg was fixed as 22 October 1947, on which date the various Lashkars were to cross into J&K territory. The invasion plan was tactically sound and, in the beginning, brilliantly executed. The main attack had by necessity to be launched frontally along the motor road. Apart from rifles, the standard weapon of the raiders, the main force was also equipped with a few light machine guns and traveled in about 300 civilian lorries.

Fall of Domel and Baramula

The main strength of the defenders was at Domel where the two approach roads from Murree and Abbottabad met before leading towards Srinagar along the Jhelum gorge. Its two out posts Lohar Gali and Ramkot were the key to the whole defence and were guarded by the 4th Kashmir Infantry, which had a mix of Muslim and Dogra soldiers.

When the raiders struck in the morning of October 22nd, traitors within the 4th Kashmir Infantry joined the raiders and gave them complete information about the strength and disposition of the defending troops and helped them send sufficient force against each piquet of defenders. That proved to be the beginning of a series of successes for the raiders before they were ultimately held, and subsequently thrown back, by Indian reinforcements over the next two weeks or so.

Between October 22nd and 26th, the raiders had run over Domel, Muzaffarabad, Uri and Baramula. Yet in their success lay the seeds of their doom. For on their way, they took to looting and raping, and the ultimate goal of the 'Holy War' was forgotten. Each man tried to grab as much wealth or as many girls as he could, and the 'infidel' Maharaja at Srinagar or the 'liberation of the oppressed Muslims' of Kashmir was last on his mind.

The advance on Srinagar was held up for a few days, and that proved crucial. In Delhi, hundreds of kilometres from stricken Baramula, it had at last been decided to save Kashmir in its hour of peril. Even as the barbaric raiders were satisfying their greed and lust in Baramula, transport planes full of Indian troops were winging their way through the azure autumn skies: Destination Srinagar.

Smashing of the J&K Siege

When the first wave of tribal warriors from Pakistan invaded the Kashmir Valley on 22 October 1947, the kingdom of Jammu & Kashmir had not acceded to either Pakistan or India. Therefore, taking the plea that it was an internal matter, India refused to send in its troops to the Valley. However, when Maharaja Hari Singh signed the Instrument of Accession with the Indian Government on the evening of 26 October 1947, Jammu & Kashmir became an integral part of the Indian Dominion legally, morally and constitutionally. Now was the time to react to the tribal invasion, which India did commendably, considering the short notice given to its military commanders.

The first troops were flown to Srinagar with hardly a couple of days planning and preparation. The liberation of the Valley in early November 1947 was a splendid feat of arms by the 161 Brigade, fighting against hordes of raiders. This single brigade managed to hold its own throughout the long winter of 1947-48 when its only line of communication was blocked by snow. Large areas in the Tithwal, Naushahra and Rajouri sectors were liberated from the invaders, and were held against repeated attacks by a vastly superior enemy. Naturally, the Indian Army also suffered setbacks, minor and major, at several places such as Jhangar, Pandu, Kargil and Skardu. But the situation was fully restored at Jhangar and Kargil. The long siege of Poonch was finally broken and Gurais & Dras areas were successfully recaptured against tremendous odds. The Army won five Param Vir Chakras (PVCs), 47 Maha Vir Chakras (MVCs) and not less than 284 Vir Chakras (VrCs), including three twin-awards of VrCs, during the J&K Operations of 1947-48.

During the long campaign, the Indian Army lost 76 officers, 31 JCOs and 996 men of other ranks. The wounded totalled 3152, including 81 officers and 107 JCOs. Apart from these casualties, J&K State Forces lost approximately 1990 officers and men. The small Royal Indian Air Force (RIAF) lost 32 personnel, including 9 officers. The enemy casualties were definitely many times the total of Indian Army and RIAF casualties. By one estimate the enemy suffered 20,000 casualties, including 6000 killed. The gallantry and skill of all ranks of the Indian Army are amply borne out in the various accounts of these operations. But the exploits and the vital role of the RIAF deserve special mention here. Its contribution to the success of the J&K operations cannot be over emphasized, and it was the one weapon to which the enemy had no answer, as the Pakistan Air Force wisely desisted from joining the fray.

Only the impromptu airlift to Srinagar in October 1947 saved the Kashmir Valley. A hundred planes landed every day on the improvised airfield at Srinagar, bringing in troops, ammunition and supplies and evacuating casualties and the refugees. The RIAF and civilian pilots of these Dakotas defied the mountains, the weather, and fatigue, to continue the airlift till the Valley was saved. Giving invaluable support to these were the fearless fighter pilots who accurately and repeatedly attacked vital enemy positions at Gurais, Zoji La, Pindras and Rajouri.

Apart from the men in uniform, civilians played a crucial role in liberating the Valley. The dedication and skill of the civilian pilots who flew to Srinagar in October 1947 was no less than their counterparts in the RIAF. Very few know that a civilian washerman, Ram Chander, won a Maha Vir Chakra for rescuing an officer wounded during an ambush, shooting down several enemy troops in the process. It was this Indian spirit and valour that saved the Valley.

India to the Rescue

It was on 24 October 1947 that the Government of India first got news of the Kashmir invasion. By that time, Domel and Muzaffarabad had already fallen to the raiders, who were fast approaching Srinagar. The Maharaja of Kashmir sent an S.O.S. message to the Indian Government on the night of October 24th. After deliberations at the highest levels, it was decided that India couldn't send its troops till J&K formally acceded to India. Maharaja Hari Singh signed the Instrument of Accession in the evening of October 26th, which made J&K an integral part of India-legally, morally, and constitutionally. The Indian reaction, from then onwards, was swift, adverse ground conditions notwithstanding.

Operation Jak

The Indian rescue operation was beset with obvious difficulties from the very beginning. Srinagar was over 480 km from the nearest point on the Indian border. Troops in East Punjab were engaged in dealing with the refugees and maintaining law and order. Hence, air transport was the only way out. Worse still, the airport at Srinagar was hardly fit to land fully laden transport planes. But that was the only option available and it had to be taken. The rescue mission was code-named, Operation Jak. The first regiment to move in was 1 Sikh, stationed at Gurgaon at the time and commanded by Lt. Col. D.R. Rai. The troops were transported in four Dakota planes that took off from Delhi on October 27th and reached Srinagar early morning the same day. The first engagement with the enemy started on October 28th. Lt. Col. Rai was the first Indian officer to fall in the battle of liberation.

It was only after the first troops had landed at Srinagar that the gravity of the situation was realised. So, the Indian Army decided to throw its full weight to drive back the invaders. On October 28th, the Delhi and East Punjab Command was ordered to carry out Phase II of Operation Jak. It involved dispatching one Brigade Group to Jammu via Pathankot.

The next day, the Eastern Southern commands were asked to spare whatever troops they could for the operation. Airlifts were undertaken almost round-the-clock airlifts to increase the troop strength. On October 30th, two fighter aircraft of the RIAF were detailed to operate from the Srinagar airstrip to provide air-support to the ground troops. In the following days, many Harvards and Spitfires were based on that airfield and they gave invaluable support to the infantry.

Meanwhile, there had been some fierce engagements with the enemy on the ground, resulting in some casualties on the Indian side. But most importantly, the advance of the invaders had been checked.

The ground troops held the enemy. Transport planes took care of the supply of troops, equipment and ration. Interestingly, apart from three RIAF planes, 33 civil Dakotas were used in these sorties. Many of them even did a double trip to Srinagar on a single day-a tribute to the morale of the pilots and crew. By November 6th, the critical phase for Srinagar was over. The raiders had lost the initiative thanks to their looting at Baramula. About 3500 Indian troops had reached Srinagar by then. They threw a ring of machine guns and bayonets around Srinagar and the airfield. Although the invaders were only about 8 km away from the city at the nearest point, it was now impossible for them to penetrate the Indian positions and capture the capital, almost in their grasp. Having strengthened their position, the Indian Army was about to begin the liberation of the Kashmir valley.

The Liberation of the Valley

According to orders from the Defence Committee of the Cabinet, Baramula was to be recaptured from the enemy by November 17th, even if the Indian Army had to incur 500 casualties. The original plan was to launch the decisive battle on November 10th, but an unexpected attack on Indian positions at Shalateng on November 7th postponed the initiative.

In a masterly battle strategy, the Indian troops flanked the invaders from three sides and unleashed murderous firepower on them. The RIAF strafed them from the air. The Battle of Shalateng was over within 20 minutes. It put Srinagar and Kashmir Valley beyond the grasp of the invaders forever. There were encounters after that, but the enemy was being driven back steadily and surely. By the evening of November 13th, Uri was captured. With that the liberation of the Kashmir Valley was complete.

The Relief of Poonch

On 20 November 1947, a column for the relief of Poonch set out from Uri, but was halted at Kahuta, 13 km short of Poonch. The Poonch garrison held out for one full year before it was finally relieved. Operation Easy was aimed at establishing the final link-up with Poonch, which had proved to be difficult throughout most of 1948.

An attempt to link up with Poonch could be made either from the south, namely, via Thana Mandi or Rajouri, or from the north via the Haji Pir Pass. Lt. Gen. Cariappa (later Field Marshal and Army Chief) gave the go-ahead for the link-up with Poonch via the south. Lt. Gen. Shrinagesh (later General and Army Chief), who had been appointed Corps Commander of J&K Forces on September 14th, ordered Major General Atma Singh to plan for a link-up accordingly.

Major General Atma Singh was further ordered to carry out Phase I (secure Pir Badesar) by October 8th; commence Phase II (demonstrate north of Thana Mandi) by October 10th; and concentrate in Rajouri the required force for Operation Easy by October 16th. On October 9th, Major General Atma Singh finalised his plan.

The force was to be under the command of Brigadier Yadunath Singh, Commander 19 Brigade, and was to consist of six infantry battalions plus one field battery and one mountain battery. It was to be divided into two columns, one column of three battalions under command of Brigadier Umrao Singh, Commander 5 Brigade, and the other column of three battalions under command of Lt. Col. Jagjit Singh Aurora (the same Lt. Gen. Jagjit Singh Aurora of 1971 War fame), Commander 1/2 Punjab. As a preliminary to the main operation, the deception plan was to be carried out about October 12 to secure Pir Badesar.

The main operation was to commence on about October 19th with 5 Brigade advancing from Rajouri and securing Pir Kalewa ridge. Lt. Col. Jagjit Singh's column was then to pass through, moving from south of Thana Mandi to secure a firm base in the area around Sangrot. Having secured the base, the intention was to advance to Potha with 5 Brigade and carry out operations from Potha for the link-up with Poonch.

Capture of Pir Badesar

Operation Ranjit: The task of carrying out Operation Ranjit for the capture of Pir Badesar was given to 268 Brigade, 1/2 Punjab, 1 (Para) Kumaon and 1/1 Gorkha Rifles concentrated south of Darhal on October 13th.

The brigade plan was for 1/1 Gorkha Rifles less one company and one platoon to lead the attack and secure Kater and the high ground north of Giran. Then 1/2 Punjab was to push on and capture Khalbahat Gala. 1 (Para) Kumaon was to take the lead next and capture Point 5432. At 2000 hours on October 14th, the brigade moved out, 1/1 Gorkha Rifles leading, and the first objective, Kater was secured without opposition. 1/2 Punjab captured Point 3978 at 0600 hours on October 15th. 1 (Para) Kumaon captured Pir Badesar by 1700 hours on the same day. Artillery played an important part in Operation Ranjit also.

After the capture of Pir Badesar, there was an important modification in Operation Easy and it was decided that the link-up with Poonch should be made via Mendhar and not via Potha. An ad hoc formation named Durga Force under overall command of Brigadier Yadunath Singh was to undertake Operation Easy and was composed of 5 Infantry Brigade, 19 Infantry Brigade, and the Rajouri Garrison. To provide air support, the RIAF No.10 Squadron of Tempests and No.12 Squadron (Transport) of Dakotas and No.1 AOP Flight of Austers were made available. As per the plan, 5 Brigade secured the vital Pir Kalewa ridge at 1200 hours on October 28th. The next important features to be secured were Ramgarh Fort and Bhimbar Gali.

Poonch Finally Relieved

Major General Atma Singh now detailed 19 Brigade Group to capture Point 5732 with a view to exploit Jhhika Gali, an enemy stronghold barring the way to Mendhar. 5 Brigade Group was assigned the task of capturing Point 4394 and securing the right flank of the main column up to but excluding Point 3295. The plan was to capture Topa area with a view to linking up with 101 Brigade from Poonch. 19 Brigade less one battalion, supported by all available artillery was to commence attack on night of November 19/20th. 101 Brigade was to start operations on the night of November 19/20th to capture Point 6005 and Point 6876 (Pir Margot Ghazi). It was expected that the link-up with 101 Brigade would take place by the evening of November 20th.

During the night of November 19/20th, 1/4 Gorkha Rifles and 5 Rajputana Rifles carried out a night march. Point 5982 was captured by 0730 hours on November 20th without much opposition. Meanwhile, the leading company of 1/4 Gorkha Rifles had also captured its objective at 0620 hours. Then exploitation began. One platoon 1/4 Gorkha Rifles was sent to Point 6793 and met the troops of 101 Brigade at 1200 hours.

1/2 Punjab passed through the positions of 5 Rajputana Rifles and captured Topa at 1500 hours on November 20th. The link-up with Poonch in November 1948 was a notable performance. The enemy ring round Poonch was broken and attempts to force the Poonch garrison to surrender were finally frustrated.

The Battle of Naushera

The capture of Jhangar on 24 December 1947 gave the enemy a tremendous advantage. It was, hence, vital to Indian strategy to recapture Jhangar. The battle of Naushahra on 06 February 1948 was decisive in this context and paved the way for the recapture of Jhangar later on. Lt. Col. R.G. Naidu, CO of 2 Jat, was put in command of Operation Satyanas for clearing the enemy from the area around Beri Pattan. The troops occupied Tung on January 23rd and crossed the Thandapaniwali Tawi the next morning. In the early hours of January 25th, as they advanced to attack Siot and Pt. 2502, they came under heavy enemy fire and had to make a retreat, but not before inflicting heavy casualties on the enemy, estimated to be 100 dead and wounded.

To weaken and disrupt the enemy's offensive, a mobile force known as 'Cheeta Force' was formed. It consisted of Stuart tanks from 7 Light Cavalry. Orders were given to this mobile force on January 24th. The plan was simple. Two small detachments of mixed armour and infantry were to be established at Amberala and Chordhaki to guard the rear; the rest of the mobile column was to push right up to area Assar-Kadala-Bhimbar to destroy the enemy base. The mobile force launched its operation at 0530 hours on January 25th. Despite earlier reverses, it was able to inflict heavy losses on the enemy at Amberala, Chordhaki, and Assar/Kadala.

Operation Kipper

Intelligence reports revealed that a strong enemy build-up was taking place at Kot. Situated about 9 km north-east of Naushahra on the highest point, Kot allowed observation over the Rajouri road to a point near Merian. It was therefore, planned to attack and capture this strong enemy position, which was a serious threat to Naushahra. Other important enemy bases in the area were at Uparla Dandesar and Pathradi. The enemy strength here was estimated to be one battalion, about 500 strong, equipped with 3" mortars, medium machine guns, light machine guns and about 400 rifles.

On January 30th, Brigadier Usman issued instructions for Operation Kipper, the code name for dislodging the enemy from Kot-Pathradi-Uparla Dandesar area and to establish a permanent picket in Kot.

The responsibility fell on 50 Para Brigade Group which included 2/2 Punjab, 3 (Para) Mahratta Light Infantry, 1 Rajput (A Coy), 3 (Para) Rajput (B Coy), 7 Cavalry (B Sqn), 1 Mahar (MMG) (Y Coy), among others. The plan was to attack Kot and Pathradi on a two-battalion front. On the left was 2/2 Punjab with objective Pt. 3227 and Kot; on the right 3 MLI with objectives Pt. 3284, Pathradi and Uparla Dandesar. The assault was timed for 0630 hours on February 1st and it was to be a silent dawn attack. The RIAF was to support the ground attack by softening the strong enemy positions.

As per a deception plan the enemy was made to believe that an advance towards Jhangar was imminent. Meanwhile, 3 MLI moved from Naushahra camp at 1915 hours on January 31st to area Pt. 2300. Enemy opposition was liquidated and Pathradi was captured by 0710 hours on February 1st. Meanwhile, 2/2 Punjab too had secured its objectives. But, the enemy launched a counter offensive almost immediately and recaptured Kot. It was after a fierce fighting that Kot was finally recovered at 1010 hours. Capture of Kot area had a significant bearing on future operations, as it was from this base that the enemy used to operate its successful efforts to cut the supply route to Naushahra. The occupation of Pathradi and Kot by the enemy would have rendered matters critical in the major attack on Naushahra that followed on February 6th.

Victory at Naushahra

Stung by the loss of Kot, the enemy launched the expected all-out attack on Naushahra on 06 February 1948. The pickets at Kot and Tain Dhar were heavily mortared between 0640 and 0715 hours. Picket No. 2 at Tain Dhar bore the brunt of the attack but they fought to the last man.

At about 0715 hours, Brigadier Usman realising the gravity of the situation sent a company of 3 (Para) Rajput to reinforce the main picket. It was the turning point of the whole battle. At Kot, fighting continued throughout the day and night of February 6/7th. Indian troops held the onslaught and beat off the enemy attacks. The estimated enemy casualties at Kot and Tain Dhar were 400 killed and 250 wounded.

The enemy also attacked the Kangota picket. This picket was heavily mortared and attacked at about 0700 hours. About a 1000-strong enemy force surrounded the picket and tried to rush it, but was beaten back in hand-to-hand fighting. Simultaneously, the enemy, approximately 5000 strong, attacked other pickets from the west and south-west.

To meet this serious threat to the Naushahra valley, Brigadier Usman decided to take the offensive and send his small reserve to attack the enemy concentration southwest of Naushahra. The valley was cleared of the hostiles by 1500 hours. In the annals of military warfare, the battle of Naushahra was par excellence a gunners battle.

The Recapture of Jhangar

Operation Bharatpur: After the victory at Naushahra on 06 February 1948, the stage was set for the recapture of Jhangar. For that it was essential to dislodge the enemy who was still holding Ambli Dhar and Kaman Gosha Gala. The responsibility to push back the enemy from Ambli Dhar fell on the 2 Jat through Operation Bharatpur, which was launched on 28 February 1948.

The plan was to launch a surprise attack at dawn after an approach march. A deceptive attack was launched in the east towards Bhata Village to mislead the enemy. The decoy worked and the enemy did not realise the threat of the main advance until 2 Jat was half way up for the attack on Ambli Dhar. Soon, Pt. 3319 on Ambli Dhar was captured and the enemy was forced to retreat to lower positions. After an hour's lull, however, there was a counter offensive by the enemy in which one Junior Commissioned Officer (JCO) and two men were killed and seven wounded. Eighty raiders were also wounded in the return fire.

Operation Vijay: By March 5th, Ambli Dhar was secured and the enemy had been cleared from Kaman Gosha Gala as well. It was now time for the final assault on Jhangar. Operation Vijay was to be completed in two phases.

In the first phase, the 19 Independent Brigade, consisting of 1 Rajput, 4 Dogra, 1 Kumaon Rifles and ancillary units, was to secure Pt. 3327 and 3283. In phase two, the 50 Para Brigade Group, consisting of 3 (Para) Maratha Light Infantry, 3 (Para) Rajput, 1 Patiala and ancillary units, was to secure Pt. 2701, Jhangar, Pt.3399 and Pt. 3374. Unknown even to the Indian troops, a squadron of the 7 Cavalry was also pushed into the operation.

The tanks arrived from Naushera camouflaged with wooden covers at night. The secret plan to push in tanks paid off, as the enemy was completely surprised by their arrival. One of the vital strategic points on the way to Jhangar was Pir Thil held by the enemy.

On March 15th, 3 MLI was sent on offensive reconnaissance to locate the enemy position in the area, but it was resisted with strength. It was now confirmed that there was an equivalent of one enemy brigade, six medium machine guns, a couple of light machine guns and two 3" mortars.

Based on the information, Brigadier Usman modified his plan and decided to attack two places on the Pir Thil feature about 360 metres apart with two battalions-the 3 MLI on the right and the 1 Patiala on the left. By March 17th, the 50 Para Brigade had captured Pir Thil Nakka and the way was now clear for the final attack on Jhangar.

The offensive started on March 18th. That day, the 3 (Para) Rajput captured Pt. 3477, following which the 50 Para Brigade, the 3 MLI and the 1 Patiala concentrated at this feature. The plan was to attack with two forward battalions-the 1 Patiala, on the right, was to secure objective ring contour and the 3 MLI, on the left, was to secure Pt. 3399 and Pt. 3574. Both the objectives were secured the same day.

The enemy fled towards Mirpur, leaving behind 46 dead and a cache of ammunition. Meanwhile, the Stuart tanks of 7 Cavalry (C Sqn), were already on their way. Brushing aside minor opposition, which resulted in the loss of one tank, the squadron along with one company of the 1 Rajput entered Jhangar at 1400 hours that day.

With the recapture of Jhangar on March 18th, the main land route leading into the Naushahra Valley was secured and the enemy's supply line was disrupted. Operation Vijay thus ended in Vijay, i.e. Victory.

The Fall of Skardu

The northern front of the Kashmir campaign included the sectors of Gurais, Skardu, Dras and Kargil, and Leh. From November 1947 to August 1948, the enemy achieved impressive successes in the region.

But equally impressive was the valour of the Indian troops who held their positions against all odds. Of particular importance was the siege of Skardu. It was at Skardu that the true spirit of a typical Indian soldier was first demonstrated. After the fall of Gilgit to the enemy in November 1947, it fell on Lt. Col. Sher Jung Thapa and his men of 6 J&K Infantry to defend Skardu.

The troops reached Skardu on December 03rd and positioned themselves inside a fort. With a total strength of about 285 men, Lt. Col. Thapa was to defend his picket against a 600-strong enemy who was equipped with modern rifles, 2" and 3" mortars and was led by professional fighters.

The enemy attacked on February 11th. From that day till August 13th, when Skardu finally fell to the enemy, it was a saga of defiance, gallantry and determination. Lt. Col. Thapa and his men repulsed waves after waves of enemy attacks. To make matters worse, the fort had hundreds of refugees men, women and children who had trusted Lt. Col. Thapa with their lives against the raiders.

The brave men held the siege for more than six months fighting not only the relentless enemy, but also ration and ammunition shortage. A major attempt to send reinforcements to the besieged men had ended in failure. There came a stage when there was just enough food to feed 70-80 mouths, but the garrison and the refugees numbered 600! Meanwhile, Kargil had fallen to the enemy.

The priority of the headquarters shifted to recapturing Kargil to establish the crucial line of communications. Lt. Col. Thapa and his men were literally forgotten. Reinforcements were few and scarce. Lt. Col. Thapa sent his last message to his commanders at 0800 hours on August 13th. That day, after holding out for six months against overwhelming odds, Skardu finally capitulated.

Offensives in the Uri Area

Uri was of great strategic importance since it commanded the routes to Domel, Poonch and Srinagar. Hence, the main objective of major offensives carried out in the Uri area was only to establish a firm base there in order to prevent the raiders from entering the Kashmir valley.

Uri had its first heavy snowfall about the middle of January 1948, resulting in this front getting more or less frozen for the time being. Activity on both sides was, therefore, confined to local patrolling only. Intelligence reports, however, showed that an enemy build-up was taking place in Uri and Mahura in order to destroy the powerhouse and to cut off the line of communication between Rampur and Uri.

By the first week of April, enemy reinforcements in this area had swelled manifolds. The Indian response had been somewhat similar and 161 Infantry Brigade-responsible for holding the area-was suitably reorganized and reinforced. Till the first week of April, both the sides were mostly involved in small raids and counter raids owing to heavy snow. With the onset of spring, vigorous offensives were launched. From the Indian perspective, the first major offensive was directed at capturing Kopra. 4 Kumaon regiment secured the objective on April 15th and Indian pickets were established there. Another major achievement during this period was the capture of Point 9062.

The Indian troops launched an attack in heavy rain. Despite slippery and steep slopes, the offensive was successful and the enemy was driven out of what was supposed to be a very strong defensive base. The threat to Mahura was finally ended when 3 Royal Garhwal secured Zambur Pattan on April 21st.

Meanwhile, a threat was developing at Kaurali where enemy in large numbers had infiltrated from Poonch. In one of the most tragic ambushes, the enemy annihilated the entire patrol party of 1 Madras, including its commander Lt. Col. Menon. A sole survivor who had escaped by hiding under a waterfall for more than three hours conveyed the tragic news to the base. The Indian troops during this period repulsed many enemy raids on various pickets. Of special significance was the fight at Nalwa-the picket described as 'Uri ka Morcha' due to its strategic importance to safeguard Uri. Jemadar Sanwal Ram who was commanding this post was awarded the Vir Chakra for successfully defending it against severe enemy onslaught.

Failure to force the Haji Pir Pass

The Haji Pir Pass, situated 22 km south of Uri along the Uri-Poonch road, was dominated on either side by high ridges, both of which were held by the enemy who was two-battalion strong and equipped with 12 medium machine guns. Despite bold attempts by the 2 (Para) Madras to evict the enemy from the ridges and break through the Pass, the objective was not secured. Overall, the strenuous efforts on the Indian forces in the Uri area met with limited success. Domel remained out of reach and Haji Pir Pass couldn't be broken through.

Operations in the Jammu Division

Operation Ranjit and Capture of Rajouri: One of the tasks assigned to Major General Kulwant Singh by Lt. Gen. Cariappa on 06 April 1948 was to carry out Operation Ranjit (earlier called Operation Mumtaz) for capturing Rajouri. The 48-km road that the Indian troops had to traverse to capture Rajouri was thickly wooded and well defended by enemy armed with machine guns and mortars.

The operation was to be completed in two phases. The first phase involved capturing Chingas, while the second phase was to capture Rajouri. The task was assigned to 19 Brigade.

To secure Chingas, it was essential to push out the enemy from the Barwali ridge. Despite heavy shelling from mortars, the enemy was forced out of his position. It was during this offensive that Captain J.N. Jatar received the Maha Vir Chakra for showing exemplary courage and presence of mind. Meanwhile, troops had also secured other objective en-route to Chingas without much opposition.

Chingas was captured on 11 April 1948. Of special mention during this period was the work done by 2nd Lt. R.R. Rane who was in-charge of clearing the road of landmines. Despite losing two of his men, and himself being wounded, he completed his task fearlessly amidst incessant enemy fire and enabled the tanks to reach Chingas. He was awarded the Param Vir Chakra for the most conspicuous gallantry.

The enemy resistance simply collapsed after the capture of Chingas. But the tanks and men had to wade across the river Tawi in water one and a half metre deep to reach Rajouri, which was captured on 12 April 1948.

Total enemy losses were estimated at 500 killed and an equal number wounded. The enemy also blew up his ammunition dump though the Indian troops captured clothing and ration stores. Three big pits around the town were full of dead bodies as a result of atrocities committed by the enemy.

i1In a well-conceived strategy to facilitate the capture of Rajouri, two brigades were to carry out diversionary operations. While 50 Para Brigade carried out its Operation Hathi successfully at a place 5 kilometre north of Jhangar, 80 Brigade did so in the Beri Pattan area. Enemy reaction to the loss of

Rajouri was to launch coordinated attacks on Jhangar and Naushera. But all these attacks were successfully repulsed by Indian troops.

Operation Birbal: While other Indian troops were busy consolidating their positions and probing enemy positions around Rajouri, 19 Brigade was planning to launch Operation Birbal to capture Thana Mandi. As per the plan, Thana Mandi was to be attacked after first capturing the feature east of Sain Samut. In a fierce battle that lasted for two and a half hours, the feature was secured but at the cost of 4 killed and 19 wounded. Thana Mandi was captured the next day, i.e. 02 May 1948 without any resistance.

3

CHIEFS OF THE INDIAN ARMY

-Field Marshal Kodandera Madappa Cariappa, OBE

Commanders-in-Chief from Inception to Independence			
Sir Robert Lockhart	Sir Roy Bucher	K.M. Cariappa	K.S. Rajendrasinhji
S.M. Shrinagesh	K.S. Thimayya	P.N. Thapar	J.N. Chaudhuri
P.P. Kumaramangalam	S.H.F.J. Manekshaw	G.G. Bewoor	T.N. Raina
O.P. Malhotra	K.V. Krishna Rao	A.S. Vaidya	K. Sundarji
V.N. Sharma	S.F. Rodrigues	B.C. Joshi	S. Roychowdhury
/V.P. Malik	S. Padmanabhan	N.C. Vij	J.J. Singh
Deepak Kapoor			

GENERAL SIR ROBERT LOCKHART, KCB, CIE, MC
C-in-C, 15 Aug 1947-31 Dec 1947
Infantry, 51 Sikhs Frontier Force

Born on 23 June 1893, Sir Robert McGregor Macdonald Lockhart was commissioned in the British Indian Army and joined 51st Sikhs Frontier Force on 08 March 1914. He served as Military Attaché in Kabul, Afghanistan from March 1934 to December 1935. He was then appointed as the Deputy Director of Staff Duties, India in December 1939 and then took over as the Director of Staff Duties, India from 1940 and held that appointment till December 1941. He was subsequently selected to serve as the Secretary of Military Department, Indian Office and held that post from 1941 to 1943. In April 1945, he was posted to the Southern Army as the General Officer Commanding-in-Chief and served in that capacity till June

1947. He was appointed as the Commander-in-Chief of the Indian Army from 15 August 1947 and served till 31 December 1947.

After the Second World War, he served on the World Scout Committee of the World Organisition of the Scout movement from 1953 to 1959. He was awarded the Bronze Wolf Award, the only distinction of the World Organisition of the Scout Movement, awarded by the World Scout Committee for exceptional services to world scouting, in 1961. He passed away in 1981.

GENERAL SIR ROY BUCHER, CB, OBE, MC

C-in-C, 31 Dec 1947-15 Jan 1949

Infantry

Born on 31 August 1895, Sir Francis Robert Roy Bucher was commissioned into the British Army on 15 August 1914 and took part in World War I with the Cameronians (Scottish Rifles) in France from 1914 to 1915.

He then joined the 55th Coke's Rifles (Frontier Force) in India in 1915 and subsequently the 31st Duke of Connaught's Own Lancers in 1916. He served with the Mahsud-a Pashtun tribe in Waziristan, Pakistan-in 1917. He attended Staff College, Camberley from 1926 to 1927 and then served as the Deputy Assistant Adjutant General in India's Deccan District from 1930 to 1932.

In 1937, he joined the 13th Duke of Connaught's Own Lancers as its Commanding Officer. He was the Commandant of Sam Browne's Cavalry (12th Frontier Force) from 1939 to 1940; the Assistant Commandant of the Indian Cavalry Training Center, India in 1940; the Assistant Adjutant General at General Headquarters from January 1941 to June 1941; the Assistant Quartermaster General at Iraq from June 1941 to March 1942; Chief Administration Officer at Southern Command, India from 1942 to 1945; the General Officer Commanding Bengal and Assam Area, India in 1946; the General Officer Commanding-in-Chief, Eastern Command, India from 1946 to 1947; the Chief of General Staff, Army Headquarters, India 1947 and finally culminating in the Commander-in-Chief and Chief of General Staff, Indian Army from 31 December 1947 to 15 January 1949. He passed away in 1980.

FIELD MARSHAL K.M. CARIAPPA, OBE
C-in-C, 15 Jan 1949-14 Jan 1953
Infantry, Rajput Regiment

Kodandera Madappa Cariappa was born on 28 January 1899 at Shanivarsanthe in erstwhile Coorg, which was centrally administered by the British. Cariappa, known as Chimma to his relatives, had his formal education in the Central High School at Madikeri, after which he pursued his college education at Presidency College, Madras. At the College, he grew up equally attached to books and plays under the guidance of renowned academicians. He was an active sportsman and played with vigour and brilliance, games like hockey and tennis. In addition to this, he loved music and had fondness for a sleight of hand tricks.

When World War I had concluded in 1918, Indian politicians of the time raised a demand to sanction Indians to the King's Commission. After strict screening, Cariappa was one among the privileged few who was selected for the first batch, which underwent rigorous pre-commission. He joined the first batch of KCIOs (King's Commissioned Indian Officers) at the Daly Cadet College in Indore and was commissioned in the Carnatic Infantry at Bombay.

Cariappa saw active service with the 37 (Prince of Wales) Dogra in Mesopotamia (present-day Iraq) and was later posted to the 2nd Rajput Light Infantry (Queen Victoria's Own) which became his permanent regimental home. He was the first Indian officer to undergo the course at Staff College, Quetta in 1933. In 1946, he was promoted as the Brigadier of the Frontier Brigade Group. It was during this time that Colonel Ayub Khan-later Field Marshal and President of Pakistan, 1962-1969-served under him.

Cariappa served in Iraq, Syria and Iran from 1941-1942 and then in Burma in 1943-1944. He spent many of his soldiering years in Wagiristan. He earned his Mentioned-in-Despatches' as DAA and QMG of General (later Field Marshal) Slim's 10th Division. He was the first Indian Officer to be given command of a unit in 1942. After command he volunteered to serve in 26 Division engaged in clearing the Japanese from Burma, where he was awarded the Order of the British Empire (OBE).

In 1947, Cariappa was the first Indian who was selected to undergo a training course at Imperial Defence College, Camberly, UK on the higher directions of war. During the traumatic period of partition, he handled the division of the Indian Army and sharing of its assets between Pakistan and India, in a most amicable, just and orderly manner. He was then the Indian officer in-charge to oversee the transition.

Post-Independence, Cariappa was appointed as the Deputy Chief of General Staff with the rank of Major General. On promotion to Lieutenant General he became the Eastern Army Commander.

On outbreak of war with Pakistan in 1947, he was moved as General Officer Commanding-in-Chief, Western Command and directed operations for the recapture of Zojila, Dras and Kargil and re-established a linkup with Leh. In all this, he showed tremendous energy in moving troops, against heavy odds and finally ensuring success.

On being appointed as the first Commander-in-Chief of an independent Indian Army on 15 January 1949, he was instrumental in;

- Integration of troops and turning an imperial army into a national army.
- Raised the Brigade of the Guards and the Parachute Regiments on an all-India caste composition.
- Raised the National Cadet Corps (NCC) and Territorial Army (TA) using troops from the Regular Army.

His career in the Army during which he had the rare distinction of being first in many spheres is a continuous tale of upward progress;

- The first Indian to be commissioned at the age of 19.

- The first Indian cadet to be commissioned from Daly Cadet College, Indore.
- The first Indian Brigadier.
- The first Indian to enter Imperial Defence College in England.
- The first Indian Officer to enter Staff College, Quetta.
- The first Indian Major General in 1947.
- The first Indian Chief of Staff.

Cariappa held no truck on commission in the Indian Army and in picturesque, forthright language remarked after the partition, "I don't care a damn if a man is a Hindu, Muslim, Sikh, Parsi or Christian as long as he plays the game to serve our country well.

This is all that matters to me." His association with the Indian Army is spread over an unbroken period of more than 29 years, during which he had wide experience of staff and command work. He lived and remained, as he said, "an Indian and to the last breath would remain an Indian. To me there is only two Sthans-Hindusthan (India) and Foujisthan (the Army)." After his retirement from Indian Army in 1953, he served as the High Commissioner to Australia and New Zealand till 1956.

Cariappa settled down amidst greenery and nature, in his own Roshanara at Madikeri after his retirement from public service. He loved the environment and the flora & fauna around him. He lived a life of simplicity and dignity, which was the hallmark of a man. He spent a lot of his leisure time educating people about cleanliness, pollution control and other essential issues.

During the 1962, the 1965 and the 1971 wars, he visited the front lines to talk to the troops and keep their morale up. Every Jawan of the Indian Army was inspired by his words. He always said, "An officer is nothing without the soldiers." He gave the following credo to the Indian officers, which remains even now the guiding spirit. He insisted that every officer carried in his breast pocket the red booklet, 'A Code of Conduct For Officers' and he would not hesitate to check accordingly. He insisted on small details, knowing full well that attention to minor matters would lead to a good future for the Army.

Apart from being a military man, Cariappa had insight about the status of the country. He is quoted as saying, "In modern warfare, a large army is not sufficient, it needs industrial potential behind it. If the army is the first line of defence, the industry is the second."

Cariappa had even said that "soldiers know the facility of wars to solve the internal problems. We ought to be ashamed that today they had more peace in war than peace in peace." Such insight has placed him above many in this field. "Army is there to serve the Government of the day, and we should make sure that it does not get mixed up with party politics. A soldier is above politics and should not believe in caste or creed," was another insight of this soldier.

He was affectionately known as Kipper and as the story goes, a British officer's wife found it difficult to pronounce Cariappa and shortened it to a convenient Kipper. The name stuck. In the years that followed, his colleagues, and others who knew him well, continued to call him Kipper. Cariappa had great concern for the nation and saw himself as an Indian first and only then as an officer of high rank, which is one of the reasons why he is still held in high esteem by his fellow men in his native Coorg and the rest of the country.

Cariappa took active part in the reorganisation of armed forces in many foreign countries. He was a much traveled man and visited parts of China, Japan, United States, Great Britain, Canada and most of the European countries. He was conferred with 'Order of the Chief Commander of the Legion of Merit' by American President, Harry S. Truman. As a token of heartfelt gratitude of the nation for the exemplary service rendered by him, the Government of India conferred the rank of Field Marshal on Cariappa in 1983. If there is one man whom the Kodavas can identify with reverence and respect it is undoubtedly Cariappa.

Field Marshal K.M. Cariappa is an unforgettable name in the history of Indian Army. Old soldiers never die, they just fade away and he has proved this proverb. He has been a legend in his lifetime and he has left an indelible impression that would inspire the people of India, for a long time to come. He was the first and the last Commander-in-Chief of the Indian Army and was a man of great discipline and integrity. He breathed his last at Bangalore at a ripe age of 94, on 15 May 1993. The legendary hero of this great country who professed duty, discipline and loyalty to the nation is now history.

In 1953, General Kodandera Madappa Cariappa became India's third High Commissioner to Australia. He was 53 and had recently stepped down from his demanding role as the first Commander-in-Chief of the Army of Independent India. He did not particularly want to go to Australia, but Prime Minister Nehru had insisted and that, of course, settled the matter. Cariappa was an intriguing choice as High Commissioner. He was a revered figure, admired for his substantial accomplishments and the high character that distinguished his army career. As India's pre-eminent soldier, he had worked and fought alongside the British and was comfortable in their company. Although adept at the silky arts of persuasion, Cariappa was a soldier who spoke his mind. He was not a diplomat by training or by inclination.

Cariappa (Kipper to his army colleagues and Carry to the world at large) was a lively conversationalist and a generous companion. An Australian novelist described him as a "tall, striking man still capable of playing a couple of useful chukkas of polo...in some ways more British than the British, but with a good deal more elasticity and charm." There was certainly elasticity, but also discipline and pride. Our novelist judged that the General had gone down well in Australia. No other High Commissioner in Canberra at the time had travelled more extensively or was better known. He visited many small country towns, places far removed from Canberra's cocktail circuit and the brittle tinkle of polite conversation. Cariappa had come to like Australia and Australians, although he had his reservations.

The Immigration Issue

In March 1956, one month before the end of his Australian mission, "Kipper" received a letter from an old army friend and India hand, Field Marshal Sir Claude Auchinleck. The "Auk" remarked on how foolishly provocative it was to allow so much of Australia to remain "empty" when land-hungry Asia was at the doorstep. Cariappa had a better understanding of the limits to population growth in Australia. He was well aware that vast deserts and unpredictable rainfall imposed severe limits on settlement.

Cariappa did not think Australia was the answer to India's over-population, but he resented the White Australia policy that restricted immigration to Europeans and he certainly made his feelings known in private. It was a time when Australia was receptive to some fresh thinking about immigration. Throughout the 1950s domestic criticism of the White Australia policy gained support in progressive circles. There were even whispers of dissent in External Affairs where some people recognised that the rigid application of immigration policy was doing Australia damage throughout Asia, not the least in India.

The only thing many Asians knew about post-war Australia was that it did not want them as immigrants no matter what their gifts or talents. Cariappa felt the insult keenly. The Indian Army had tied the Japanese down in Burma, a crucial contribution to Australian security during the war. Many of his ex-army colleagues from these campaigns would make excellent settlers, but rather than accept them Australia had thrown open its doors to European immigrants, including Italians and others from former enemy countries. These were welcomed, but no Indians need apply.

The policy was particularly galling because Cariappa was frequently told of Australia's new appreciation of its Asian neighbours. In the 1950s, strenuous efforts were made to show that Australia was Asia-friendly. Government ministers readily claimed that Colombo Plan students studying in Australian universities experienced no racial intolerance and no "colour bar".

Australia's Future Lay in Asia

Richard Casey, the Minister for External Affairs, took charge of the hospitality offensive. A former Governor of Bengal, Casey was committed to the White Australia policy intellectually and pragmatically. He believed in racial homogeneity and knew that the quickest way to end a political career in Australia was to criticise restrictive immigration. However, Casey also recognised that Australia's future lay in Asia. He used neighbourly allusions to describe the Commonwealth as a family, exchanging confidences, sharing a joke and speaking frankly when required, a grouping drawn together by shared experiences.

The irony was that at Independence Lord Louis Mountbatten had been required to use all his persuasive powers to keep India within the Commonwealth family. It is less well known that he also attempted to secure some relaxation of the White Australia policy on India's behalf. Had they known of it, ordinary Australians would have condemned this strategy. It was precisely the kind of trade-off that made them suspicious of the titled elite who, they believed, ran the Empire. They suspected the top people didn't think much either of the White Australia policy or of white Australians for sticking to it so vehemently. A suspicion developed that Cariappa was working hand in glove with those who wanted to see an end to the restrictive immigration programme.

Conspiracy theories do not require much nourishment in order to flourish. From the late 19th Century some Australians suspected that Britain would put the commercial interests of its "polyglot" Empire before the Australian ideal of a racially pure continent set aside for the development of the "higher races". One prominent zealot declared that it was Australia's "sacred duty" to breed "a pure race in a clean continent". This seemed an ideal that Britain did not understand and would not want to defend.

The Shadow of Suspicion

That Cariappa moved freely among people like Claude Auchinleck and Viscount William Slim, Australia's Governor

General, fuelled suspicion. He was also a great hit among titled Australians and particularly, so it seems, among titled women. This set more raw nerves quivering. In the demonology of the time, there is no more a menacing figure than the suave "oriental" with an impressive command of English. We encounter one of the worst (or finest) examples of the type in Madge Peterson's The Lure of the Little Drum, set in India just before the First World War. The villain is the sinister Ishaq Khan. He is tall, handsome, accomplished and, most worrying of all, Oxford educated. Beautifully shaped sentences roll from his tongue and, inevitably, the exquisite but susceptible Esther falls for his charms. The harem and an early and humiliating death await her. Khan (unaccountably) is not interested in Esther's shapely profile. His purpose is to degrade "what we white men hold so dear, our women".

Cariappa may well have thought that being a handsome, accomplished and beautifully spoken member of the Commonwealth would be well-received in Australia and proof that educated Indians could make a positive contribution to Australian development. He may have hoped that he could win over public opinion. Cariappa's charms certainly worked wonders in some quarters, but this may have deepened suspicions in others. The Ishaq Khan principle reveals that certain accomplishments were considered threatening. Cariappa was a dangerously seductive figure. He was a war hero and a thinker deeply versed in British and in Indian traditions. He could expound the Upanishads and execute a perfect fox trot. If the occasion required, he could do both simultaneously. He was witty and charming over drinks and could be wonderfully theatrical as he flourished his personally monogrammed Sobranie black Russian cigarettes (ordered in batches of 1,000 from London). And he was unattached.

Australian upper class ladies, some with titles, began to fall at his feet. Edith, a resident of one of Sydney's best suburbs, explained to "Dear Carry" that she was studying international affairs, paying particular attention to Australia's Asian neighbours. By "close study and personal associations" she hoped to banish English prejudice from her system. Some weeks later she writes again. Somehow the Marabar Caves had found their way to Australia. Edith appealed to Cariappa to overlook a recent episode in which she had behaved as a "silly ass" for "intimating any undue personal feelings towards you". We do not know how Cariappa responded to being the object of Edith's bold experiment in self-improvement.

In some eyes these may have been suspicious conquests, part of a cleverly laid plan to turn susceptible British Australians like Edith against the White Australia policy and have Australia opened up to immigration from India. Here was another potent apprehension, deeply embedded in Australia's white history: the flood from the north, the obliterating "yellow wave" sweeping an insecure white Australia right off the map.

The contradictory pressures shaping the post-war world and the now multiracial British Commonwealth were not easily contained. Cariappa quickly discovered this when in June in 1954 he visited northern Queensland. This was a voyage into tropical Australia and the famous "empty north", a part of Australia acutely sensitive to its lack of population. Public opinion in Queensland was stridently opposed to Asian immigration of any kind. After a long and tiring trip Cariappa returned to Brisbane where he agreed to grant an interview to the Brisbane *Courier Mail.*

The Brisbane Controversy

What Cariappa said is now difficult to ascertain. He was reported to have said that Australia's restrictive immigration policies might drive India and Pakistan out of the Commonwealth and into the hands of the communist powers. He added that Australians were more interested in the colour of a person's skin (tapping the back of his hand for effect) than in their hearts and minds. He rejected the fond talk about the Commonwealth family when it was clear that Australia preferred any white immigrant to the Commonwealth's coloured ex-servicemen.

The *Courier Mail* story was soon picked up nationally and reported overseas, including in India. For white Australia diehards, Cariappa's statement was all the proof they needed that secret plans were being hatched to do away with the White Australia policy.

Yet although Cariappa was always prepared to make it clear in private discussions that the White Australia policy was repugnant and offensive, there is no evidence that he or the Indian government ever wanted to force the issue. Although Cariappa was roundly condemned in some quarters, to his supporters his Brisbane comments seemed to state an obvious truth: all the efforts to win over the neighbours and create a friendly image in the region were negated by the White Australia policy. It could not be explained away, no matter how hard Casey and others tried.

Cariappa was shaken and angered by the Brisbane controversy. He thought of returning to India, but believed this might be interpreted as an official rebuke and a recall. The old soldier in him refused to surrender. He would not give his Australian critics this comfort. Cariappa also found more indirect means of making his case about the Commonwealth family. He was instrumental in founding the Commonwealth Club in Canberra and as he travelled Australia he made a point of visiting war memorials. In the small town of Gundagai, Cariappa and his Sikh driver found the local memorial overgrown with weeds. These two spectacular figures got to work and soon had the memorial looking ship-shape.

The story found its way into the papers and became another part of the Cariappa mythology. No one could reasonably object to a soldier paying his respects to fallen colleagues, but few could have missed his point that India had been a loyal friend in the Second World War. Cariappa's impact is not easy to assess, but he gave heart to those agitating for immigration reform and consistently drew attention to the logic of Australia seeing itself as part of Asia. In simply being who he was he made white Australia re-consider its embarrassingly insular and offensive prejudices. And more than any other figure in Australia at the time, he spoke out for and embodied the newly independent India.

GENERAL MAHARAJ K.S. RAJENDRASINHJI, DSO
C-in-C, 14 Jan 1953-31 March 1955
COAS, 01 April 1955-14 May 1955
Armoured Corps, 2 Lancers

General Maharaj Kumar Shri Rajendrasinhji (also known as Maharaj Shri Ranjitsinhji and Rajendrasinhji Jadeja) assumed charge of the Indian Army, as the 2nd Chief of Army Staff, on 14 January 1953. Born on 15 June 1899, he attended Rajkumar College at Rajkot in Gujarat and then joined the Royal Military Academy (RMA) at Sandhurst on 10 September 1919. Commissioned into the Indian Army in 1921, he joined the 2nd Royal Lancers in 1922 as a Second Lieutenant.

He held various ranks and offices in the British Indian Army and served with distinction during the Second World War. He was also deputed to serve as Military Attaché in Washington D.C. in 1945-46. He took over as the Commander-in-Chief of the Indian Army on 14 January 1953, a post he held until 31 March 1955. Since the President of India was appointed as the Commander-in-Chief of the Indian Armed Forces, his designation was changed to the Chief of Army Staff on 01 April 1955.

In 1941 he went to North Africa, to serve as a squadron commander in his regiment. Early in that year the 3rd Indian Motor Brigade, of which the 2nd Royal Lancers was a part, was surrounded at Mechili by vastly superior German and Italian forces. As a last desperate measure the encircled regiments decided to force their way through the enemy and into the desert.

The then-Major Maharaj Rajendrasinhji, with two squadrons of his regiment, were acting as rearguard and had to wait for their divisional headquarters to move out. Most of his regiment was overwhelmed by a German tank attack, although his own squadron was not seriously involved. It was then that he charged with his men straight into the enemy, crashing through their battery of guns. After shaking off pursuit, they hid themselves in the hills for the rest of the day. Moving out once more at night they eventually reached the place of safety, but not before having a couple of skirmishes with the enemy. His squadron fought the actions successfully and brought back 60 prisoners. For his courageous leadership and determined action he was awarded the DSO (Distinguished Service Order), the first Indian to be honoured with such an award in World War II.

The Independence of India in 1947 caused an upheaval in both the security situation and the dynamics of the Indian Army. The partition of India meant the division of the Indian Army, which was concurrently called upon to deal with several critical security situations arising from the partition of the country and the integration of the princely states. Also during this period, British officers who held most of the senior ranks in the Indian Army were gradually disengaged, being replaced with Indian officers. During this critical period, Rajendrasinhji was called upon to shoulder many onerous responsibilities and received rapid promotion in rank commensurately. He was made Brigadier in 1946, Major General in 1947 and Lieutenant General in 1948. He served successively as General Officer Commanding (GOC) of Delhi and East Punjab (1947-48), GOC Eastern Command (1948) and GOC Southern Command (1948-53). Operation Polo, which resulted in the integration of Hyderabad State with India, was executed during his term in office as GOC Southern Command.

Addressing a passing-out parade at the National Defence Academy in Dehra Dun on 09 June 1953, General Maharaj Rajendrasinhji advised the newly-commissioned Army officers to remember that loyalty, duty, discipline, physical & mental fitness and a thorough knowledge of their military profession were the most important attributes expected of an officer and their achievements will require really hard work through their Army career. He also said, "To-day you are on the threshold of your careers as officers of the Indian Army. Tomorrow you will become members of a brotherhood that has a code of honour and sense of duty unequalled in any other profession in the world. See to it that your responsibilities and obligations to this brotherhood do not find you lacking in spirit or energy. Your loyalty to your country and the Army must be the dominating factor. Keep abreast of your profession, and ensure that you keep pace with new weapons and their effects in applied military science.

The men who respect your professional knowledge, and have confidence in your leadership will follow you anywhere. You must be the leader of your men and cannot afford to lag behind being out of condition. Go out shooting, trekking, mountaineering, go in for games that develop sound judgment, decision-making and team work, because these are the qualities that will make your career a success."

General Rajendrasinhji served in the Indian Army with distinction for 34 years till his retirement on 14 May 1955. Married to Maya Kunwarba in 1928, he had three children. He passed away on 01 January 1964.

General Rajendrasinhji's Medals & Decorations

- First Indian commissioned officer to be awarded the DSO during World War II
- India General Service Medal (1941)
- Africa & Burma stars
- Defence & War medals (1945)
- Officer of the Legion of Merit of the USA (1948)
- Indian Independence Medal (1947)
- George V Silver Jubilee Medal (1935)
- George VI Coronation Medal (1937)

GENERAL S.M. SHRINAGESH
COAS, 14 May 1955-07 May 1957
Infantry, Kumaon Regiment

General Satyawant Mallannah Shrinagesh assumed charge of the Indian Army, as the 3rd Chief of Army Staff, on 14 May 1955. He was the eldest son of Dr Shrinagesh Mallannah, who was the personal physician to the Nizam of Hyderabad. Born in 1903 at Kolhapur, Maharashtra he went to a public school in England and entered Cambridge University in 1921.

Among the earliest batches of Indians to be nominated for the Sandhurst Military Academy in the U.K., he won the Quetta Cup for the best man at arms entering the Indian Army in 1923. He was subsequently commissioned into the 19th Hyderabad Regiment (presently known as the Kumaon Regiment) on 30 August 1923. After a brief association with the North Staffordshire Regiment, he was posted to the 2/1 Madras Pioneers with which he served mostly in Burma until it was disbanded. In 1933, he joined the 4/19th Hyderabad Regiment and served in Singapore as its adjutant. In December 1939, he was posted as an Instructor at the Indian Military Academy, Dehra Dun.

From 17 December 1942 till 28 August 1945, he was the Commanding Officer of the 6/19th Hyderabad Regiment (now 6th Kumaon). He then officiated as the Brigade Commander of the 64th Indian Infantry Brigade of the 19th Indian (Dagger) Division in Burma from August 1945. He was then appointed as the first Indian Commandant of the Kumaon Regimental Centre in Agra on 02 October 1946 and served in that capacity till 12 December 1946. He was then chosen to lead the 268th Infantry Brigade British Commonwealth Occupation Force (BCOF) in post World War II Japan and served in that post till 1947. He was also Brigade Commander of the famous Lushai Brigade in Burma in 1947. He was selected to go to Germany as Deputy Chief of the Indian Military Mission in November 1945. In that capacity, he also worked as the Economic Adviser & Consul looking after the interests of Indian nationals in Germany and locating missing Prisoners of War (POWs).

On his return from Japan, he was promoted to Major General and was appointed the General Officer Commanding of the Madras Area. From January 1948, he was appointed as the Adjutant General at the Army Headquarters and held that post till August of the same year. He also commanded the 5th Corps (later designated as 15th Corps). He was appointed the overall commander of all troops in Jammu & Kashmir during the 1947-48 Indo-Pak War and held this command till the ceasefire on 01 January 1949. Promoted to the rank of Lieutenant General in 1950, he was chosen as the GOC-in-C Western Command on 15 January 1949. He was then appointed as the GOC-in-C Southern Command and held that post, till he assumed charge as the Army Chief on 14 May 1955.

General Shrinagesh retired on 07 May 1957, completing 34 years of distinguished military service. Post retirement, he served as the Governor of Assam from 1959 to 1962, then as the Governor of Andhra Pradesh from 1962 to 1964 and finally as Governor of Mysore (now Karnataka) from 1964 to 1965. From 1959 to 1957, he also served as the Principal of the Administrative Staff College in Hyderabad. He passed away on 27 December 1977.

GENERAL K.S. THIMAYYA
Padma Vibushan, DSO, MD, ADC
COAS, 07 May 1957-07 May 1961
Infantry, Kumaon Regiment

General Kodandera Subayya Thimayya assumed charge of the Indian Army, as the 4th Chief of Army Staff, on 07 May 1957. Timmy, as he was better known, was a graduate of the Royal Indian Military College in Dehra Dun, a necessary stepping stone for a commission in the Indian Army. He was commissioned into the Army in 1926 and was attached to the Highland Light Infantry. He was soon posted to the 4/19th Hyderabad (the name changed to Kumaon in 1946) Regiment. He cut his soldiering skills on that famous training ground in the Northwest Frontier (present-day Pakistan), battling recalcitrant Pathan tribals.

Timmy's merits were soon recognized and just before World War II he was posted as an Adjutant at the University Training Corps in Madras, as a fitting example for young Indian undergraduates interested in joining the Indian Army, of what a good soldier should be. Due to an illness he was evacuated to India in 1939, just as World War II broke out, and was posted as the Second-in-Command of the Hyderabad Regimental Centre. He did however serve during the war and his record as a company commander, battalion commander and brigade commander came to the fore in operations against the tenacious Japanese in Burma.

He did his Staff College in Quetta and was posted to the 26th Infantry Division as a Grade II Staff Officer. His infantry division was conducting jungle warfare training and was preparing to go into Burma to face the Japanese Army during World War II. In Burma, he was posted to his old battalion as a Commanding Officer, which he led with outstanding success in battle. For a short while the battalion was under the command of the 3rd Command Brigade, with Brigadier C R Hardy at the helm, who during the height of a battle presented a trophy to the 8/19th Hyderabad. It was a green beret-the command's head dress-with a little typed message on a card, "We cannot buy anything here but we would like you to accept this as a token of our great admiration for the bravery and achievement of your battalion." He was also promoted to the rank of Brigadier in the field! For his outstanding service in battle, he was awarded the much coveted Distinguished Service Order (DSO) and also Mention-in-Despatches.

His innate talents of professional soldiering and leadership were soon recognized by Field Marshal Sir Claude Auchinleck, the Commander-in-Chief of the Indian Army. He was specially selected to lead the 268th Indian Infantry Brigade as part of the British Commonwealth Occupation Force in Japan after World War II. He got this assignment due to his outstanding battle experience as a Brigadier and being the only Indian to command a battle formation in the field. As an independent brigade, the 268th had done excellent work in the Burma Campaign and it had to represent, in Japan, the might & valour of the Indian Army. India made great contributions in stopping and later defeating the Axis forces and had raised the greatest volunteer fighting force in all of history, with more than two million men. More than two-thirds of the Allied land forces in South-East Asia were men of the Indian Army and among them were the original battalions of the 268th Brigade. It was now to be commanded by Timmy, who had won great honour and renown in the fighting against Japan.

Timmy proved to be an outstanding commander and his diplomatic skills emerged as he had to deal with General Douglas MacArthur, the Supreme Allied Commander of the Southwest

Pacific Theatre, the other Allies and the vanquished Japanese. His popularity was to be seen to be believed and he was most suited by his personality, charm of manners and unassailable reputation, to impress on the Japanese the calibre of Indian commanders. He represented the country during the surrender of the Japanese in Singapore, followed by the surrender of the Japanese in the Philippines. At the ceremony of Japanese surrender in Singapore, Timmy signed on behalf of India. He was awarded the 'Keys to Manila' when he was sent to the Philippines. As Indian Independence approached, he was recalled to India by Field Marshal Sir Auchinleck for greater things.

He returned to India in 1947, during the Partition, as member of the committee to agree to the allotment of weapons, equipment and regiments that were to remain in India, or to be allotted to Pakistan. Soon after the commission was completed, he was promoted to the rank of Major General and was then assigned the command of the Fourth Infantry Division and also to take over the Punjab Boundary Force, dealing with the exodus and intake of refugees fleeing to their respective countries. His next appointment was command of the 19th Infantry Division in Jammu & Kashmir to drive the raiders and the Pakistan Army out of the Kashmir Valley. He succeeded in driving them beyond Uri and he ordered Stuart Light Tanks of the 7th Light Cavalry to the dizzy heights of the Zoji La Pass, to drive out the entrenched raiders and Pakistan Army regulars from the dominating heights.

He established the best of relations with Sheikh Abdullah and Bakshi Ghulam Mohammad and even Prime Minister Nehru, but his pleas to give him three more months to drive the raiders back to Muzzarfarabad fell on deaf ears and instead, Prime Minister Nehru went to the United Nations (UN). The rest is history.

Thereafter, Timmy served as the Commandant of the prestigious Indian Military Academy, Dehra Dun. The experience gained by him in Japan stood him in good stead when he was specially selected by the United Nations to head the Neutral Nations Repatriation Commission in Korea. It was a very sensitive and delicate task dealing with unruly Chinese and Korean prisoners. Here again, through sheer charisma, impartiality, firmness and diplomacy, he completed this task to the satisfaction of the world body. He returned to India and served as the Chief of the Southern Command and took over the reins of the Indian Army on 07 May 1957.

In 1959, he handed his resignation in protest to Prime Minister Nehru due to Defence Minister V.K. Krishna Menon's blatant interference in purely Army matters. Fortunately for the Indian Army, and the nation, Prime Minister Nehru persuaded him to withdraw his resignation and he continued as the Army Chief till his retirement on 07 May 1961, completing 35 years of distinguished military service.

After retirement from the Indian Army, the UN sought his services yet once again when he was appointed as the Commander of UN Forces in Cyprus (UNFICYP) in July 1964. He carried out this ticklish issue with consummate diplomatic skill earning the confidence of both parties. Alas, he passed away during his tenure as UNFICYP in December 1965 and his mortal remains were flown to Bangalore for the last rites. Of all the eulogies for him, the late Lieutenant General Premindra Singh Bhagat, VC (Retd.) summed it up best, "A General Thimayya is not born in every generation. The likes of him there will seldom be a soldier. The General is a man's man, the Army his soul and his soul the Army."

General Thimayya or Timmy, also more familiarly known by us as Dubbu, were old family friends. When he visited us, he used to come roaring into the colony, in his Ford car, with a couple of piglets strapped to the carrier of his car. In the evenings, he would drive my younger sister Bolly, my younger brother Bunny and myself at great speed and go around a huge tree located near Sivasamudram's famous landmark, twin waterfalls. On Christmas Day in 1926, there was a big party at the local club and we all left for the party including Dubbu. At the party, when everybody were enjoying themselves, one of the persons got up to sing. However his voice sounded a little better than a fog horn. Dubbu, in his enthusiasm to silence the singer, threw a potato at him which landed straight in his open mouth. There were roars of laughter amongst the revellers.

In 1926, after his commission as an officer in the Indian Army, he was posted to the Highland Light Infantry, then based at Bangalore. As the champion athlete of his Regiment, his fellow British officers wanted him to be a member of the Bangalore Club. However the recommendation of the British Officers were turned down by the Club's Committee, as at that time, no Indian could be a member. In protest, his fellow British Officers all resigned en-bloc from the club. In 1935, he married my elder sister Nina, who had returned to India after her education in France. In May 1935, his battalion was located at Quetta (present-day Pakistan) which suffered a devastating earthquake and Nina helped in comforting the homeless refugees of the earthquake. She was awarded the KAISER-I-HIND medal for her social work at the tender age of nineteen, the youngest to do so.

In 1941, I served as a Sepoy in the Regiment of Artillery at Muttra (today known as Mathura), a short distance from Agra. In 1942, I was selected for an Officers' Commission and did my training at the Royal Indian Military Academy, Dehra Dun and was then later commissioned into the 19th Hyderabad Regimental Centre at Agra. Dubbu's younger brother Freddy (later killed in action in Jammu & Kashmir), a very great friend of mine, was also posted to Agra. We young officers were billeted in a huge house which had a large drawing cum dining room surrounded by four large bed rooms and bathrooms. Freddy and I stayed in one of those rooms and we had local servants who polished our shoes, saw to the upkeep of our uniforms and the washing of our linen. However the food in the officers' mess was insipid and we were getting fed up of eating it all the time.

We young officers decided to have a party. There were ten of us. On a Saturday night, we went to the mess, nibbled at the food, said goodnight to Colonel Campbell who was surprised at our sudden departure. Our civilian bearers were told that they had to lay out a sumptuous meal of biryani, chicken, parotas, veggies and dancing girls (for which Agra was famous) for all of us, including the musicians as well. All of us, including the lovely dancing girls who were from Jaisalmer, the musicians, food and drink, and our bearers to act as servers, were having one whale of a time when at about 11 o'clock at night, Colonel Campbell and the Second-in-Command, Major Thimayya appeared.

Everything came to a standstill. The girls stopped singing and shaking their hips. The musicians were paralysed and we were frozen and thought to ourselves, "Now we have had it." Women were strictly forbidden to enter any Army bachelor quarters. Colonel Campbell asked as to why we were so silent, but there was not a single peep from any of us. He turned around to Dubbu and said, "Don't you think we should join them?" and Dubbu, ever ready for fun, agreed whole heartedly. We were so relieved and all of us had a blast that night, with the Colonel and the Major joining in, shaking their legs or dancing with the beautiful girls. The party got over at 2 o'clock in the morning, with Colonel Campbell and Dubbu having to stagger home, but not before we put them both in a tonga. The next time Dubbu and I met was in Rangoon, when he was on his way to Singapore to represent the Indian Army for the surrender of the Japanese. He was then a Brigadier with a DSO and a Mention-in-Despatches. From the surrender at Singapore, he went on to Manila, where he received the keys to the city. Later on, he was to command the 268th Indian Infantry Brigade as part of the British Commonwealth Occupation Force in Japan after the Second World War.

Dubbu was called back to India in 1947, as the partition of India was in progress, and was promoted to the rank of Major General. I too landed in India from Burma, whilst the partition riots were in full ferocity. I had to report to Army HQ in New Delhi for my posting orders, and was told that I was to report to Dubbu as his ADC in Jalandhar. Upon reaching Jalandhar, I stayed at the Officers Mess and waited for four days to report for duty. I was getting impatient doing nothing, and was longing to report back to my unit. On the fifth day, I received a message ordering me to report to Major General Thimayya at his residence immediately. A truck was waiting to collect me and

I quickly hopped in and reported to the General. I saluted him and said, "Captain Cariappa reporting for duty as ADC Sir!" He then asked, "Who sent you as my ADC?" I replied, "Sir, I did not want to be an ADC. I am too senior for the job, and I should be with my battalion at this time with all the disturbances going in due to the massive flow of refugees from Pakistan and those also moving in great hordes from India." He then told me that I had to be his ADC for the moment and until he found a suitable replacement, I had to stay put. The official interview ended and then we sat down and chatted about our home affairs. During my stay as his ADC, nobody at the Divisional Headquarters knew we were related. It was always "Yes Sir" and "No Sir" with Dubbu and at my farewell party (after finding my replacement) where everyone knew the rest of my family, they were surprised to know that we were related.

Dubbu had two responsibilities. He was the GOC 4th Infantry Division and also of the Punjab Boundary Force, and he maintained direct, personal contact with his counterpart in Pakistan. He made frequent official visits of the border areas and led huge Muslim refugee columns to Pakistan and did the same with Indian refugee columns, by having them follow his vehicle along the route. He was tremendously popular and well respected on both sides, but that still did not stop the carnage between the citizens of India and Pakistan.

The route was lined by the most ghastly sights and the stench of rotting human flesh in the thousands was unbearable. After completing that task in true 'Thimayya' fashion, he was posted as the Commandant of the Indian Military Academy and then later on as Quarter Master General (QMG) at Army HQ in New Delhi. In that post, he sorted out the 'Baniya System' that was prevalent in all units whereby the local contractor supplied all wants of the men in the matter of food, drink, cigarettes and civilian clothing. He stopped all contractors and units were made to run their own canteens with profits going to the unit itself. Today, it has become a very big organisation called the Canteen Department and is headed by a Major General, with all canteen items sold at a very cheap rate, the profits going to all units every year, some of which is used to finance officers, jawans and families who are in need of financial assistance and medical treatment.

In 1953, the United Nations appointed him as the Chairman of the Neutral Nations Repatriation Commission in Korea to solve the problem of the North and South Korean POWs. He was awarded the Padma Vibushan for his services rendered during his UN tenure, was promoted to the rank of Lieutenant General and took over as the GOC Western Command and later on as the GOC Southern Command. After his retirement from the Indian Army, he was appointed as Commander of UN Forces in Cyprus (UNFICYP) in July 1964. His old regiment, the Highland Light Infantry, was under his command and the young officers of the regiment were surprised when he went around mentioning the names of the soldiers he knew, as many of them were the sons of soldiers who had served with him early on in his army career.

During his tenure as Commander of UNFICYP, he was called on by President Dr Sarvepalli Radhakrishnan and was told that he would be reinstated into the Indian Army and would be appointed as Chairman, Chiefs of Staff Committee. Unfortunately, he passed away before it could come into effect. Back in 1947, he was recommended by Admiral Lord Mountbatten, the then Governor General and by Prime Minister Nehru to take over as the Army Chief, but Defence Minister Gopalaswamy Iyengar opposed it, as he said that Dubbu was very young (in his early forties) and his talent would be wasted if he had to retire after doing his tenure as Army Chief. On his death at Cyprus, the regiment that did the Honour Guard and sounded the last post was the Highland Light Infantry, the regiment that he first served in. The Government of Cyprus, named a road after him in their nation and published a stamp in his name.

The late Lieutenant General Harbaksh Singh, PVSM, VC (Retd.) who served under Dubbu in several military operations and as his staff officer later on, had this to say about Dubbu, "I had an exceptional opportunity to study General Thimayya not only as a soldier on the battlefield in Jammu & Kashmir, but also during peace time as his Principal Staff Officer, when he was Army Commander, Western Command. I was able to see him both as a military leader as well as a man. In his official dealings, he would not let his personal interests or prejudices weigh with him. Yet whether in office or outside, he was always relaxed, jovial, friendly and freely exuding goodwill and bonhomie.

People were generally fond of him as a man. He was fond of the nicer things of life and was often seen enjoying himself in five-star hotels and restaurants in the metropolis of Delhi. He once told me, when he was COAS in Delhi, that one morning Panditji (Prime Minister Nehru) sent for him in his office, and obviously tutored by Intelligence Staff, suggested that he should not be seen at public places late at nights as it created a bad impression. To this he humorously replied, 'Panditji isn't that better than planning a coup in the middle of the night?' Panditji, I believe, laughed it off-such was his confidence in the General's integrity."

Dubbu's death was a great loss to our country and his achievements are sadly not lauded by our countrymen. Our people have not realised what an outstanding soldier and diplomat he was. A person who was loved by his soldiers and greatly respected in international circles. He always set a very high example of courage and steadfastness under the most dangerous conditions in the battlefield and that is why he was so loved and respected by all ranks under his command. He was undoubtedly a born leader of men, if there was one. He instantly won the confidence of his subordinates through his forthrightness, practical approach to problems and an even handed attitude to both his seniors and juniors alike.

He had the knack of getting the best out of those who served under him and soon established his relationship with them as their hero. His greatest quality as a military leader was that he never sought credit for himself, but always gave it is to his subordinates, and that is why they were ready to do their best for him. His human relationship was the epitome of his popularity and general acceptance among the public. He was by nature generous and forgiving and he never thought ill of any one, nor was any one inimically inclined towards him, barring one or two of his contemporaries who were victims of professional jealously. As the old saying goes and is still very much valid, "A prophet has no value in his own country."

GENERAL PRAN NATH THAPAR

COAS, 07 May 1961-19 Nov 1962

Infantry, Bengal Infantry & Punjab

General Pran Nath Thapar assumed charge of the Indian Army, as the 5th Chief of Army Staff, on 07 May 1961. Born on 08 May 1906, he was educated at Government College in Lahore and was commissioned into the 1st Punjab Regiment from the Royal Military Academy at Sandhurst in 1926. As a regimental officer, he spent nearly ten years with the 1st Punjab Regiment and later attended staff courses at Quetta (in present-day Pakistan) and at Minley-Manor in England.

During the Second World War, he saw service in Burma in 1941, followed by a tenure in 1943-44 in the Middle East and Italy. In 1945, he was appointed as the Assistant Military Secretary, General Headquarters in India. Later on, he was selected to serve on the Army Reorganization Committee. After victory over Japan in 1945, he commanded the 1st Battalion of his parent regiment in Indonesia during the national trouble in that country in 1946. Later he commanded the 161st Indian Infantry Brigade in East Bengal.

On the advent of partition and during its first turbulent months, General Thapar served as the Director of Military Operations & Intelligence at Army Headquarters from August 1947 to December 1947. In November 1947, he was promoted to Major General and officiated for a few months as the Chief of General Staff and later appointed as the Military Secretary, a post he held till August 1949. This was followed by his appointment as the Master General of Ordnance from August 1949 to April 1950. He served as the Colonel of The Rajputana Rifles from 18 July 1949 to 20 July 1963.

General Thapar commanded an Infantry Division for about four years and was promoted to the rank of Lieutenant General in 1954 as Commander of a Corps. He held this appointment till December 1955 when he was selected to attend the Imperial Defence College in London from January to December 1956. On successful completion of the course, he was appointed as the General Officer Commanding-in-Chief, Southern Command and later took over as the General Officer Commanding-in-Chief, Western Command on 25 May 1959.

He hails from a distinguished family and brought to his high office a wealth of experience & knowledge gained on various fronts during his 35 years of service. He was forced to resign from the Indian Army on 19 November 1962, after the debacle of the 1962 Indo-China War. A keen tennis and golf player, he was at one time the Defence Services' tennis champion. After retirement, he was appointed as Indian Ambassador to Afghanistan from August 1964 and held that appointment till 01 January 1969. He passed away on 23 January 1975, at the age of 69.

GENERAL J.N. CHAUDHURI, OBE
COAS, 19 Nov 1962-07 June 1966
Armoured Corps, 16 CAV and 7 LC

General Joyanto Nath Chaudhuri assumed charge of the Indian Army, as the 6th Chief of Army Staff, on 19 November 1962. Born on 10 June 1908, he received his early education at St. Xavier's College in Calcutta and later at Highgate School in London. Obtaining a nomination to the Royal Military College at Sandhurst in 1926, he was commissioned into the Indian Army in February 1928 and subsequently joined the 7th Light Cavalry. In 1940, he went overseas with the 5th Indian Division and saw service in Sudan, Eritrea, Abyssinia (present-day Ethiopia) and the western deserts of Africa. He rose from the rank of Captain to Lieutenant Colonel within a span of two years. He was present at the capitulation of the Italian Forces in Italian-controlled East Africa. For his services he was awarded the Order of the British Empire (OBE) and was thrice Mentioned in Dispatches.

Recalled to India, he was appointed as the Senior Instructor at the British Staff College in Quetta (in present day Pakistan) and in 1941 led a regiment of the Indian Armoured Corps on a trek of 3,000 miles to join the fighting in Burma. The regiment, which then went on to lead the allied march to Rangoon, won great renown for its part in the fighting. At the end of the Burma campaign, he saw service in French Indo-China with his regiment in Java, Indonesia. In 1946, he was promoted to the rank of Brigadier in Malaya (a part of Malaysia which lies on the Malay Peninsula) and in the same year was selected to command the Indian Victory Contingent to London. Following a course at the Imperial Defence College at England in 1947, he returned to India and was appointed Director of Military Operations & Intelligence at Army Headquarters in New Delhi.

In February 1948, he was promoted to the rank of Major General and became the officiating Chief of the General Staff. In May 1948, he took over command of the 1st Armoured Division which played a major role in the 1948 Hyderabad Operations. Following Operation Polo in 1948, **he** was appointed as the Military Governor of Hyderabad State and from where he also functioned as Chancellor of Osmania University and Chairman of Deccan Airways. In the years following, he occupied important military posts and led an Indian Military Delegation to China.

In 1949, he was appointed as the first Colonel Commandant of the Electrical & Mechanical Engineers. In January 1952, he was appointed as the Adjutant General, Army HQ and in January 1953, he again took over as the Chief of the General Staff. On 19 November 1962, he was promoted to the rank of General and took over as the Chief of Army Staff (COAS). A facet of his talents and interests was demonstrated during his term as COAS, where he founded and was first president of the Delhi Symphony Society-an organization designed to promote Western music in New Delhi. He retired on 07 June 1966, after completing 38 years of distinguished military service. For his services to the nation, he was presented with the Padma Vibhushan-India's second highest civilian honour-by the President of India.

Six weeks after his retirement from the Indian Army, he was appointed as the Indian High Commissioner to Canada on 19 July 1966. He was married and had two children. In addition to being a distinguished military man, he displayed notable talent as a writer and literary critic. He wrote two books on military themes and was also the military correspondent and literary reviewer for one of India's leading newspapers. He passed away on 06 April 1983, at the age of 75.

OPERATION POLO: THE 100-HOUR WAR

The State of Hyderabad comprised most of the Deccan Plateau. Having risen from the ruins of the Mughal Empire it like many other states was a Hindu majority state with a Muslim ruler called the Nizam. Established in the 18th century by Nizam-ul-Mulk Asaf Jha, it came under British protection as per the Subsidiary Alliance of Wellesley. In 1947 the Nizam of Hyderabad was Nawab Mir Osman Ali Khan, a man of vast wealth. Dreaming of an independent state he sought Dominion status from the British only to rebuffed by Lord Mountbatten. The Indian Government was averse to a forced takeover and agreed to conclude a Standstill Agreement. It was hoped that this would open negotiations and the eventual peaceful accession of the state. However this only emboldened the Razakars a militant organization led by Kasim Razvi. Helped by the manipulations of the Nizam and his men, the Razakars aided by the communists let loose an orgy of violence,

THE INITIAL SKIRMISHES

The Razakars went on a recruiting spree including many from outside the state. There was an orgy of political murders and Hindu villages were razed. By the spring of 1948, they become bold enough to raid the Union territory. On September 6th, a police post near Chillakallu village came under heavy fire from Razakar units. A squadron of Poona Horse and a company of 2/5 Gorkha Rifles were sent to investigate. They too came under fire. The tanks then chased the Razakars to Kodar, in Hyderabad territory. Here they were opposed by the armoured cars of 1 Hyderabad Lancers. In a brief action the

Poona Horse destroyed one armoured car and forced the surrender of the state garrison at Kodar. Since the trouble began the Razakars had attacked about 70 villages in the state, 150 attacks outside the state, killing, raping and looting. The Nizam was given a last warning to rein in the Razakars.

LAST DITCH EFFORTS

The Nizam instead continued to insist that the conditions were normal and that his own troops were capable of maintaining law and order. Then hoping to get the UN to intervene, a delegation of his advisors left for UN headquarters via Karachi. This raised the possibility of the same power politics that plagued the case of Jammu & Kashmir. It was time for decisive action.

The first plans for a military operation were outlined by Lieutenant General E N Goddard, GOC-in-C Southern Army Command. This envisaged the capture of Hyderabad the state capital with a dual thrust by 1st Armoured Division, from Vijayawada in the East a distance of 250 km and Sholapur in the West, a distance of 300 km while small units will pin down the Nizam forces on the border.

The ORDER OF BATTLE

Hyderabad had a large army, with a tradition of hiring mercenary forces. This included Arabs, Rohillas, Pathans and Uttar Pradesh Muslims. The State Army consisted of 3 armoured regiments, a horsed cavalry regiment, 11 infantry battalions and artillery. There were supplemented by irregular units with a horse cavalry, four infantry battalions (Saraf-i-Khas, Paigah, Arab and Refugee) and a garrison battalion for a total of 22,000 men. Finally there were the Home Guards and Razakars. They were commanded by Major General El Edroos-an Arab.

The Razakars totalled about 200,000 although only 25% were armed with modern small arms and the rest with muzzle loaders and swords. The final plan for Operation Polo was based on the Goddard Plan. It envisaged two major thrusts: a western thrust through the Sholapur-Hyderabad axis and an eastern thrust along the Vijaywada-Hyderabad axis. Smaller thrust were to be made from the South to protect the railway lines of communications and from the North in the Jalna area. The Indian Task force, commanded by Major General J N Chaudhuri (later General and Chief of Army Staff) for the thrust from Sholapur, consisted of four operational groups:

Strike Force:

9th Dogra-Lt. Col. Ram Singh

Skinner's Horse minus one squadron (Stuart tanks)-Lt. Col. Kamla Nand

1 Troop Div HQ Squadron (Shermans)

Battery 1st Field Regiment (self-propelled)

1 Forward Air Control team

Smash Force:

1st Armoured Brigade (Brigadier S D Verma)

3rd Cavalry minus one squadron (Shermans)-Lt. Col. D C Basapa

17th Horse minus one squadron (Shermans)-Lt. Col. K Jangshamsher Singh

One troop-Skinner's Horse

1st Field Regiment less one battery (self-propelled)

2nd Battery-40 Medium Regiment

One Company-9th Dogra

Engineer and Administrative

Kill Force:

7th Infantry Brigade (Brigadier Gurbachan Singh)

2nd Sikh

3rd Grenadiers

14th Rajput

9th Para Field Regiment

Engineer and Administrative

Vir Force:

9th Infantry Brigade (Brigadier Apji Randhir Singh)

3rd Punjab

2/1 Gorkha Rifles

34th Anti-Tank Regiment

Engineer and Administrative

The advance from the Vijaywada was led by Major General A A Rudra and consisted of:

2/5 Gorkha Rifles

1 Squadron minus a troop of 17th Horse

1 troop from 19th Field battery + Engineers and ancillary units

Besides these forces four infantry battalions were to neutralise and protect lines of communication. Two squadrons of Tempest aircraft were available from Pune to provide air support. The overall control was in the hands of Lieutenant General Rajendrasinghji, DSO (later C-in-C and COAS, IA). The date was fixed for September 13th and all foreign governments especially the US, British, Canadians and Australians were asked to evacuate their national embassies. At 0500 hrs on the morning of the 13th, the Pakistan Army was informed about the decision.

Last Minute Discussions

It is interesting to note that General Sir Roy Bucher (C-in-C, IA) was opposed to the military action, and if agreeable was for an attack from the south, even though Lt. Gen. Rajendrasinhji was in favour of the western approach. A cabinet meeting was organised for September 12th to take a final decision. Among those who attended were Prime Minister Nehru, Home Minister Patel, Defence Minister Baldev Singh, Gopalswamy Iyengar, General Bucher, Lt. Gen. (later Field Marshal and C-in-C, IA) K M Cariappa and Air Marshal Sir Thomas W. Elmhirst (C-in-C, IAF).

As the decision was being finalised, Gen. Bucher stood up and said, "Gentlemen, you have taken a decision in a difficult matter. I must give you my warning. We are also committed in Kashmir. We cannot say how long it will take so we will end up having two operations on our hands. This is not advisable, so as your C-in-C I ask you not to start the operations." He further offered his resignation if his advice was not heeded.

There was a silence while a distressed and worried Nehru looked around. Patel replied, "You may resign General Bucher, but the police action will start tomorrow." A angry General Bucher stormed out, and coincidentally the next few days saw a rise in the Kashmir operations.

The War Begins-september 13

The first obstacle was the Naldurg fort which stood on the Sholapur-Secunderabad road about 19 km from the state border. Behind it was the Bori river with a bridge vital for the passage of Indian armour. The fort was defended by the 1 Hyderabad Infantry, some irregulars and a pair of 25 pounders. The task of capturing the bridge was given to 7th Brigade consisting of 2 Sikh, 3 Grenadiers and a battery from 34th anti tank regiment, a detachment from armoured reconnaissance and some Engineers. It started on the night of 12th Sept and moved to an area 23 km South of Naldrug in Indian territory.

Here the column split with one going for the bridge and the other for the guns. Achieving complete surprise the bridge was secured intact. The main column set of at 0400 hours. Led by 1 Armoured Brigade it consisted of 3 Cavalry less 2 squadrons, 17 horse less a squadron, 1 Field regiment less a battery, 7 Field Company, 14th Rajput, 4 Gwalior and a company of Dogras. Brushing aside the odd sniping and the occasional 25 pounder it linked up with the 7th Brigade. Meanwhile 2 Sikh made a dash for Jalkot 8 km east of Naldurg. Havildar Bachittar Singh commanding a platoon saw 2 vehicles coming from Naldurg. In spite of the withering fire he ran forward and succeeded in capturing the vehicles with their escorts. Latter during the day an entrenched Hyderabadi position opened up with Bren guns. Havildar Bachittar Singh led a skilful charge.

25 metres from the post he was hit on the thigh. Still he crawled forward and silenced the post with 2 grenades. Refusing to allow any medical help he kept encouraging his men till the end. He was awarded the Ashok Chakra.

The armoured columns of 1 Armoured brigade now reached Jalkot around 0900 hours. Chaudhari now asked the 3rd column to pass through and continue advancing. Under Lt Col Ram Singh this column consisted of 1 Horse (less a squadron), 1 battery of 1 field regiment, 1 battery of 40 medium regiment, an Engineer detachment, 9 Dogra less a company and some ancillary units. Brushing aside the resistance they made it to Umarge, 61 km inside Hyderabad, by 1515 hours. The Razakars in the town resisted but were quickly overpowered.

The 4th column was in charge of clearing the Northern flank of the main advance. Under 9th Brigade it consisted a squadron of 3rd Cavalry, a troop from 18th cavalry, a troop from 9 Para field regiment, 10 Field company engineers, 3/2 Punjab Regiment, 2/1 Gorkhs Rifles, 1 Mewar Infantry and ancillary units. Its task was to capture Tuljapur, 34 km NW of Naldurg.

This straddled the Sholapur Osmanabad road and connected to Naldurg by road. A battalion group consisting 2/1 Gorkha rifles, a battery of 9 Field regiment, a squadron of 3rd cavalry and a detachment of engineers advanced from Barsi and crossed the border at 2000 hours. By dawn they had isolated Tuljapur by stationing a company each on the Tuljapur-Osmanabad road and the Tuljapur-Naldurg road. A ridge commanding the plateau below was held by 200 Razakars and 1 Hyderabad infantry. There was a stubborn resistance for two hours, even though the issue was never in doubt.

Another group of 9th Brigade consisting of 3/2 Punjab, Mewar Infantry, a troop of 18th Cavalry, a battery from 9 Field regiment and some Engineers advanced along the Sholapur-Tuljapur road. Though the tanks got bogged down, the Punjabis continued to lead the advance and linked up with the Gorkhas at 1530 hour. Further movement towards Lohara was given up due to the swollen nulla on the way. After the units linked the

Mewar infantry was given the task of mopping and holding to Tuljapur. Thus ended the first day with the Indians battering the Hyderabad forces and inflicting heavy losses. A number of men were captured including a British mercenary tasked with blowing up the Naldurg bridge.

Meanwhile the column from Vijayawada leading the Eastern thrust was making good progress. The opposition was in the form of 2 armoured units of Humbers and Stagehounds. The task of neutralising it was given to 4 battalions: 9/2 Punjab, 3 Sikh LI, 6 Jat and 6 Kumaon. Some support was provided by 17 Poona Horse. The force was commanded by Lt Col Amrik Singh. The advance began at dawn on Sept 13 and by 0830 hours they had reached Kodar. Leaving the 9/2 Punjab to guard Kodar. Lt Col Singh pressed on to reach Mungala by afternoon.

On the Southern borders of Hyderabad, the Indian aim was to ensure the safety of the rail communications that passed through the area. The bridges at Kurnool, Tungabhadra and Hospet were the responsibility of units under Brigadier N V Bal. Headquartered in Guntakal he had the 5/5 Gorkha Rifles, 1 Mysore Infantry and Mysore Lancers (on horses). He had two armoured trains for patrolling. These units did not encounter much resistance except at Hospet, where a company of the Mysore Infantry ran into trouble.

A sugar factory by the bridge was occupied by a large number of Razakars and Pathans. Twice the company took over the factory only to be beaten back by large numbers of the defenders. A company of the 4th Rajputana rifles trying to aid the Mysoremen was itself in trouble when the train in which they were travelling got derailed. However the stubborn resistance could not hold out against determined Indian efforts.

A company of 5/5 Gorkha rifles left Guntakal for the Tungabhadra bridge in the early hours of 13th Sept. The bridge was guarded by a strong contingent of the Hyderabad forces, its flanks covered by Bren gun posts. A section led by Nail Narbahadur Thapa engaged the defenders. Under heavy fire he dashed across hundred yards of open ground between him and the Bren gun position and decapitated its crew with his khukri. With it all resistance collapsed. Naik Narbahadur Thapa got the Ashok Chakra.

Day 2-september 14

Maj Gen Chaudhuri's aim was to reach Rajasur, 48 km east of Umarga. However the road passed through an 8 km defile near Talmud. Here the hills on both sides of the road were covered with scrub. Furthermore the ground at the end of the defile rose sharply providing a good vantage point for artillery observers. Air recce had indicated well defended positions. The Indian Air Force was called in and a couple of strikes by IAF Tempests caused the Hyderabadis to abandon their positions. With Rajasur falling in the afternoon. a small detachment was sent to take care of Kalyani which was held by some Razakars.

Meanwhile in the Kodar area the Hyderabad army had dug an anti tank ditch. The ditch was filled up and as the advance continued heavy fire was encountered from some low hills 6 km short of Suriappet. The fire was coming from units of 1 Lancer and 5 Infantry but fight as well as they did they could not hold long against the veterans of the Burma campaign the 2/5 Gorkha rifles. The cost was 35 Hyderabadis dead and 49 captured for 2 Gorkha soldiers killed. Meanwhile a column of 3/11 Gorkha Rifles and a squadron of 8th cavalry advanced on to Osmanabad from the North. However its main defences were in the South and provided stiff resistance to a column from 9th Brigade which advanced from Tuljapur. Heavy street to street combat took place as the Razakars fought doggedly.

Major General D S Brar was given the task of taking Aurangabad. An important military and civil centre its early capture was essential. Major General Brar organised six columns for this purpose. A column comprising 3/5 Gorkha Rifles, 2 companies of 17th Sikh, a squadron of Stuarts and armored cars from Armoured Corps School, 20 Field Battery and Engineers and ancillary under Lt Col P S Thapa was tasked with taking the city. Moving along the Nangaon-Aurangabad axis, it brushed aside the odd opposition and entered Daulatabad fort by the afternoon. As the column reached the city outskirts the civil administration came out to surrender. A column consisting of 3 Sikh, a company of 2 Jodhpur infantry and some tanks from 18 Cavalry marched to Jalna. Here the Hyderabadi forces resisted stubbornly before giving up.

Day 3-september 15

The action here continued till early morning when the elements from 9th Brigade were joined in by 8th cavalry. The action left 75 Razakars killed and 84 taken prisoner. Once this was over a company of 3/11 Gorkhas were left behind with some tanks to hold the city while the rest of the forces moved to Latur. By afternoon they reached Mominabad. The 3 Golconda Lancers who held it, after some initial half hearted resistance threw in the towel.

Suriapet was strafed by the IAF in the morning, followed by a rapid advance by the 2/5 Gorkhas. The Hyderabadis had withdrawn but a few dozen Razakars were captured in mopping operations. The retreating Hyderabadis partially destroyed the Musi Bridge. But they neglected to lay covering fire and it was repaired and the advance resumed. The only other action was at Narkatpalli where a Razakar battalion was decimated.

The column led by 1 Armoured was cautious as it approached Zahirabad and Bidar. This were well defended and the aim was to take over Homanabad and launch probing operrations towards Zahirabad and Bidar. Homanabad fell at 0800 hours with only sporadic resistance. Leaving the 9th Brigade to mop up, the armoured units moved towards Bidar but soon ran into a swollen nullah. The other column led by Ram Singh advanced about 16 km towards Zahirabad before halting for the day.

Day 4-september 16

Ram Singh's forces moved out towards Zahirabad in the early hours of the morning to capture the junction where the road from Bidar met the Sholapur-Hyderabad road. If that fell he was to turn north towards Bidar while the armoured column moved towards Zahirabad. The armoured columns was slowed down by a mine field which were cleared in due time. Ram Singh's forces encountered fire at the junction. Some time into the fighting the armoured column joined up and Ram Singh's units disengaged and moved north, leaving the fighting to the armoured column. All along the route there was sporadic resistance by Hyderabadi forces and by nightfall Ram Singh's men were a few kms short of Bidar. Meanwhile the armoured column met with determined resistance from the Razakars. Within the built up areas the Razakars enjoyed a brief advantage till the 75mm guns of the tanks were brought into play. By nightfall the forces had moved 15 kilometres beyond Zahirabad.

Day 5-september 17 the War Ends

On Sept 17 in the early hours the Indian Army entered Bidar. With the Nizam forces being routed from all directions, the Government resigned. The forces led by the 1 Armoured Regiment were at Chityal about 60 km from the capital. Another column took over Hingoli. With no escape route and no foreign aid coming, the Nizam went on the air and asked his remaining forces to cease fire by 1700 hours. He banned the Razakars and allowed Union troops into Secunderabad and Bolurum. The next day Major General Chaudhuri rode at the head of an armoured column to Secunderabad and at 1600 hours the Hyderabad Army represented by Major General El Edroos surrendered.

Major General Chaudhuri took over as Military Governor. Over the next few days mopping operations continued against the Razakars with their leader Razvi arrested on Sept 19. On November 24th, Major General Chaudhuri handed over control to a civilian Governor following the Nizam's accession to the Union. The Indian Army suffered 66 killed and 97 wounded. The Hyderabad State forces had 490 killed and 122 wounded. The Razakars suffered even more.

GENERAL P.P. KUMARAMANGALAM, DSO

COAS, 07 June 1966-07 June 1969

Regiment of Artillery

General Paramasiva Prabhakar **Kumaramangalam** assumed charge of the Indian Army, as the 7th Chief of Army Staff, on 07 June 1966. Born on 01 July 1913, he completed his early education at Eton College and graduated from

Woolwich College in England. He was the last of the King's Commissioned Indian Officers trained at the Royal Military Academy, Sandhurst and was the second Indian Officer to be commissioned into the Regiment of Artillery on 19 August 1933.

During the Second World War, he participated in the operations in the Middle East and was awarded the Distinguished Service Order (DSO) as a Major for action in Libya on 27 May 1942. He was taken Prisoner of War (POW) in Italy in 1942, however he did not stay long and escaped. However his luck ran out and he was caught again and imprisoned, this time in Germany. At the end of the war in 1945, he returned to India and become a Brigadier in 1948.

General Kumaramangalam took over as the General Officer Commanding–in-Chief (GOC-in-C), Eastern Command in May 1963. In November 1964, he was appointed as the Deputy Chief of Army Staff (DCAS) and on 15 January 1965, he became the Vice Chief of Army Staff (VCAS). He also served as the Adjutant General and the Commandant of the Defence Services Staff College (DSSC) at Wellington, before becoming the Army Chief on 07 June 1966.

General Kumaramangalam was the first gunner from the Regiment of Artillery, to serve as the Army Chief. His tenure as Army Chief was marked by an unpublicised, but exhaustive, re-organisation of the Indian Army which included up-gradation of weapons and training & tactics based on the lessons learned from the 1965 Indo-Pak War. He served in the Indian Army with distinction for 36 years till his retirement on 07 June 1969. For his services to the nation, he was presented with the Padma Vibhushan-India's second highest civilian honour-by the President of India in 1970.

General Kumaramangalam was an avid polo player and a keen cricketer. He was also a member of the Marylebone Cricket Club, a prestigious cricket club in England; the President of the Indian Polo Association and Equestrian Federation of India and a Fellow of the Royal Horticultural Society. He was the Senior Colonel Commandant of the Regiment of Artillery from

05 July 1959 to 04 July 1969 and the Honorary Colonel Commandant from 05 July 1969 to 30 June 1975. On retirement as Army Chief, he was elected President of the World Wildlife Fund-India during its formative stages. He passed away on 13 March 2000, following cardio respiratory failure, at the age of 87.

FIELD MARSHAL S.H.F.J. MANEKSHAW
Padma Vibhushan, Padma Bhushan, MC
COAS, 07 June 1969-15 Jan 1973
Infantry, 8 Gorkha Rifles

Field Marshal Sam Hormusji Framji Jamshedji Manekshaw assumed charge of the Indian Army, as the 8th Chief of Army Staff, on 07 June 1969. Born in Amritsar, Punjab on 03 April 1914, he completed his schooling in Amritsar and Sherwood College, Nainital. He then joined the first batch of 40 cadets at Indian Military Academy (IMA), Dehra Dun on 01 October 1932. He passed out of the IMA in December 1934 and was commissioned as a Second Lieutenant in the Indian Army. He held several regimental assignments and was first attached to the Royal Scouts and later to the 12 Frontier Force Rifles.

During World War II, he saw action in the Burma campaign on Sittang river and has the rare distinction of being honoured for his bravery on the battle front itself. During World War II, he was leading a counter-offensive against the invading Japanese Army in Burma.

As he charged forward with his men, a Japanese soldier suddenly emerged from the bushes and fired at him, wounding him seriously in the stomach. Fortunately, Major General D.T. Cowan spotted Manekshaw holding on to life and was aware of his valour in face of stiff resistance from the Japanese. Fearing the worst, Major General Cowan quickly pinned his own Military Cross ribbon on to Manekshaw saying, "A dead person cannot be awarded a Military Cross."

Having recovered from those near-fatal wounds in Burma, Manekshaw went for a course at Staff College, Quetta and later also served there as an instructor before being sent to join 12

Frontier Force Rifles in Burma under General (later Field Marshal) Slim's 14th Army. He was once again involved in a fierce battle with the Japanese, and was wounded for a second time. Towards the close of World War II, Manekshaw was sent as Staff Officer to General Daisy in Indo-China where, after the Japanese surrender, he helped rehabilitate over 10,000 POWs. He, then, went on a six-month lecture tour to Australia in 1946, and after his return served as a First Grade Staff Officer in the Military Operations Directorate at Army HQ in New Delhi.

Manekshaw showed acumen for planning and administration while handling the issues related to partition in 1947, and later put to use his battle skills during the 1947-48 Jammu & Kashmir Operations. After command of an Infantry Brigade he was posted as the Commandant of the Infantry School and also became the Colonel of 8 Gorkha Rifles (his regimental home) and 61 Cavalry. He commanded a Division in Jammu & Kashmir and a Corps in the North East, with a tenure as Commandant of Defence Services Staff College (DSSC) in between. As GOC-in-C Eastern Command, he handled the tricky problem of insurgency in Nagaland and the grateful nation honoured him with a Padma Bhushan-India's third highest civilian honour-in 1968.

Manekshaw succeeded General Kumaramangalam as Chief of Army Staff (COAS) on 07 June 1969. His years of military experience were soon put to the test as thousands of refugees from the erstwhile East Pakistan started crossing over to India as a result of oppression unleashed from West Pakistan. The volatile situation got worse, and soon erupted into a full-scale war in December 1971. During the military campaign, Manekshaw showed uncommon ability to motivate the forces, coupling it with a mature war strategy. The war ended with Pakistan's unconditional surrender, and the formation of Bangladesh. For his selfless service to the nation, he was awarded the Padma Vibhushan in 1972 and was conferred with the honorary rank of Field Marshal on 01 January 1973. He retired a fortnight later, on 15 January 1973, after completing nearly four decades of military service.

Some of his achievements as COAS are;

- Prepared the Army for a well-planned and a well executed operation against Pakistan in 1971, leading to the creation of Bangladesh.
- As Chairman of Chiefs of Staff Committee, he welded the Army, Navy and Air Force into a well-knit team.
- Taking of over 90,000 Pakistan POWs, thereby paving the way for favourable negotiations.

SAM BAHADHUR

The man eventually destined to be free India's first Field Marshal was born on 03 April 1914 at Amritsar. How did a Parsi couple settle for the holy city of the Sikhs? I once asked him and was told that in 1899, his father recently qualified as a doctor and just married, could make no professional headway in Bombay, and was advised to try his luck at Lahore in the Punjab. With his young wife, he set off by train for Lahore.

The long dusty and hot journey took five days and by the end of it, his young wife, who had never left the comforts and civilization of Bombay, was in hysterics and cried to go back. Poor Dr Manekshaw did all he could to comfort her, but as the train steamed into Amritsar, with her first sight of the Sikhs the young bride screamed her lungs out and refused to go any further. So they left the train at Amritsar, and there they stayed for forty-five years.

The Manekshaws had six children, four boys and two girls, and Sam was the fifth child. Sam had his schooling at Nainital's Sherwood College. After completing his schooling, he should have gone to England to pursue higher studies; this was the promise made to him by his father but, fortunately for the Indian Army, Dr Manekshaw felt that this particular son was far too young to be on his own in a foreign country, even with his two elder brothers already studying there. So he was admitted to the Hindu Sabha College, Amritsar. If he had gone abroad, he often reminisces, he would have become a doctor. "What doctor?" I queried, and was told "Gynaecologist."

After a stint in Hindu College, he applied for and was accepted for entry into the first batch of the newly opened Indian Military Academy at Dehradun for training Indians for commissioned rank in the British Indian Army. He received his commission on 04 February 1934 and, after an attachment as was the practice then with a British Infantry Battalion, the 2nd Battalion the Royal Scots, he joined the 4th Battalion, 12 Frontier Force Regiment, commonly called the 54th Sikhs. In 1937, at a social gathering in Lahore he met his future wife, Silloo Bode; they fell in love and were married on 22nd April 1939. Silloo is a graduate of Bombay's renowned Elphinstone College and also studied at the JJ (Jamsetjee Jeejeebhoy) School of Arts there. A voracious reader, a gifted painter and an extremely intelligent and interesting conversationalist, she has made an admirable wife and a wonderful mother.

The outbreak of the Second World War saw the 4/12 Frontier Force Regiment in action in Burma with the famed 17 Infantry Division. Sam was separated from his family for over three years and this separation was the cause of a celebrated example he was later to give while answering questions put to him in his capacity as Chief of the Army Staff by the Pay Commission. The question, which triggered off the reply was, why should the army continue to get separation allowance? This, to clarify, is a token sum every officer and enlisted man gets when his unit moves to a non-family station thus necessitating separation. I say 'token' because the name is a misnomer; whereas it is meant to cover the expenditure incurred in running two establishments, the amount paid is, in fact, a pittance. For example, an officer used to get just seventy rupees a month and the men an even smaller amount. The answer to explain the need was "After my marriage, I went off to war and didn't see my wife for three long years, and when I returned I found I had a brand-new daughter, and the only reason I am sure the child is mine is because she looks just like me." Needless to say, the Pay Commission broke up in laughter, but went away convinced. The separation allowance continues.

On 22 February 1942, occurred the much publicised event when Sam Manekshaw was wounded. The retreat through the

Burma jungle ended abruptly for him on 22 February 1942, when seven bullets from a Japanese machine gun whipped through his body. The young captain who had just led two companies in the courageous capture of a vital hill was awarded the Military Cross. "We made an immediate recommendation," a senior officer explained, "Because you can't award a dead man the Military Cross." His orderly Sher Singh evacuated him to the Regimental Aid Post where the regimental medical officer, Captain G M Diwan, treated him overruling his protestations that the doctor treat other patients first. Sam was evacuated to the hospital at Pegu where he was operated upon, and then evacuated further to Rangoon, from where he sailed for India in one of the last ships to leave that port before it fell to the Japanese. He still carries the scars of this wound and I am not quite sure whether it is that or regular exercise that keeps his stomach in — to the envy of people much younger than he.

I was to see a great deal of Sher Singh during my tenure in Delhi. He and some other grizzled old veterans of the 4/12 Frontier Force Regiment were frequent visitors to Army House and South Block. The entire staff including all guards and sentries, had strict orders that if a man said he was from the 54th Sikhs he was to be led straight to the Chief, whatever the time or whatever the Chief happened to be doing. Consequently, these gentlemen would turn up whenever it suited them with a string of requests that ranged from wanting a bag of sugar for a daughter's marriage (easy to solve) to asking that a relative or friend's relative be given immediate out-of-turn promotion. When I patiently attempted to explained the impossibility of the latter request and others like it, the worthy would bristle and inform me: "In the British time if the Jangi Lat gave an order it was executed without question." No amount of explanation that times had changed and that such Nadirshahi orders would now invite representations which could not possibly be answered, would pacify them and they would go away and complain to the Chief about the incapable and unhelpful Colonel Sahib he had from the Gorkhas.

The war over, saw Sam working in the Military Operations Directorate at Army Headquarters, first as a General Staff

Officer Grade I, and later as Director of Military Operations. It was from here that he oversaw the fighting that broke out between India and Pakistan, over Kashmir, the two nations that until so recently had been one. It was also under his direct supervision, when the cease-fire was declared, that the famous line called the Cease Fire Line was drawn. Many, many years later, by a strange coincidence, while he was Chief of the Army Staff, it was he whose brainchild it was to scrap the Cease Fire Line and call it the Line of Actual Control. Promotions followed in rapid succession and 1959 saw Sam as commandant of the Defence Services Staff College. There his outspoken frankness got him into trouble with the Defence Minister, V K Krishna Menon, and his protégé of the time, the late Lieutenant General B M Kaul; a court of inquiry was ordered against him. Despite persistent questioning I have not been able to ascertain from him the reasons and the facts that led up to a situation where the Indian Army could have lost its most brilliant up-and-coming general officer: he just refuses to talk, calling the entire episode, just another phase. Be that as it may, the court of inquiry that was convened with the late Lieutenant General Daulet Singh, then Western Army commander, as presiding officer, exonerated Sam, but before a no case could be announced, fate intervened in the shape of the Chinese hordes that swept over what we had always considered the impregnable Himalayas.

The Indian Army, that proud, disciplined and distinguished force that had fought and triumphed in practically every battlefield of the world, was outmatched, out manoeuvred and outfought; its remnants streamed back dazed and humiliated leaving among the lush green mountains of the North Eastern Frontier Agency and the stark white to Ladakh its dead, its wounded and its pride. The North Eastern Frontier Agency (NEFA), now called Arunachal Pradesh, was where we suffered our worst defeat, and it was to 4 Corps that providence ironically decreed and Army Headquarters ordered Sam Manekshaw to succeed Lieutenant General B M Kaul, the man who had almost ruined his professional career. He took over 4 Corps on 28th November 1962 on promotion to lieutenant general, and the same day addressed a conference of what must surely have been a very shaken group of staff officers. He entered the room with his usual jaunty step, looked as if he were meeting each eye trained on him and said, "Gentleman, I have arrived! There will be no more withdrawals in 4 Corps, Thank You," and walked out.

But the charisma that surrounds the man had preceded him and soldier and officer alike knew the 'chosen one' had arrived and henceforth all would be well. It was as if the dark and oppressive atmosphere had suddenly been lightened and Sam was the bearer of the light.

On 04 December 1963, Sam took over as Army Commander in the west, the second rung from the top. One of his Brigade Commanders was H S Yadav, the man who had been the principal prosecution witness in the case cooked up against him in 1961. At a party in an officers mess in Kashmir one evening, talk veered round to Yadav, and the senior brass, knowing the background and not averse to making a few points with the Army Commander, started on what each planned to do to catch or embarrass Yadav. The Army Commander heard this for some moments and then butted in ('before I got sick' as he told me later) with "Look chaps, professionally, Kim Yadav is head and shoulders above most of you, so forget about trying to catch him out. He just lacks character and there is nothing anyone of you can do about that."

At a meeting in Delhi a few months later, Chavan, then the Defence Minister, asked him his views on which army command Sam considered most important, challenging and threatened. Eastern, said Sam, as it had the Chinese in the North, East Pakistan in the South and on its flank insurgency rampant in Nagaland and the Mizo Hills and, if all that was not enough to fill the hands of the incumbent, the troubled state of West Bengal certainly would.

Chavan thought over the answer for a few moments and then asked if Sam would like to accept the challenge of taking over that command. He accepted immediately. Eastern Army had to keep one wary eye directed north on the Chinese; another eye had to be kept on erstwhile east Pakistan which lay in its gut, it had to fight insurgency in Nagaland which later spread to the Mizo Hills, and finally it had to watch over the politically volatile states of Assam and West Bengal. It was, therefore, no bed of roses, and the job of lower formations was not facilitated by the army commander's personally coming on the telephone every now and then and 'grilling' staff officers and commanders with endless questions about detail.

I remember an occasion in Shillong where I once asked the senior staff officer why he was looking a bit off-colour. He told me he had just finished a telephone conversation with the army commander who had wanted answers to so many questions that, 'I am now in orbit.' His mastery of detail was fantastic and, as I was to learn later, he could quote an answer given verbally or in writing months previously to correct someone who was saying something else.

A battalion employed in the Mizo Hills, paying perhaps a little more attention to the welfare of its troops and, in the process, a little less than desirable to the operational side received a rude reminder that 'someone up there' was watching, very keenly, every move that was made. A parcel of bangles was delivered to the Commanding Officer-with the compliments of the Army Commander with a cryptic note: "If you are avoiding contact with the hostile give these to your men to wear." Needless to say, the next few weeks saw a flurry of activity by this battalion resulting in another, more soothing message: "Send the bangles back."

He was officiating as Army Chief in 1967 when the Chinese had their first clash with the Indian Army since 1962. This occurred at the 14,000 foot high pass, Natu La, in Sikkim where the Chinese learnt to their cost that the Indian Army of 1967 was a different kettle of fish from that of 1962. He was summoned to a meeting of the Cabinet where, as he recalled later, everyone present at the meeting was vying with the others to present to the Prime Minister his grasp of the situation and offering one suggestion after another as to what should be done. After hearing most of the speakers, the Prime Minister enquired whether the officiating army chief, until then a silent spectator, had something to say. "I am afraid they are enacting Hamlet without the Prince," he said. "I will now tell you exactly what has happened, and how I intend to deal with the situation." He then proceeded to do so.

Bengal in those days was a very troubled state where anarchy was prevalent, and law and order was almost on the way out. Sam was traveling to Dum Dum airport, Calcutta, once when he found the road blocked for traffic by a huge crowd being harangued by one person.

The outrider and the staff officer accompanying him both advised a detour, but this would have meant running away and would have been noticed by the locals. So he got out of his staff car instead, and started walking up to the speaker who, he discovered to his disquiet as he approached, was a 'huge fellow, well over six feet tall.' Anyway, hiding his mounting uneasiness, he put his hand out and announced, "I am Sam Manekshaw." This unsettled the other person somewhat as he had probably anticipated an argument. He too, put his hand out and mumbled his name. He was then asked to clear the road, as otherwise "I shall miss my plane." The speaker, by now completely confused, hastened to obey, and the last glimpse the Army Commander had of his latest acquaintance was of that worthy helping to clear the road.

By then Sam Manekshaw had become one of the most popular and well-known officers in the Indian Army. Stories of the many admirable qualities he possessed and did not hesitate to display were legion. Always an unconventional dresser, he once met Lieutenant General Kulwant Singh, at that time commanding Western Army and an awe-inspiring man, in a jacket that could best he described as a cross between a regulation shirt and bush shirt.

When the Army Commander pointed this out he was asked: "Have you come to see my formation or my dress?" While he could stand up to his superiors, he always stood by his subordinates. Service with him, it was rumoured, was certain to bring rewards in its wake. But, helpful as he was, he never consciously helped a subordinate at the cost of someone else. In other words, 'No throat was cut.' I once asked him if he was aware of the jealousy his so-called favourites aroused among others. He replied he was aware of this but as his 'favourites' were all competent officers he defied anyone to point a finger at them as far as their professional competence was concerned. On another occasion I asked him why he could not 'see through' the slick types who fawned and flattered him, and why he acceded to their requests. "Oh, I see through them all right," he replied. "I detest them, but I make use of them."

He was human and approachable to a fault. Once, so a story goes, while he was a Corps Commander, a junior officer on his staff asked for some leave, and the request was turned down by the officer's immediate superior.

The officer then tried the indirect approach and made his problem known to the Corps Commander who called the man's immediate superior the next day and said, 'Look, I have had a letter from this youngster's father asking that the boy be sent on a spot of leave as there is some family problem to sort out. I am sure we can spare the bugger for a few days, let him go, we won't miss him.' The officer got his leave; no feathers were ruffled and everyone was happy, which brings us to his next great quality, the ability to run a very happy and contented team. His professional qualities ensured that the team was also a competent one. He was believed to finish his own work in an hour and spend the remainder of the time walking from one office to another, sitting down with the harried junior staff and helping them sort out the problems they were working on.

They said he never raised his voice, but even a mild reproving look from him with a 'Sweetheart, this won't do,' was enough to shake the stoutest heart. Sharply critical, but always constructively so, there was nothing his eye ever missed or his fantastically retentive memory ever forgot. He forgave easily, being basically a kind man. While he was Chief of the Army Staff, at an 'at Home' he attended in Rashtrapati Bhavan, as the guests came out into the Mughal Gardens he found himself walking beside Mr V K Krishna Menon, of whom mention has been made earlier. Polite to a fault, he wished Mr Menon the time of day and also enquired how the latter was progressing health-wise. He then turned to Mrs Manekshaw, who was also walking in line, and asked her: "Darling, you remember, Mr Menon?" Mrs Manekshaw, not quite as forgiving as her spouse, at least on this occasion, replied brusquely: "No, I don't."

A Legend Turns 90

In the company of generals, children, politicians, journalists and illustrious members of the global Parsi community and with traditional Zoroastrian rituals, Field Marshal Sam Hormusji Framji Jamshedji Manekshaw, India's first and only living field marshal, celebrated his 90th birthday in New Delhi on 03 April 2003. Manekshaw, his legendary wit and charm intact, cut his birthday cake with a silver khukri, the favourite dagger of the legendary Gurkha soldiers, as the large gathering sang *Happy Birthday to You*. The hero of the 1971 war with Pakistan, which resulted in the birth of Bangladesh, made no speech at the evening function organised by the Parzor Foundation, a UNESCO-supported initiative for the preservation and promotion of Parsi Zoroastrian culture and heritage.

But he was visibly overwhelmed by the gathering and its affection. Defence Minister George Fernandes, Tourism Minister Jagmohan, the three Service Chiefs, numerous retired war heroes and several former service chiefs were present at the function. Defence Minister Fernandes pointed out that Field Marshal Manekshaw not only created history, but also created a nation. Everyone who knew Manekshaw had a tale or two to recollect, as the crowd gathered to share some delightful Parsi snacks. Field Marshal Manekshaw, who almost lost his life during World War II in Burma and won a Military Cross for bravery, was the first Indian officer to command the Gurkhas after Independence.

A documentary — In War and Peace: The Life of Field Marshal Sam Manekshaw, MC — was screened as the Parzor Foundation celebrated his life as a mark of the contribution of the Parsi community to India and a celebration of India's multiculturalism. The documentary, which has India's favourite soldier narrating his life to his grandson Jehan, details his legendary career. Delhi's military circles has been abuzz for the last week with anecdotes of the exploits of Sam Bahadur, as Manekshaw was known to his troops.

In 1962, in the midst of the humiliating defeat against China, Manekshaw took over the Tezpur-based 4 Corps and famously told his troops, 'Gentlemen, there will be no more withdrawals.' In 1971, he prevailed upon Prime Minister Indira Gandhi to give him six months to wait out the monsoon and prepare for the invasion of East Pakistan, bulldozed the finance ministry to give the military extra funds, and skipped major cities to take Dacca and create Bangladesh.

Despite his age, Manekshaw did not disappoint Delhi on this visit. On 02 April 2003, at the Battle Honours Mess, he was at his witty best as he quipped, "Officers, you have kept up the great tradition of the Indian Army... [pause] of having beautiful wives." When the wife of a former army chief asked Field Marshal Manekshaw how he managed to remember the first names of most army wives, he remarked there are two things no honourable man should forget: His wife's birthday and the first name of the women around him. The Field Marshal now lives in the Nilgiri Hills in south India, looked after by a loyal Gurkha family.

The Courage to Say No!

At the start of this year, a popular journal featured a leading article on prominent living Indians who, in the 20th century, had inspired India's younger generation. I have no comments about those listed but was disappointed to note the article did not include the name of Field Marshal Sam Hormusji Framji Jamshedji Manekshaw. Was this an unfortunate lapse?

Did the editor consider the soldier unworthy of inclusion? Was this another example of the tendency in democracies to only remember their military leaders in times of danger and forget them in peacetime? I'm not sure of the answers to these questions. Today, Sam Manekshaw celebrated his 90th birthday.

Senior Army officers celebrated the occasion in Delhi and many newspapers published summaries of the Field Marshal's distinguished career. I have no desire to add to this paean of praise. However, one incident in Manekshaw's distinguished career bears repetition. Readers may recall that, on 25 March 1971, when political events in East Pakistan had taken a turn for the worse, the Pakistan Army cracked down on Bengali intellectuals and leaders, killing over 50,000 of them. Millions of refugees began fleeing into India to escape from this organised genocide. The exodus of refugees placed an unbearable financial burden on India and strained the fabric of social structure and political stability in eastern India.

Then Prime Minister Indira Gandhi toured the border in order to see for herself the unprecedented and desperate situation prevailing in the region. On her return from Calcutta, she drove straight to South Block and walked into the operations room of Army Headquarters. After giving her firsthand assessment of the situation in East Pakistan and the Indian border, she turned to Manekshaw and bluntly asked, "What can the Indian Army could do in this situation?" Manekshaw, in his inimitable cryptic style, replied, "Nothing." Gandhi's entourage, consisting of a few ministers and bureaucrats, were shocked at the General's abrupt answer. No one had ever dared to respond to the PM in this manner. The Army Chief went on to explain it took time to launch military operations and the Army was not ready. The PM said, "I want the army to launch an offensive into East Pakistan as early as possible. You should be prepared to attend a Cabinet meeting in two days' time and outline your plans."

Later, Manekshaw attended a Cabinet meeting where the PM repeated she wanted the armed forces to invade East Pakistan as quickly as possible so that a pro-Mujibur Rehman government could be installed and millions of refugees returned to their homes. The General explained there were over 90,000 Pakistani troops in East Bengal and he needed to move two army corps into the area, one into Bengal and the other into north-east India. These moves could not be completed in less than two months. The PM kept quiet but her ministers protested and said the economic and political situation in the states adjoining East Pakistan had become intolerable and he must act more quickly. Manekshaw ignored the protests. He turned to the PM and said, "Even when my troops are in position in June, I do not recommend we launch any operations for two reasons. Firstly, the monsoon would be raging at the time. Secondly, the Himalayan mountain passes would be open and I will not be able to withdraw troops from the northern borders for operations against East Pakistan. Moreover, India must guard against the prospect of fighting a war on two fronts. That would present me with problems far more complex than what had been the bane of the German general staff for more than 50 years across two world wars. It would be unwise to rely on diplomatic assurances that the Chinese would not react in support of Pakistan. We must wait for the snow to block the northern passes."

Manekshaw recommended the earliest India should launch military operations was in November. This statement was met with an uproar of indignant protests. The PM again kept quiet but her ministers said such a prolonged delay was unacceptable. Manekshaw told the Cabinet the monsoon in that region was very severe. He quietly explained how the whole area of Bengal, East Pakistan and northeast India becomes a virtual lake. All road transport would cease. If India launched operations in June, the results would be disastrous. He would rather resign than act against his professional judgement. The PM ordered the general to move his formations into position and be ready by June. Operations would then be launched depending on the circumstances. The Cabinet meeting was called to a close. Throughout the months that followed, a whispering campaign of calumny was mounted against Manekshaw.

His critics talked of the General having cold feet and no stomach for a fight (The fact that Manekshaw had won the Military Cross for bravery in Burma during World War II, where his stomach had taken a full burst of machine gun fire, meant nothing to these people). The army's state of unpreparedness became a cocktail circuit joke. Manekshaw's daughter faced continuous pinpricks from her friends (daughters of senior bureaucrats and police officials), who made fun of the army's lack of guts. They suggested if the army was not up to this task, the BSF should be allowed to clear up East Pakistan.

Manekshaw was well aware of all that was being said against him. He kept his cool. While he managed the movement of troops, essential supplies and armaments to the east and dealt with the politicians in Delhi, he gave the Eastern Command a free hand to plan the operations in detail. Meanwhile, the armed forces built up the minimum required administrative and communication facilities around East Pakistan. The delay also enabled the arming and training of the Bengali guerrilla freedom fighters, the Mukti Bahini. The delay witnessed the establishment of a formal Bangladesh government in exile inside India, enabled the government of India to finalise a Treaty of Friendship with the Soviet Union and neutralise interference from both China and the US. By late October, as the intensity of the rains decreased, the media once again clamoured for military action. Armchair strategists had a field day publishing various tactical scenarios on how best to overcome Pakistan's defences. A late monsoon made cross-country movement difficult until the last week of November. By this time, the performance of the Bengali freedom fighters had gained momentum. They dominated the countryside in East Pakistan and had confined the Pakistani army into several garrison towns, cut off from Dacca. The morale of the Pakistan army in East Bengal was very low. On the other hand, thanks to thorough planning, our troops were properly located and well prepared. Thus, when the Pakistani air force carried out a pre-emptive strike on the Indian airfields on 03 December 1971, from West Pakistan, Indian forces around East Bengal were itching to go into action and were able to end the campaign in a fortnight and capture over 90,000 Prisoners of War.

Two historical events of far-reaching consequence, though widely separated by time and space, have striking similarities. General Manekshaw's refusal to be hustled into attacking East Pakistan during May and June 1971 bears a marked similarity to the refusal by Marshal Kutuzov, the Commander-in-Chief of Russian armies, to defend Moscow against Napoleon in 1812.

Both came under increasing pressure from their governments — the czar in Kutuzov's case and Indira Gandhi in Sam's case. One refused to defend and the other declined to attack. By refusing to defend Moscow against Napoleon, Kutuzov saved the Russian armies and eventually saved Russia. By declining to attack East Pakistan in May-June, Manekshaw preserved India's honour.

Both resolutely held on to their professional assessments of the military situation and nothing could make them budge from that position. All are now agreed that had India attacked East Pakistan in June 1971 it would have been an unmitigated disaster for the Indian Army. Had it been a lesser army chief than Sam Manekshaw, the government would have stampeded him into on the offensive as it so easily did in the 1962 war against China, Operation Blue Star in Amritsar and the misadventure in Sri Lanka.

Indian troops won their last great victory against a foreign army of importance in 303 B.C. when Chandragupta Maurya's army defeated Seleucus Nicator. After 2300 years of unremitting defeats of Indian armies against every invading army, Sam Manekshaw made the country experience the glow of a stunning victory against the Pakistan army in what is now Bangladesh. That will remain Field Marshal Manekshaw's unique position in Indian military history.

Sunbeam Rapier

In fluent Nepalese, Sam Manekshaw, India's first Field Marshal, instructed Sule Bahadur, his trusted and loyal aide from his beloved Gurkha Regiment, to bring home his Sunbeam Rapier from the Staff College in Coonoor. It took an hour for Sule Bahadur to return but time flew by as the eloquent Manekshaw regaled us with stories of his illustrious life in the army. Manekshaw joined the army at a time when motorised transport was non-existent. "When I joined my regiment, we only had mules and horses and we began getting motorised three-tonners in 1936. The first time we used tanks was in 1948 when we opened the Zoji La Pass to get to Ladakh. I was then Director of Military Operations."

During his early years in the army, Manekshaw developed a fondness for driving and wanted a car that was more than just transport. So after his course in the Imperial Defence College in London, he returned with a Sunbeam Rapier which he bought for the princely sum of 600 pounds. It cost him another 100 pounds to ship the car to India and 6000 Rupees in customs duty. "In those days one pound was worth 12 or 13 Rupees, so the total cost to me was around 15,000 Rupees."

Manekshaw was posted all over the country but his Rapier followed him wherever he went. "Almost immediately after I got back from London, I was given the command of a division in Kashmir, so I drove the Rapier up there. It was wonderful driving it in the hills as I had enough power from its twin-carb engine. I would drive from Kashmir to Bombay regularly but with no air-conditioning, the summer heat would be scorching." When Manekshaw was posted back in the Nilgiris he would drive back to Bombay regularly for his holidays.

The Rapier went to the East as well when he was posted in Calcutta as Eastern Army Commandant. "It's given me excellent service and all it has required is normal maintenance from a regular garage. But when I came to Coonoor, I got TVS to do a really good job and get it into shape. It's a bit heavy on petrol in the hills but still runs without missing a beat."

The Rapier was driven mostly by Manekshaw himself, except for the last four to five years when he stopped driving. "My eyesight is not so good now and neither is my hearing. Besides I have a bad temper, so I've stopped driving altogether." Besides the occasional spin with Sule Bahadur in the Rapier, Manekshaw's regular transport is a Daewoo Cielo.

"Since I don't drive anymore I don't care what car I have, as long as it is comfortable and the air-conditioning works well." Manekshaw also has an old Maruti 800 which belonged to his late wife, Silloo. "That is my wife's car, which she used almost till the day she died. Now the Gurkhas use it for shopping and the odd errand. Occasionally I use it myself when I have go down to the market, which is pretty congested to take a big car."

Manekshaw loved bikes as well and bought a James motorcycle from a British Officer for 1600 Rupees in 1947. Just two days before partition, his good friend Major Yahya Khan, who went on to become President of Pakistan, begged Manekshaw to sell him the bike. "What will I use?" asked Manekshaw. To which Yahya replied, "Sir, you will get everything in India, we will get nothing in Pakistan." Manekshaw agreed to sell the bike for a Thousand Rupees and said, "Okay, Yahya take it!" Yahya looked at his superior and said, "Sir, I haven't got a thousand. I will send it to you." Manekshaw was never paid the thousand rupees but says, "Yahya made up for it by giving me the whole of East Pakistan!" Sule Bahadur was back with the Rapier, which meant it was time to end this interview and get on with the photography. I was amazed at the condition of the car. Original paint, original upholstery, not a bit of rust and the engine sounded crisp and healthy. The 1958 Sunbeam was remarkably well kept for its age. Just like the 90-year-old Field Marshal himself.

GENERAL G.G. BEWOOR, PVSM
COAS, 15 Jan 1973-31 May 1975
Infantry, 11 Gorkha Rifles and 2 Dogra

General Gopal Gurunath Bewoor assumed charge of the Indian Army, as the 9th Chief of Army Staff, on 15 January 1973. Born at Seoni, Madhya Pradesh on 11 August 1917, he is an alumnus of the Royal Indian Military College (RIMC) in Dehra Dun and was commissioned into the Indian Military Academy (IMA), Dehra Dun in July 1937. Whilst at the IMA, he was awarded the Gold Medal for being best all-round cadet and the coveted Sword of Honour. He was commissioned into the 2nd Green Howards Regiment on 15 July 1937 during operations in Waziristan (present-day Pakistan). He later joined the 5th Baluch Regiment and spent his World War II days in Burma, fighting the Japanese. He served with the 5th Baluch till July 1945. He attended Staff College, Quetta in 1945 and subsequently served as the Under-Secretary (Military) of the Viceroy's Co-ordination Council in 1946. He was the only Indian officer to be given this coveted appointment.

He was the Secretary of the Army Partition Committee in 1947, which determined the allotment of weapons, equipment and regiments that were to remain in India or to be allotted to Pakistan. Since his parent regiment-the Baluch-went to Pakistan, he was transferred to the Dogra Regiment and promoted to Lieutenant Colonel in December 1947. Earlier, he took over command of 2 Dogra in October 1947. With a view to imparting basic military training to school and college students, he was appointed as the Director of the NCC (National Cadet Corps) in April 1948 as a Colonel.

On promotion to the rank of Brigadier in July 1951, he was initially appointed as Commander 'Chand Sector' and later as Commanding Officer of the 80th Infantry Brigade in Jammu & Kashmir. In August 1953 he served as the Director, Personnel Services at Army HQ. He was appointed as the first Chief of Staff at the Western Command HQ in Shimla in February 1959 and had the unique distinction of becoming the youngest Major General of the Indian Army at the age of 42 years and six months. He assumed the appointment of the Colonel of the 11 Gorkha Rifles on 25 May 1960. He was then appointed as the GOC of the 27th Infantry Division in February 1961 at Jalandhar. Later he moved this division to Kalimpong (West Bengal) in the wake of Chinese aggression during the 1962 Indo-China War. In June 1963, he was appointed as the Director of Military Training at Army HQ and remained there till November 1964.

He was promoted as General Officer Commanding 33 Corps at Siliguri in November 1964. He moved to Army HQ in May 1967, as the Deputy Chief of Army Staff (DCAS) and held that appointment till June 1969. As DCAS, he was awarded Param Vishist Seva Medal (PVSM) for his meritorious services. In July 1969, he assumed the appointment of General Officer Commanding–in–Chief, Southern Command. During the 1971 Indo-Pak War, he was awarded the Padma Bhushan-India's third highest civilian honour-for conducting successful operations in the Rajasthan Sector. He took over as Army Chief on 15 January 1973 and held that appointment for two years and four months till his retirement on 31 May 1975. He served as the Honorary Colonel of the Dogra Regiment up to 11 August 1979. After retirement, he served as the Indian Ambassador to Denmark, from February 1976 to March 1978. He served as a member of the Senate of the University of Pune, for two years from August 1979 onwards. He was also on the Board of Directors of Kirloskar Oil Engines & Vickers Sperry of Pune. Besides, he was often invited to give talks on leadership and military matters by various educational societies. He passed away on 24 October 1989.

GENERAL T.N. RAINA, MVC
COAS, 31 May 1975-31 May 1978
Infantry, Kumaon Regiment

General Tapishwar Narain Raina assumed charge of the Indian Army, as the 10th Chief of Army Staff, on 15 May 1975. His early education was done at Ludhiana, Punjab because his father-Pandit B.N. Raina-was posted there as a head postmaster. Commissioned into the Kumaon Regiment on 12 April 1942, he took part in the Burma Campaign of World War II and was Mentioned–in–Dispatches for gallantry. During his Burma campaign, he was injured a grenade accident which resulted in the loss of an eye. He had a glass eye in place for the rest of his career in the Indian Army.

He commanded the 14th Kumaon (now the 5th Mechanised Infantry) from September 1957 to September 1959. He then commanded the 114th Infantry Brigade from 1959 to 1962, during the Indo-China conflict of 1962 and was awarded the Maha Vir Chakra (MVC) for showing great courage and leadership qualities in organizing the defences of Chushul. He later became the Brigadier General Staff of the 33 Corps in Siliguri, West Bengal. He also served as the Deputy Adjutant General at Army Headquarters and as GOC of the 25th Infantry Division.

In 1971, he was the GOC II Corps in the Khulna sector. He was awarded the Padma Bhushan -India's third highest civilian honour-for his contributions during the 1971 Indo-Pak War. He was General Officer Commanding–in-Chief of Western Command from 1974 to 1975. He was the Chief of Army Staff from 01 June 1975 to 31 May 1978. He was the Colonel of the Kumaon Regiment and the Naga Regiment from 16 May 1971 to 31 May 1978.

During his tenure as Army Chief, the Central Government led by Prime Minister Indira Gandhi imposed national emergency in India. Before the imposition of the emergency, it is believed that Prime Minister Gandhi asked for the Indian Army's support in the venture, but General Raina told the Prime Minister that the Indian Army would not be used to further her ends but obey only those orders of a legally construed government. This was considered a crucial moment that kept the Indian Army out of politics at a critical juncture. He retired on 31 May 1978, after completing more than 36 years of service to the Indian Army and the nation. He was married to Marie Antoinette Raina, a French woman. He was appointed as the Indian High Commissioner to Canada in February 1979. He passed away on 19 May 1980 in Ottawa, Canada during his tenure as the Indian High Commissioner.

GENERAL O.P. MALHOTRA, PVSM
COAS, 31 May 1978-31 May 1981
Regiment of Artillery

General Om Prakash Malhotra assumed charge of the Indian Army, as the 11th Chief of Army Staff, on 31 May 1978. Born on 06 August 1922 in Srinagar, Kashmir he was commissioned into the Indian Army as a 2nd Lieutenant in the Regiment of Artillery, in November 1941, at the young age of 19. He quickly rose up the ranks, which led to commanding a number of artillery regiments between November 1950 and July 1961. Later on in his army career, he became an instructor at the Defence Services Staff College (DSSC), Wellington and also served as the Military Attaché at the Indian Embassy in Moscow, Russia for three years from June 1962 onwards.

General Malhotra commanded an Artillery Brigade from August 1965 to January 1966 and then took over command of a Mountain Brigade. After being promoted to Major General in September 1967, he commanded an Infantry Division for two years. He was then appointed as GOC 4 Corps in the Eastern

Sector in September 1969, a post which he held till May 1972. He was then appointed as GOC 11 Corps at Jalandhar for two years and was later appointed as GOC-in-C Southern Command in Pune. He was awarded the Param Vishist Seva Medal (PVSM) for service of the most exceptional order in 1976. Prior to his appointment as the Chief of Army Staff, he served as the Vice Chief of Army Staff. He retired on 31 May 1981, after completing nearly 40 years of distinguished military service.

General Malhotra served as the Ambassador of India to Indonesia from 1981 to 1984. He was appointed as the Governor of Punjab in 1990, when militancy in the state was at its height. A resigned as Governor of Punjab in August 1991. A keen sportsman, he was the President of the Equestrian Federation of India for nine years and was the Founding President of the Asian Equestrian Federation. He has also been the President of the Delhi Golf Club in New Delhi. He is a Trustee of the Nehru Trust for the Indian Collections at the Victoria & Albert Museum and has served as the President of India's largest NGO (Non-Governmental Organisation)-The National Association for the Blind-in New Delhi. In 1994, the University of Jammu conferred upon him the Degree of Doctor of Letters (Honours Causa). He is an active member of Kiwanis International in India. He is presently the Chairman of two charitable organizations-Shiksha and Chikitsa.

GENERAL K.V. KRISHNA RAO, PVSM
COAS, 31 May 1981-31 July 1983
Infantry, Mahar Regiment

General Kotikalapudi Venkata Krishna Rao assumed charge of the Indian Army, as the 12th Chief of Army Staff, on 31 May 1981. Born on 16 July 1923, he was commissioned into the Indian Army on 09 August 1942. He took over command of the 3rd Mahar on 14 July 1956. He commanded a brigade in the Ladakh Sector during the 1965 Indo-Pak War.

During 1969-70, he commanded a Mountain Division in the Jammu sector. He always displayed a gift for leadership under fire and the high point came during the 1971 Indo-Pak War, when in a series of brilliant manoeuvres, his division captured the Sylhet area and liberated the north-east sector of Bangladesh. He was awarded the Param Vishisht Seva Medal (PVSM) for his most laudable command of the Mountain Division. In 1974, he took over a Corps in Jammu and was later appointed as the Deputy Chief of Army Staff (DCAS) in 1978.

Subsequently he served as the General Officer Commanding-in-Chief, Western Command in 1979. He attained the highest rank in his military career when he became Chief of Army Staff in 1981. He was the Colonel of the Mahar Regiment from June 1968 to June 1983. He presently serves as the Honorary Colonel of the Mahar Regiment.

Post retirement, General Rao was appointed as the Governor of Nagaland, Manipur and Tripura from June 1984 to 1989. He helped restore order to what was fast becoming a chaotic situation, with rising insurgency and political disarray. He was then appointed as the Governor of Jammu & Kashmir and he served from 11 July 1989 till 19 January 1990 and then for a second time from 13 March 1993 till 02 May 1998.

GENERAL A.S. VAIDYA
Padma Vibhushan, PVSM, MVC (Bar), AVSM
COAS, 31 July 1983-31 Jan 1986
Armoured Corps, Deccan Horse

General Arunkumar Sridhar Vaidya assumed charge of the Indian Army, as the 13th Chief of Army Staff, on 31 July 1983. Born on 27 January 1926, he was commissioned into the Indian Armoured Corps in 1945 and saw battle during the Second World War. He was the seventh post-independence commander of the 9th Deccan Horse, one of the oldest armoured regiments in the Indian Army. He commanded this regiment in the Battle of Asal Uttar during the 1965 Indo-Pak War and led the 2nd (Independent) Armoured Brigade in the Battle of Shakargarh during the 1971 Indo-Pak conflict.

During the 1965 Indo-Pak War, then Lieutenant Colonel Vaidya was in command of the Deccan Horse. From September 6th to 11th, his unit fought a series of actions in Asal Uttar and Cheema, both in Punjab. He showed inspiring leadership and remarkable resourcefulness in organising his unit and fighting against heavy odds and inflicted severe casualties on the Pakistan Army's Patton tanks. With untiring effort he moved from sector to sector with complete disregard for his personal safety, thereby inspiring his troops by his personal example. He was instrumental to a large extent in stemming thrusts by Pakistani armour in the battle of Asal Uttar and later at Cheema. For his exceptional bravery he was awarded the Maha Vir Chakra (India's second highest medal for gallantry).

During the 1971 Indo-Pak conflict, then Brigadier Vaidya was commander of an armoured brigade in the Zafarwal sector on the western front. He moved his brigade swiftly to get to grips with the Pakistan Army and took the enemy tanks by surprise. He employed his tanks relentlessly & aggressively and helped the division to maintain constant pressure & momentum of advance against the Pakistan Army. In the battle of Chakra and Dahira, the going was difficult due to hostile terrain combined with minefields. In a cool and confident manner, he undertook the crossing through the minefield and moved forward, disregarding his own personal safety. Through his inspiring leadership, the entire squadron pushed through the lane and quickly deployed itself to meet the Pakistan Army's counter-attacks.

During the Battle of Basantar in the Shakargarh sector, also during the 1971 Indo-Pak conflict, Brigadier Vaidya again displayed his professional skill and superb leadership. He got his tanks through one of the deepest minefields, expanded the bridgehead and repulsed a strong enemy counter-attack. In this battle, 62 Pakistan Army tanks were destroyed. Throughout, he displayed outstanding courage, great professional skill, indomitable will, foresight and imagination in fighting against the enemy in keeping with the best traditions of the Indian Army. For this he was awarded a second Maha Vir Chakra (known as the Bar to MVC).

Elevated to the rank of Major General in 1973, he held the appointments of Director Military Operations, Chief of Staff at

Headquarters Southern Command and as Commandant Armoured Corps Centre & School. Promoted to the rank of Lieutenant General in January 1980, he held the appointment of Master General of Ordnance and later as the General Officer Commanding of a Corps before being elevated to the appointment of General Officer Commanding-in-Chief of Eastern Command in June 1981. His tackling of the insurgency problems in his command has been particularly praiseworthy. He was awarded the Param Vishisht Seva Medal (PVSM) in 1983 for distinguished service of the most exceptional order.

General Vaidya took over as the Chief of the Army Staff from 01 August 1983 to 31 January 1985. During his tenure as Army Chief, he planned Operation Bluestar in 1984-a controversial military action against militant Khalistan separatists who barricaded themselves in the Sikh's most holiest shrine-the Golden Temple in Punjab. He described the operation as the *most difficult and painful* decision of his career. He retired on 31 January 1986 after completing more than 40 years of service and retired to a quiet life in Pune. He was assassinated by Khalistan separatists on 10 August 1986, in retaliation for the Indian Army's attack on the Golden Temple. He was posthumously awarded the Padma Vibhushan-India's second highest civilian honour-for his tireless service to the nation.

An outstanding military leader, General Vaidya gave the Indian Army a very sound leadership and brought with him an aura of gallantry, valour and remarkable reservoir of combat experience befitting the head of the army. He had the distinction of being among the most decorated soldiers in the defence services.

OPERATION BLUESTAR, 05 JUNE 1984

As a result of the uniqueness of this operation, and the circumstances under which it occurred, the BHARAT RAKSHAK Team would like to clarify the purpose of this article. This article is not against Sikhs or Sikhism. It is purely meant to report the Indian Army's action at the Golden Temple against heavy odds. We do not intend to discuss the causes, the misrules, the politics, the scheming that led to this mess in the first place. This sad event hurt both the Indian Army which went in with a heavy heart and the patriotic community of Sikhs who have given so much to India.

"We went inside with humility in our hearts and prayers on our lips." General K. Sundarji

For the last three years Punjab was gripped by terror. The Pakistan-backed terrorist movement had acquired monstrous proportions. Not a day went by without massacres of Hindus, Sikhs, migrant workers and those who opposed the terrorists diktats. From Golden Temple, the most sacred symbol of Sikhism and seat of its religious power, hit lists were drawn up and death squads were dispatched under the guidance of the malevolent figure Jarnail Singh Bhindranwale. The chanting of the gurbani was now drowned by the staccato bursts of gunfire. Prominent Sikh figures were assassinated in the Golden Temple when they went to pray there. Pushed to the wall, the Indian Government under Mrs. Indira Gandhi, gave the signal for the most complex and largest anti-terrorist action in the world.

May 30 to June 2

As the death toll from extremist actions climbed, the Government started holding frequent consultations with the Army. On May 30th, units of the 9th Infantry Division based at Meerut, started moving in on to Amritsar and other important towns. Para-Military forces were placed around the temple. The extremists responded with heavy exchanges of fire lasting for hours. Meanwhile newly fortified positions were coming up all around. On June 1st, curfew was clamped and troops and para-militaries fanned along the 12,168 villages of Punjab. The Akalis were threatening a food movement agitation, designed to stop the movement of food grains to other states.

Last minute attempts to get the moderate Akalis to reach an agreement came to a naught. The state was then put under siege. Lt. Gen. Ranjit Singh Dayal, Chief of Staff Western Command was brought in as security advisor to the Punjab

Governor. Men of the 12th Bihar Regiment fanned to take positions across the roof tops. Soon they realised that they were vulnerable to grenade attacks from the top of the 18th century towers and water tank.

The Biharis were moved to sandbagged windows in vacated houses. Similarly, men from the Garhwal Regiment and The Brigade of The Guards were moved on the other side of the temple. Tanks fanned out to guard sensitive villages to prevent communal killings.

June 3

By now the whole state has been secured. The Biharis watched the area of the clock tower, the main entrance and Brahm Buta Market, the Garhwalis, the Guardsmen and Punjabis overlooked the Chowk Parag Dass, Chhati Khui, Atta Mandi, Baba Atal and Buddhi Lutt Bazaar. The aim was to apply psychological pressure to break the extremists resolve. Officers used loud-hailers to ask them to surrender peacefully. The reply was automatic gun fire. The jawans replied with bursts of automatic fire of their own. The extremists responded with grenade and heavy machine gun fire from the top of water towers.

June 4

It was now evident that this was no rabble army, but a determined insurgent army fired up with religious fervour. It was decided to deal with them effectively. 106mm jeep-mounted RCLs were brought in to fire at the pillboxes. But the concrete pillboxes proved hard to crack and it was decided that stronger firepower was needed. A 3.7" howitzer was brought in. This was a risky move, as the artillery had to be elevated almost vertically and a miss would mean it would land on the top of houses.

Thus the two elevated 18th century Bungas on either side of the langar, and the elevated water tank to the rear of the Teja Singh Samunsari Hall were targeted. The firing lasted five minutes, at the end of which the pillboxes were blown to pieces with sandbags and the sniper's bodies flying apart.

Maj. Gen. Brar, Lt. Gen. Sundarji and Gen. Vaidya: Tough Act

By now the senior commanders, Maj. Gen. Brar and Lt. Gen. Sundarji, had realised there was no way to avoid bloodshed. Brar went in and spoke to all the troops. Spending 30 minutes ate each location he explained the difficult and terrible mission at hand. It was not against Sikhs but against terrorists. This was to be a volunteer mission. Not one of the many Sikh officers, JCOs and ORs, opted out.

The die was cast for Operation Bluestar. The operation was to be launched in the following phases:

I-Initial Operations:

(a) BSF to secure Hotel Temple View by 9 pm, June 5th.

(b) CRPF to secure Brahm Boota Akhara by 10 pm, June 5th.

II-Phase 1

(a) 10 Guards to secure Northern Wing of the Temple Complex by 1 am, June 6th.

(b) 1 Para-Commandos:

- (1) Secure a foothold in the Akhal Takht at the earliest and not later than 1 am, June 6th.
- (2) Secure a foothold in Harmandir Sahib with divers and neutralise demolitions, if any, by 11:30 pm, June 5th.

(c) Special Frontier Force (SFF) to isolate Akhal Takht and secure western flank by 1 am, June 5th.

(d) 26 Madras to secure southern and eastern wings by 1:00 a.m., June 5th.

(e) 9 Kumaon to secure Guru Ram Das Serai and SGPC building by 1:00 a.m., June 5th.

III-Phase 2

(a) Mopping up all areas secured in Phase 1

IV-Phase 3

(a) 9 Kumaon-extend operations to secure the rest of hostel complex.

(b) Units of 10 Guards, SFF and 1 Para Cdo to secure rest of Temple Complex and check prisoners.

Others: 12 Bihar was to continue to cordon of the Temple with CRPF units under its command and provide fire support to any target within its span of observation.

MECHANISED UNITS

Armour: 16 Cavalry

(a) Three tanks to enter through the main temple entrance, initially for close protection for 10th Guards but thereafter for support to infantry, paras and SFF with machine gun fire.

(b) Three tanks to enter the langar area and provide machine gun fire for the 26 Madras.

Mechanised Infantry: 8 Mech Btn

(a) Four BMPs to carry para-commando/divers.

(b) Four BMPs and three Skot APCs to support the 26 Madras and Paras.

Reserves: 15 Kumaon-2 companies as backup for 9th Kumaon and 2 companies for any contingency tasks.

Central Rendezvous and Logistics Control-City Kotwali.

Divisional Tactical HQ-Roof Top outside Temple complex.

H-Hour for operation launch 10 pm, June 5th

One last minute attempt was made to avoid bloodshed. A senior civil administration member and a senior army officer through a public address system asked militants and devotees to come outside. From 4:30 pm to 7:00 pm the attempts continued. Only some 129 devotees many of them very sick were let go. The other hapless ones were held hostage inside, one used as a deterrent to the army.

1. Akal Takht
2. Darshani Deori
3. Harmandir Sahib
4. Sarowar
5. Parikrama
6. Main Entrance (Clock Tower)
7. Hotel Temple View
8. Brahm Buta Akhara

9-10. Ramgaria Bungas (Towers)

11. Guru Ramdas Langar -
12. Guru Ramdas Serai / Akal Rest house
13. Water Tank
14. Seraiside Entrance
15. Teja Singh Samundari Hall
16. Manji Sahib Congregation Hall
17. Guru Nanak Niwas
18. Baba Atal Gurudwara
19. Rear Entrance
20. Sikh History Library

At 7:00 pm troops started moving up to take their appointed positions. From the surrounding balconies, people watched the rumble of trucks and tanks, as night fell and a darkness of gloom settled in the city. In order to prevent a violent backlash there was a total shutdown of he telecommunication and electric system.

Punjab was virtually cut off from the rest of India. Initial operations went through as planned with the both the Hotel Temple View and Brahm Boota Akara secured with little resistance. It was however not surprising as they were isolated and only existed to provide early warning of the army's approach. However the battlements on the top of the clock tower were proving harder to knock out and thus H-hour was postponed by half an hour. At 10:30 pm the first phase of Operation Bluestar commenced.

THE TEMPLE COMPLEX

Main Entrance-North Side

At H-hour, the men of 10 Guards, under Lt. Col. Mohammed Israr geared up to maintain their reputation as one of the world's finest troops. At 10:30 pm, the leading elements of the 10 Guards moved through the main gate. Immediately they came under heavy and accurate machine gun fire, cleverly sited through wired enclosures on either side of steps. While some troops broke through the trap and reached the ground floor, others cleared the machine gun nests. For those who made it across the steps, another nightmare awaited.

For the couple of minutes they were caught in the open, before taking the cover of the Parikrama but then they were fired upon from the Parikrama itself. 20 soldiers were mowed down in the initial assault. Captain Jasbir Singh Raina, who had three days before done a recce of the temple was severely wounded in the leg by a burst of machine gun fire. This young Sikh officer in tremendous pain refused to evacuate but was eventually ordered to do so. Unfortunately he lost the use of the leg. The troops started inching their way towards the Akal Takht but were fired upon from the southern side.

Meanwhile each room had to be cleared along the Parikrama, many by hand-to-hand combat. Militants would come out and lob a few grenades and rush back in. As troops cleared a room and moved forward they found militants again appearing from the rooms. Unknown to the Army, was an elaborate structure of concealed manhole and underground passages. Meanwhile a machine gun site was fitted about 12 inches from the ground. This low sitting meant even crawling troops were hit. While this was going on, another group of men were preparing with cool and calm, that comes with being an elite unit. These men clad in black dungarees, with bullet proof vests made last minute checks on their specialised weapons. The Indian Army's youngest units-the Para Commandos-was about to be blooded.

Their objective was to get a foothold in the Akal Takht and a foothold in Harmandir Sahib with the help of divers.

As they slipped in and made a dash across the Parikrama they met a similar fate to the Guardsmen. The Parikrama was exposed to fire from all four sides. Realising their predicament, the commandos dashed from pillar to pillar trying to cut off the suppressing fire. As they reached the Akhak Takht their misery was compounded by the devastating machine gun fire from the fortified Akal Takht, as well as the Harmandir Sahib and the area of Darshani Deori-Toshakana. Caught between the Sarovar on one side and the fortified concrete building on the other, the commandos had no option but to inch their way by fire and movement.

The Guards were asked to bring fire down on the northern side from whatever portions of the northern side they had secured. Meanwhile the senior officers were barking orders to ensure that under no condition was any fire to be returned on Harimandir Sahib. It is incredible that the orders were obeyed. The commanders were to note later that they never expected the troops to obey such orders. The mission of the divers to slip across the Sarovar was aborted as they would have not survived the murderous fire.

By midnight the Guards had secured the eastern half of the North Wing but the Western side was only 75% secured. Due to the severe casualties suffered by the first two companies, the third company was pressed in. Rather than wait for the complete clearance of the ground floor they were asked to secure a foothold on the first and second floor. This was deemed necessary to provide some sort of fire to the bogged para commandos and the SFF. One platoon climbed to the first floor using aluminium ladders. They then moved methodically clearing the rooms one by one by lobbing grenades and spraying it with fire. Another platoon likewise moved from the first to the second floor and started clearing the rooms. Troops moving up from the ground floor were suddenly fired upon by militants through an opening in the wall next to the staircase. Some casualties resulted, but the troops quickly wiped them out. By now 145 militants lay dead along with 19 Guardsmen. By 1 am, the Guards had secured their objective and could now bring covering fire for the beleaguered commandos.

The Para Commandos were still inching their way to the Akal Takht. This five-storied building was heavily fortified with all windows, balconies and other openings closed with brick masonry and sandbags, with small loop holes through which machine guns were being fired and grenades being lobbed. Together with a double storied building, the Nishan Sahib building and the Darshani Deori, they transformed the quadrangle into an ideal killing field. The leading team of para commandos made a desperate dash for the Darshani Deori. The foothold was needed to launch the CS canisters. Of the 35 men, only 12 made it. The remainder, including team leader Major Prakash Chand Katoch, were cut down. The SFF started with 50 men, had already 17 casualties (three dead). With midnight approaching, casualties mounting and the objectives far from being achieved, the situation was desperate.

Serai Entrance-Eastern Side

On the eastern side, the 26 Madras was expected to enter and then sweep the southern side of any resistance. The entry from the southern side was ruled out because of the narrow passage not allowing for entry of any vehicle. But two companies of 9 Garhwal were stealthily brought in, as backup near the Southern entrance. But they had been delayed by a steel gate which was much more formidable then expected. It needed a tank to ram it down. At H-hour, 26 Madras started to move in but came under a withering fire from atop the Langar, Guru Ram Das Serai, SGPC building, Manji Sahib and Gurdwara Baba Atal Rai. In addition the steel gate was proving difficult to break. 30 metres from the gate they came under fire from medium machine guns from the Deori itself. A section went ahead to lob grenades and clear it, but could not succeed. At this moment a sniper's bullet hit Lt. R.P. Ropiera killing him.

As casualties mounted, the CO-Lt. Col. Panikker, changed his original plan quickly and moved some of his troops in an opening on the south west side. This gave some relief but progress was slow as they had to fight it room by room, like the Guardsmen on the other side. At 11 pm, with 26 Madras behind schedule, the Garhwalis were asked to move in from the south side and secure a foothold on either side of Atta Mandi. They could then assist 26 Madras by laying down suppressive fire and allow 15 Kumaon to launch an attack on the Akal Takht from the south west. The committing of the reserves was decided based on the fact that the Guards were now more or less in control of the northern side. Garhwalis moved with little difficulty and by 1:30 am had secured the ground and upper floors of the southern gate. The 15 Kumaon, under Lt. Col. N.C. Pant, was in the process of building to launch an attack on the Akal Takht.

At 2 am the overall picture was as follows:

1. The 10th Guards suffering heavy casualties, had more or less secured the northern wing. Sporadic militant activity from concealed chambers was still a problem.
2. 26 Madras had stalled, but was now gaining ground between the eastern and southern wings. However there was still heavy opposition.
3. 2 companies of 9 Garhwal had secured a foothold in the southern gate.
4. 1 Para Cdo and SFF had bogged down within reach of the Akal Takht.

Reorganising

At this point Brigadier A.K. Dewan, an armoured corps veteran and Dy GOC of 15 Division had come to see if his troops (9 Garhwal) had reached their location. Brar placed Dewan in charge of 26 Madras, 15 Kumaon and the two companies of 9 Garhwal, and created an ad hoc task force. By 2:30 am, Brigadier Dewan took charge of the Garhwalis and Kumaonis while 26 Madras had still to join up. Meanwhile Maj. Gen. (retd.) Shahbeg Singh realising that the only way to win was to hold of the Indian Army till dawn, poured in an even higher volume of fire. Brar now sought Sundarji's permission to use tank fire to neutralise the Akal Takht's concrete defenses. Lt. General

Sundarji watching the proceeding from the Divisional Tactical HQ, agreed and relayed the request to New Delhi.

Meanwhile reports started trickling of volatile Sikh masses gathering on the outskirts of Amritsar. In the meantime, in order to help the SFF and Paras, a tank was brought in and asked to switched on its search light. It was hoped that this would temporarily blind the defenders as well as allow the SFF and Paras locate some of the defences. But unfortunately this move failed as the Xenon lamps filament burned out in a couple of minutes. When this happened, another tank was moved in followed by a third. Thus all 3 tanks were in the Parikrama. Meanwhile at 4 am, a Skot APC was brought in. Since it is a wheeled vehicle, the tank had to roll back and forth on the steps and crush the marble slabs. Only then could the APC be safely brought in. The APC was then supposed to take a squad right up to the Akal Takht.

The Guards were asked to fire a few 84mm Carl Gustaf rocket rounds at the Akhal Takht to precede the arrival of the APC. As the APC was approaching the Akal Takht, it was hit by an RPG-7 anti-tank launcher from the Akal Takht. This came as a complete shock as none had been expected. As the APC squad dismounted and retreated, the driver was shot by a sniper. By now dawn was approaching and soon the troops in the Parikrama would become sitting ducks. At 5:10 am the clearance to use tanks came from Delhi. The 3 tanks in the Parikrama, were asked to line up their machine guns on the Akhal Takht. Dewan had meanwhile readied for an assault, and the first Madrassis were trickling having cleared the southern wing.

The first assault was led by 'A' Company of 15 Kumaon. Led by Major B.K. Mishra, a group of men reached the footsteps of Akal Takht, the first group to make contact. As they climbed the stairs, a machine gun opened up from the inside and all seven men were mowed down. More machine gun fire rained from the base and the buildings on both side and the Kumaonis were thrown back with heavy casualties. It was clear that the tank machine gun fire was not enough. The Kumaonis fell back to reorganise, having suffered 7 killed and 23 wounded. 2

companies of 26 Madras were now asked to pick up where the Kumaonis left. In the darkness there was confusion as Kumaonis and Madrassis got mixed up. It was realised that the 2 machine guns at the entrance had to be eliminated for any chance to move in on the Akal Takht. A section of troops were asked to volunteer for this dangerous task. The group was led by Lt. Jyoti Kumar Dang and was formed into two sub groups.

One group led by Subedar K.P. Raman Ravi and 4 ORs was to destroy the bunker covering the staircase by hurling pole charges. Another led by the Lt and4 ORs was to rush the first floor and silence the MG there. As the groups reached the Akal Takht, 8-9 fortified machine guns opened up. Valiantly the two groups moved forward. Subedar Ravi and his men reached the bunker and were about to launch their charges when they were cut down by machine gun fire. Lt. Dang and his men also managed to reach the first floor only to be cut down by machine gun fire. Two of the wounded men managed to crawl back. Lt. Dang, although wounded, tried to pull the wounded Subedar Ravi with him but had to give up due to the heavy fire. The barbarism of the terrorists now came through. Subedar Ravi was dragged back, attached with sticks of dynamite and blown up in full view of the other troops. In spite of this, discipline still held. 26 Madras had suffered 14 dead and 49 wounded.

Progress of Operations in the Golden Temple

It was 7:30 am and daylight was well upon us. The temple complex marble was a sea of olive green and red as dead army personnel and terrorists lay sprawled all over. The Temple of God, was a full fledged fortress. With no other option the Generals authorised the tanks to use their 105mm main guns. The high explosive squash rounds smashed into the Akal Takht throwing up flames and masonry. This subdued the machine guns. Except for a few machine gun bursts it was now calm. All troops were asked to stay in the building they had secured and wait till dusk before launching an attack to clear the Akal Takht of any remaining militants.

In response to reports of angry mobs approaching Amritsar, 15 Infantry Division moved in and sealed of the routes leading to Amritsar. At 11 am a large number of militants rushed out of the Akal Takht on to the Parikrama and fled towards the gates. Most were cut down. Seeing that the troops were not firing on the Harmandir Sahib some of them jumped in the Sarovar and tried to swim towards it. They too were killed. This led to a group of militants emerging from the Akal Takht, waving white flags. Now the Akal Takht suddenly went silent. To the army commanders it indicated that either the top leadership of Bhindranwale, Maj. Gen. (retd.) Shabegh and Amrik Singh had either escaped or been killed.

The Hostel Complex

The main buildings of the Hostel Complex were the Guru Ram Das Langar, Guru Ram Das Serai, Teja Singh Samundari Hall, Guru Nanak Niwas, Manji Sahib and Baba Atal Gurdwara.

(1) Guru Ram Das Langar: double storied heavily fortified building commanding a view of the side entrances and open area leading to Parikrama.

(2) Guru Ram Das Serai (Akal Takht Rest House): 3 storied building, 228 rooms and seven halls.

(3) Teja Singh Samundari: houses the offices of SGPC and occupied by Longowal, Tohra, Ramoowalia and others.

(4) Guru Nanak Niwas: 4 storied building with fortified roof tops, 85 rooms and one hall.

As mentioned earlier the operations was in the hands of 9 Kumaon. The operation was to commence at 10 pm, with the simultaneous launch of the Paras and SFF. It had three Vijayantas, six BMPs and three Skot APCs to provide machine gun support. In addition they were to break open the gates to help 26 Madras to enter the eastern gate. On schedule, 9 Kumaon moved into the Guru Ram Das Serai. A company was deployed on each of the floors with the fourth held in reserve. The troops encountered opposition from each of the floors although it was lighter than the temple complex. Many a place hand to hand combat resulted. The troops secured all corners and stairwells, as the rooms were to be cleared later in mopping operations.

By 1:30 a.m. the building was isolated from the rest of the complex. Two companies were left behind to secure it while the rest led by Lt. Col. K. Bhaumik moved to clear the Teja Singh Samundari Hall. Now initial briefings had indicated a large number of devotees and Akali leaders in the building. In the dark Bhaumik realised that it would be impossible to separate the militants. He decided to block the exits and ask them to surrender. The building was isolated by 2:30 am and an emissary sent to establish contact with Tohra and Longowal. Both men had initially vowed to defend the Temple to their death but now agreed to surrender.

Major H.K. Palta with a few men went into meet the leaders which also included Ramoowalia, Akali Dal secretary Gurcharan Singh, SGPC member Bagga Singh and head of the Akhand Kirtani Jatha, Bibi Amarjit Kaur. The leaders were fearful that they might be targeted and needed protection. As the troops started leading them out a group of 350 devotees rushed out to join them. At this, the terrorists threw hand grenades in the crowd and sniped at them. Total chaos reigned as the Kumaonis tried to control the situations. While Major Palta managed to get Tohra, Longowal and Kaur in an APC, snipers got Gurcharan Singh and Bagga. It was 5 am, when things were under control. About 70 innocent devotees were killed or injured in the indiscriminate fire.

With 1 company left behind, the Kumaonis tackled the Guru Nanak Niwas. The clearing operations continued. Every now and then devotees would try to escape only to have the militants throw grenades at them and open fire. By morning, the Kumaonis had 600 hundred prisoners and controlling them absorbed manpower. By 10 am, the Hostel Complex was fairly secured by 9 Kumaon. There were terrorists holed up in manholes, tunnels and concealed basements. The only are of resistance continued to be the langar. The militants continued to pour machine gun fire and hurl grenades. The Kumaonis fired back with everything at their disposal. At one point the wheat and kerosene caught fire sending huge columns of smoke. Gas cylinder caught fire and exploded intermittently. This fighting however was a rearguard action allowing some 40

Babbar Khalsa activists to escape. By the early hours of the morning on June 7th, the fighting suddenly died down. Perhaps they had learnt the fate of their leaders in the Akal Takht.

Mopping Operations, 7th-9th June

Now the job of clearing the many rooms, concealed tunnels and basements began. A number of them were captured and handed over to the Punjab Police and intelligence agencies. Meanwhile other units began cleaning the remains of the battle. The snipers continued to take pot shots. When President Zail Singh was visiting the complex a sniper's round hit his bodyguard Lt. Col. M.P. Choudhary of the SFF in the arm. The sniper was spotted on the terrace and was gunned down. After his departure two companies of 10 Dogra joined 9 Kumaon, in the flushing operations. At this point a burst of gunfire from the area around the bunga wounded four soldiers. While the rest fanned out to search for the militants, Captain Ramphal of the Medical Corps and his nursing assistants were attending to the casualties.

Suddenly a group of militants emerged from a concealed tunnel and grabbed Captain Ramphal and 2 soldiers of 10 Dogra. As the alarm was raised, the SFF and 10 Dogra got into position to clear the tunnel. The militants were asked to surrender. Their responses was to ask for the Head Priest Gianin Sahib Singh. When he was brought in the militants demanded that he come in. The scared Head Priest refused to go in and troops got ready to blast in. A demolition party crawled up and fixed explosives to the grill at the entrance. When it was blown up the SFF charged in and in the firefight, killed 7 militants inside only to find that the three soldiers had been executed in a inhumane manner. Their limbs had been chopped of. Search revealed cash, weapons and survival rations stashed away.

Behind the Akhal Takht, a lone militant jumped down and tried to make a getaway. He was caught and his turban fell away to reveal a wad of currency notes. Further interrogation revealed him to be one of many criminal elements which had taken refuge in the temple. He further indicated that many others were dumping valuables in the well behind during the course of the fighting. 12th Bihar and the Engineers lowered an anchor in the well. The first attempt pulled up 19 weapons and cash. As naval divers joined the search it revealed Rs.20 lakhs in cash sealed in trunks, gold and silver biscuits, transmitters and weapons and ammunition. A weapons manufacturing unit was discovered in a room at the top of the Deori with grenades, country pistols and rifles in various positions of manufacture. All this added to the ability to convert the holy Golden Temple into an armed fortress.

The army suffered 83 dead and 248 wounded. A total of 492 terrorists and others were killed and 86 wounded. About 1500 people were captured, including a number of Pakistanis. Thus ended the Indian Army's toughest operation. However a number of terrorists had fled to the countryside and the army had to launch Operation Metal to move around Punjab. These operations were relatively minor. The operations indicated the need for a specialised unit for such operations and led to the formation of the National Security Guards. Thus the next time around it was the NSG which was involved in Operation Black Thunder I and II at the Golden Temple along with the Punjab Police. It would take a few more years before a reinvigorated Punjab Police led by K.P.S. Gill and backed by the army, would break the back of the terrorist movement.

GENERAL K. SUNDARJI, PVSM, ADC
COAS, 01 Feb 1986-30 April 1988
Infantry, Mahar Regiment

General Krishnaswamy Sundarji (formal name was Krishnaswamy Sundararajan) assumed charge of the Indian Army, as the 14th Chief of Army Staff, on 01 February 1986. Born on 28 April 1930 at Chenglepet in Tamil Nadu, he joined the Madras Christian College only to leave it before receiving a degree. Dr A.J. Boyd, who was then the highly distinguished principal of the college, was sorry to see him leave. He was commissioned into the Mahar Regiment in April 1946 and saw action in the North-West Frontier of Undivided India and later on in Jammu & Kashmir. In 1963, he served in the UN Mission in the Congo, where he was Chief of Staff of the Katanga Command and was mentioned in dispatches for his bravery. Later, he commanded the 1st Mahar from November 1963 to November 1965 and his battalion saw action in the plains during the 1965 Indo-Pak War.

During the 1971 Indo-Pak War, General Sundarji was the Brigadier General Staff of a corps in the eastern theatre and made valuable contribution in operations culminating in the liberation of erstwhile East Pakistan into Bangladesh. In March 1974, he was promoted to the rank of Major General and took over command of an infantry division in the plains. He was chosen by General KV Krishna Rao to be part of a small team for reorganizing the Indian Army, especially with regard to technology. He came to head the Mechanised Infantry regiment, which he had himself shaped, by inducting various battalions from the Indian Army's premier regiments. He was then appointed as the Deputy Chief of Army Staff in August 1981, where he threw himself into the Indian Army's modernisation activities.

General Sundarji was a graduate of the Defence Services Staff College (DSSC) at Wellington, the Command and General Staff College at Fort Leavenworth in the US in 1967-68, the Senior Officers Preventive Maintenance Course at Fort Knox, Kentucky and the National Defence College in New Delhi. He held an Master of Arts in International Studies from Allahabad University and a Master of Science in Defence Studies from Madras University. After graduating from Wellington, he held various command and staff appointments, including that of Chief of Staff, Katanga Command and took part in combat as part of the UN forces in the troubled African state of Congo. He was Mentioned-in-Despatches for his distinguished UN tenure. He was also awarded the PVSM in 1978 in recognition of his distinguished service of the most exception order. He took over as the GOC Western Command in 1984 and was involved in the politically-sensitive Operation Bluestar, to flush out Sikh militants holed up in the Golden Temple at Amritsar.

General Sundarji was amongst the most farsighted armoured corps commanders in the Indian Army. Despite being commissioned in the infantry, he was a keen student and admirer of tank warfare. He pioneered various operational guidelines, challenged his commanders to push the men & machines to the limits. In various exercises, he is known to have ordered tanks full speed up sand dunes in the Thar desert at 70° degrees Celsius. Amongst other things, he designed the flamboyant all-black uniform of the Indian Armoured Corps. Post his transformation of the Armoured Corps, he went on to create the Mechanised Infantry. With emphasis on speed, technology and mobile weaponry it is now an integral part of the Indian Army's Strike Corps. He is also credited for shaping modern Indian Army thinking. In his stint as the Commandant of the College of Combat in Mhow, he practically rewrote the Indian Army war manual with emphasis on speed, decisive action, technology and his abiding love-armour.

As Army Chief, his operations at Sumdorong Chu in 1986-known as Operation Falcon-has been widely praised. The Chinese had occupied Sumdorong Chu and General Sundarji used the Indian Air Force's new air-lift capability to land a brigade in Zimithang, north of Tawang. The Indian Army took up positions on the Hathung La ridge, across the Namka Chu river, where India had faced a s humiliating defeat in 1962. The Chinse responded with a counter build-up and adopted a belligerent tone. Western diplomats predicted war and some of Prime Minister Rajiv Gandhi's advisers blamed General Sundarji's recklessness. But General Sundarji stood by his steps, at one point telling a senior aide, "Please make alternate arrangements if you think you are not getting adequate professional advice." The confrontation petered out.

Among the Indian Army's most articulate Generals, he guided and conducted the Indian Army's largest military exercise for its time, codenamed Operation Brasstacks, near the Indo-Pakistan border in Rajasthan. Conducted between December 1986 and January 1987, the exercise involved two armoured divisions, one mechanised division and six infantry divisions. The stated objective of Operation Brasstacks was to test new concepts of mechanization, mobility, and air support devised by General Sundarji. A man of immense wit, charm and style, he was also known as the 'scholar warrior' and a visionary with a brilliant mind.

Handsome with high cheekbones and a pugnacious jaw, and with his cap worn at a rakish angle, he fitted the glamorous image of the soldier and was married to Vani Sundararajan. He was afflicted by an ailment of the central nervous system and was hospitalised during March 1998. He passed away on 08 February 1999, at the age of 69.

OPERATION BRASSTACKS

Operation Brasstacks was a military exercise undertaken by Indian Army in Rajasthan during November 1986 and March 1987. It was one of largest mobilization of armed forces in the Indian subcontinent. Many regard this as one of the most critical point in relationship between India & Pakistan with regard to nuclear war.

The exercise's closeness to the border and the magnitude of it caused a situation where a war between India Pakistan looked imminent. There is still a considerable debate about the entire exercise as many believe that India in fact was preparing for a war against Pakistan.

Indian Army Rationale and Moves

The Indian army chief at that time was Krishnaswamy Sundarrajan populary known as Sundarji. Sundarji advocated modern methods of warfare and professionalism in the Indian army. According to Sundarji, Operation Brasstacks was carried out to test new concepts of mechanization, mobility, and air support.

The scale of the operation was bigger than any NATO exercise and the biggest land exercises since World War II. According to retired Lt General PN Hoon of the Indian Army, Operation Brasstacks was a mobilization of the entire army of India. The entire exercise took place in the deserts of Rajasthan instead of the sensitive regions of Kashmir and the then restive Punjab. At one point of time nearly 400,000 Indian troops were deployed directly across the Pakistani state of Sindh leading to Pakistani fears that India was displaying an overwhelming display of conventional superiority and was in fact planning to invade Pakistan and dismember it by surgical strikes.

Pakistani Response

Pakistan's response was to mobilize its own forces near the Indian state of Punjab. The then president and army chief of Pakistan, General Zia ul Haq viewed the exercise as a direct challenge and threat to Pakistan and issued commands to his armoured units to move to the front lines.

By mid January, both the Indian army and the Pakistan army were facing eye ball to eye ball on the frontiers. The situation could have potentially lead to a war between the two *de facto* nuclear weapon states (India had already conducted a nuclear test in 1974 and Pakistan was also believed to possess nuclear weapons at that time).

Nuclear Saber-rattling

The nuclear threat was brought into the picture by the Pakistani nuclear scientist A Q Khan. Khan stated in an interview to Indian journalist Kuldip Nayyar that Pakistan would retaliate with the nuclear bomb towards any offensive move by India against Pakistan.

This threat by Pakistan was considered to have prevented an all out aggression by Indian army. India responded that it was re evaluating its options after this disclosure by Khan. Khan in fact retracted his comments after a few days.

End of Operation Brass Tacks

According to events that played out and stance taken by the Indian army, Operation Brasstacks was only an exercise and not supposed to be a provocative one. The media was involved after this and intense diplomatic maneuvres followed preventing any further escalation in hostilities.

Indian Prime minister Rajiv Gandhi and Pakistani President Zia ul Haq involved in Cricket diplomacy to resolve this issue towards a peaceful end.

GENERAL V.N. SHARMA, PVSM, AVSM
COAS, 30 April 1988-30 June 1990
Armoured Corps, 16 Light Cavalry

General Vishwanath Sharma assumed charge of the Indian Army, as the 15th Chief of Army Staff, on 30 April 1988. General Sharma belongs to a distinguished military family whose members have served in the Armed Forces for two generations and produced three Generals. He is the son of Major General Amarnath Sharma who retired as the Deputy Director General of Medical Services.

His oldest brother is none other than the late Major Somnath Sharma, who was awarded Independent India's first posthumous Param Vir Chakra-the highest medal for gallantry-on 03 November 1947 for the Battle of Bagdam in Kashmir in October 1947. His older brother, Lieutenant General Surindranath Sharma, retired from the Army as Engineer-in-Chief and his younger sister, Kamla Tewary, is a doctor retired from the Army as a Major. Lieutenant General Surindranath Sharma's youngest son, Major Gautam Shavnik, continues the long time family tradition of serving in the Indian Army.

General Vishwanath Sharma was educated at Sherwood College, Nanital and later at the Prince of Wales' Royal Indian Military College at Dehradun. He joined the 5th Regular Course at the Indian Military Academy (IMA), Dehra Dun and was the first recipient of the Rajputana Rifles Gold Medal for tactics and leadership. He was commissioned into the 16 Light Cavalry on 04 June 1950 and was on the rolls of this Armoured Regiment for 16 years. He has held important commands, staff appointments and instructional assignments. As a young Major, he saw action during the 1965 Indo-Pak War in the Lahore sector.

As a Lieutenant Colonel, he commanded the 66 Armoured Regiment and was later appointed as an instructor at the Defence Services Staff College, Wellington. During the 1971 Indo-Pak War, he served as the Colonel General Staff Operations of an Armoured Division. On promotion to Brigadier, he commanded a mountain brigade in an insurgency affected area and was awarded the Ati Vishisht Seva Medal (AVSM) for distinguished service. Later he commanded an armoured brigade in the Rajasthan desert was appointed Brigadier General Staff of a Strike Corps in the Western sector. In 1980, he was promoted to Major General and commanded a mountain division in the eastern sector. He then served as Deputy Director, General Military Operations at the Army HQ. He was promoted to Lieutenant General and took over command of a reserve Corps in the western sector in 1984.

General Sharma was awarded the Param Vishisht Seva Medal (PVSM) for rendering distinguished services of the most exceptional order in March 1986. He was later appointed Commandant of the prestigious College of Combat at Mhow. He is a graduate of the Defence Services Staff College (DSSC), Wellington and the National Defence College (NDC), New Delhi. He has had vast experience in serving in all border regions with their varied terrain and types of operations. He is considered an authority in both mobile operations and mountain warfare. He took over as General Officer Commanding-in-Chief, Eastern Command on 01 June 1987. He is the Colonel of the 66th Armoured Regiment and was appointed as the Honorary Army ADC to the President on 25 July 1987. He retired on 30 June 1990, after completing 40 years of distinguished service to the nation.

GENERAL S.F. RODRIGUES, PVSM, VSM
COAS, 30 June 1990-30 June 1993
Regiment of Artillery

General Sunith Francis Rodrigues assumed charge of the Indian Army, as the 16th Chief of Army Staff, on 30 June 1990. Born in Mumbai on 19 September 1933, he was educated at St Xaviers High School in Mumbai. He joined the Joint Services Wing of the Indian Military Academy in 1949 and was commissioned into the Regiment of Artillery in December 1952. An alumnus of the Defence Services Staff College, he commanded a Mountain Artillery Regiment from 1970 to 1971 and during the 1971 Indo-Pak War served as a General Staff Officer at a Corps HQ. In 1972, he was awarded the Vishisht Seva Medal

(VSM) for distinguished service during the 1971 Indo-Pak War. He commanded a mountain brigade in high altitude from June 1975 to December 1977. In 1978, he attended a course at the Royal College of Defence Studies in the UK.

After serving as the Chief Instructor (Army) at DSSC for about three years, he took command of a division deployed in high altitude on becoming a Major General. In 1981, he earned his Master's Degree in Defence Studies. After a stint as the Chief of Staff of a Corps from 1983 to September 1985, he took over as the Director General Military Training (DGMT), on promotion to the rank of Lieutenant General in 1985. The next year, he took over the command of a corps in the northern sector, a post which he served for about three years. He was appointed as the Honorary ADC to the President in 1987 and in 1988, was decorated with the Param Vishisht Seva Medal (PVSM).

He served as the Vice Chief of Army Staff (VCOAS) from 01 November 1987 to 20 April 1989, when the Indian Peace Keeping Force (IPKF) was deployed in Jaffna, Sri Lanka during Operation Pawan. He served as the GOC-in-C Central Command from 21 April 1989 to 31 October 1989 and later as the GOC-in-C Western Command from 01 November 1989 to 29 June 1990. He took over as the Chief of Army Staff (COAS) on 30 June 1990 and retired from service on 30 June 1993.

He is known among his compatriots as a visionary and a strategist. It was during his tenure that the Army started inducting women officers. His tenure, however, was not totally without controversy. A remark made by him that good governance of the country was also the Army's business, led to a debate in Parliament.

Post retirement, he served as the Director of the International Centre, Goa for nearly six years. He also served two terms on the National Security Advisory Board. He has also been engaged in social and literary pursuits and has also been delivering talks on strategic issues. He takes a keen interest in education and empowering children to achieve their potential. He was on the Executive Council of Goa University for seven years and on the Managing Committee of the Goa Chamber of Commerce & Industry. He was appointed as the 32nd Governor of Punjab on 09 November 2004 and is the second former Army Chief, after General Om Prakash Malhotra (Retd.) to hold that appointment. He is also a long standing member of the Goa Planning Board and is on the Board of Governors of the Goa Institute of Management. He is married to Jean Rodrigues and they have two sons and a daughter.

THE INDIAN ARMY IN SRI LANKA, 1987-90

Introduction-The Origins of the Sri Lankan Civil War

After Sri Lankan independence there was a steady rise in Sinhala chauvinism. Like in many other countries, where a majority ethnic group is upset by the advancement of a educated and hard working minority the result was a "Sinhala only" policy. This drove the Tamils out of traditional job and opportunities. As the educated class had no land to fall back, frustration began building up. A methodical Sinhala wedge was driven between Vanni and Trincomalee district. With all major industries being handed to Sinhalas, the only economy to fall back on was smuggling.

The Tamils were initially influenced by the Indian Freedom movements leadership like Gandhi, Nehru and Bose. But as the Indian method of peaceful mass resistance, satyagrahas, etc did not work the militancy of Netaji Bose provided the new approach.

To this day Netaji Bose is talked about in glowing terms. The high education state, accentuated political awareness, strong traditional pride and a growing sense of loss created an explosive mix. It led to the formation of various militant groups like the LTTE, ERPLF, EROS, etc. As the state responded heavy handedly the militants started hit and run tactics on the Sri Lankan Army and para-militaries. One such ambush caused the deaths of 13 soldiers. This triggered of major anti-Tamil riots in Colombo and elsewhere resulting in the massacre of hundreds of Tamils. This completed the separation of the two sides and a bitter civil war started.

Operation Poomalai-India Intervenes

The civil war in Sri Lanka between the Sinhalese majority and the Tamil minority had escalated. The situation had deteriorated to such an extent that in Jaffna, there was large scale casualties amongst civilians. The Indian Government tried to coerce the Sri Lankan government into halting the offensive against the LTTE (Liberation Tigers of Tamil Eelam). An initial attempt to send food and medical supplies, by boat, was prevented by the Sri Lankan government. This led to Operation Poomalai (Garland). On 4 June 1987, five AN-32s escorted by four Mirage 2000Hs air-dropped 24 tonnes of relief supplies.

This led to the Indo-Sri Lanka accord, to establish peace and normalcy in Sri Lanka on 29 July 1987. This was to be upheld by an Indian Peace Keeping Force (IPKF). The first phase envisioned the supervision of the surrender of arms by the various militant groups. Soon some 24 AN-12s and AN-32s flew into Palaly carrying two Indian Army battalions constituting the IPKF. On July 30th, Lieutenant General Depinder Singh, the Indian Army's GOC-in-C Southern Command flew into Jaffna to discuss arrangements with the Sri Lankan forces. The next few days saw the bulk of an infantry brigade comprising the Sikh Light Infantry, the Maratha Light Infantry, the Mahar Regiment plus supporting elements had landed in northern Sri Lanka. By August, the 54th Infantry Division under the command of Maj Gen Harkirat Singh and the 340th Indian Inf Bde had landed in Sri Lanka.

The composition was;

- 54th Infantry Division (Maj. Gen. Harkirat Singh GOC, Brigadier Kulwant Singh, Dy GOC):-
  - o Divisional Reserves
    - * 10 Para Commando (Jaffna)
    - * 65 Armoured Regiment
  - o 91 Infantry Brigade (Jaffna)
    - * 5 Madras Bn

    * 8 Mahar Bn
    * 1 Maratha LI Bn

- o 76 Infantry Brigade (Brigadier I.M. Dhar) (Munnar, Vavuniya, Mulliativu)
- o 47 Infantry Brigade (Trincomalee-Batticoloa-Amparai)
- o 340 Ind. Inf. Bde. (Trincomalee)

THE PROBLEM

The initial phase of the agreement called for the disarmament of the various militant groups followed by the formation of the Interim Administrative Council. This was to have proportionate representation from various groups but the LTTE wanted to dominate it. Part of this fascist outlook was the massacre of political rivals and Sinhalese groups. A group of captured LTTE militants committed suicide in the custody of the Sri Lankan Army. These gave the LTTE the excuse it wanted. The turning point was;

1. Automatic and mortar fire on IPKF post at Tellipallai
2. Ambush of CRPF convoy near Tellipallai (4 Jawans killed)
3. The kidnapping of five unarmed para commandos on their way to collect provisions. These men were brutally killed by 'neck lacing'. i.e. they had burning tires placed on their necks.

A political decision was taken to disarm the LTTE if necessary by force. Meanwhile on October 8th, the LTTE carried out mortar and machine gun attacks on IPKF patrols. Following a high level Defence Ministry meeting on October 10th, the IPKF commenced its operations, code-named 'Pawan' on the night of 11/12 October 1987.

Operation Pawan-The Battle for Jaffna

The rules of engagement for this operation were strict and once again tied the Indian Army's hands. Use of artillery, heavy weaponry and offensive air support was forbidden to minimise civilian casualty and damage to property. The Indian Army's plan was to cripple the LTTE guerrilla network by capturing its headquarters in Jaffna City, a task the Sri Lankan Army had tried this for many years but had not succeeded. Pushed by the political/bureaucratic establishment the Army made a hasty plan. However it had only 91st Brigade under Brigadier J. Ralli consisting of only three battalions. One was at the front, one at point Pedro and one west of Palaly.

Furthermore each battalion was staffed to only 50% and had none of its heavy weapons as they had not been expecting a fight. The IPKF push into the city was contested by the LTTE at every nook and corner. It had to fight against heavily armed guerrilla, in a heavily built up and densely populated urban area already fortified and extensively mined during the three years of war with the Sri Lankan Army. Both sides took heavy casualties. Furthermore all the approach roads were pitted with Claymore mines or huge drums filled with explosives, buried in the ground. The whole area was flooded with IEDs (Improvised Explosive Devices) which could be detonated by remote or radio control from over a kilometre away.

One such explosion killed 29 IPKF personnel. The attack took place along five axis to the city. A bold plan to make a heli borne assault on Jaffna University to capture the LTTE leadership was made. The plan involved a company of 10 Para Cdos. to act as path finders. They were to be followed by a company of Sikh LI. If all went to plan the heli borne troops would be linked with troops coming by land. On the night of 11/12th October 1987, the plan was put to effect. But unknown to the Indian troops, was the fact that the LTTE had sophisticated Japanese radio sets which were monitoring IPKF communications.

Heavy and sustained machine gun fire pinned down the commandos killing six of them instantly. The Mi-8s were damaged but made it back to base. A further flight of helicopters brought in a platoon from the Sikh LI. These came under even more intense fire. As the men from the Sikh LI ran out of ammo, they made a valiant bayonet charge. All but one perished.

The commandos had conserved their ammo but were close to running out. Still they managed to hold out the entire night. Next morning their battalion commander, Lt. Col. Dalbir Singh personally led a column of T 72 tanks to relieve them.

At this point the major operational base for the IPKF was Palaly airbase. This was a hub of LTTE activity and therefore a constant battle to secure it from guerrilla attacks. The IPKF was badly overstretched. On October 15/16 it halted its advance to stabilize its front. A massive airlift was undertaken to reinforce it with 3 brigades and heavy equipment. These included T-72s and BMP-1s. The improvised controllers worked round the clock to fly in troops and equipment. While the IL-76s and An-12s moved the heavy equipment the AN-32s, Hs.748s and Indian Airlines B737s brought in the troops. So heavy was the traffic that the runway in Tamabaram (Madras) cracked with the repeated take offs and landings. The Mi-8s and Mi-25s, as well as Cheetahs, were flown in. By end of October the IAF flew 2200 tactical transport and 800 helicopter sorties.

36 Infantry Division:

* 115 Infantry Brigade (Jaffna)
* 72 Infantry Brigade (Jaffna)
* 4 Bn of 5 Gorkha Rifles
* 13 Sikh LI Bn
* 41 Infantry Brigade (Jaffna)
* 5 Rajputana Rifles
* 18 Infantry Brigade
* 5 Para Bn

Independent:

* Elements of the 65 Armoured Regiment (Jaffna)

Now reinforced the fighting resumed. In some areas the anti-personnel mines were countered by rolling BMP-1s and T-72s over them. But there was another weapon in the LTTE arsenal which the IPKF found hard to combat-snipers. Located in buildings, treetops and even coconut palms, equipped with powerful telescopic infra-red sights they took a heavy toll. Helicopters flying below 2000 feet were shot at damaging five, although all were recovered. By selectively killing officers and radiomen the LTTE would bring advances to a grinding halt. Take the case of 4/5 Gorkhas. As part of 72 Brigade the battalion was supposed to move up to Jaffna and link up with the heli borne troops at the Jaffna University campus. There, it followed the T-72 tanks and rescued the Para Commandos. But while the tanks moved out, the Gorkhas bringing up the rear came under fire from four temples dominating the main road crossing in Uramparai.

Under orders not to fire back at temples, the Gorkhas tried to close in. The battalion adjutant, Major N.J.D. Singh-a tough Manipuri-was hit on the head and died instantly. Another company commander, Major Anil Gardner had the entire flesh of his leg blown off by a Claymore mine. Major A.A. Verghese the other company commander and the only Tamil speaker in the whole unit, went into a house full of crying women and children to comfort them.

As he turned to leave an old woman shot him in the back. It became disastrous, when Lt. Col. I.B.S. Bawa was shot just under his heart. Along with the other wounded he was moved to a dried up well, the only cover available. With the helicopters unable to come in because of withering fire the wounded had to wait for tanks to fight their way through. By the time they made it at 4:30 p.m., Lt. Col. Bawa died. Only two Officers in the battalion survived trough the fighting, One was the second-in-command Major Randhir Singh.

The other was a young subaltern, Lt. Raj Sinha, who had joined the Army in 1984 and experienced this battle after three years of service. Lt. Sinha was running from post to post seeing that the wounded were taken care of and fighting with the LTTE with whatever was left of the battalion along, with bullets whizzing past him, He could never imagine why the bullets went past him without hitting him. With just these two officers at the helm, the battalion became unfit for further operations till officer reinforcements were flown in. Elsewhere a BMP-1 of the 72 Brigade with Colonel D.S. Saraon was blown by a mine killing him and the entire complement of nine men. The IPKF was forced to improvise by having its officers avoid pips of ranks, wearing slouch hats and carry oversize back packs. As advances got bogged down, the battalions should have taken the time to manoeuvre around the defenders. Instead, due to pressure from New Delhi more troops were thrown into the furnace. But the mines continued to harass the IPKF. Frustrated, the IPKF cut off power to Jaffna to counter it.

To compound the IPKF's problems, it was impossible to distinguish between the Tigers and civilians. Many a times they would open fire on a IPKF unit, hide their weapons and merge with the civilians. Sepoy Govindan, Madras Regiment, says, "It was impossible to say who was a Tiger and who was not. Everyone male or female above the age of 10, could be armed and dangerous. We saw little girls producing guns from under their frocks and shooting at us. How do you fight them?" The turning point came when IMSF commandos broke out of the besieged Jaffna port and cleared the heavily mined Navanturai Coastal Road. This allowed the crucial link up between 1 Maratha Light Infantry in the fort under Colonel T. Brar and the advancing troops of 41st Brigade. This sealed off the Nallur area.

It took two weeks of bitter and hard fighting for the IPKF to wrest Jaffna and other major cities from the LTTE. Unfortunately many of the LTTE had ex-filtrated out of Jaffna. All this time the Mi-25s were not authorised to be used. Finally as patience ran out, the order to use these powerful gunships was given.

In its debut at attacking LTTE entrenchments in Chavakacheri it was used to devastating effect. For only a handful of IPKF casualties, Chavakacheri was wrested from the LTTE. Contrast to the 600+ casualties in Jaffna, this speaks monuments of the political leadership of India. Battered in Jaffna, the LTTE fled southwards. Its hard core fighters moved to the safety of the jungles by skirting the coast of Jaffna from Point Pedro to Elephant Pass, sheltered by the impenetrable jungles and criss-crossed waterways of the Nittkaikulam jungles.

Shifting to the Jungles

With the LTTE slipping into the jungles the overstretched IPKF began to build up for the long haul ahead. The 36th Infantry Division along with 2 additional brigades was brought in. It took over responsibility for the Trincomalee-Batticaloa and Vavuniya sectors while the 54th Division consolidated in Jaffna. Then in Feb 88 the 4th Mountain Division and 57 Infantry Division came in and took over Vanni and Batticaloa sectors from the 36th. The Jaffna sector was the smallest, about 60 km by 30 km) with a population of 200,000. About 16 to 20 battalions were employed in this sector. Then began the daily rituals of mine and IED explosions, unearthing of arms and shootouts with groups of LTTE men. The town of Jaffna was under the charge of Brigadier Manjit Singh. A tough and temperamental individual, he would lead some of his operations from a BMP.

His impatience with his command led him to sack two of his COs, his Brigade Major and his Signal Officer. But his personal bravery and dynamism was beyond reproach and was later decorated with the MVC. He held Jaffna well although there was always tension in the town. When his Brigade was pulled off the task was passed on to Brigadier JS Dhillon. A man of few words Dhillon moved in quickly. He used his forces intelligently constantly thinking of changes. Small units scurried around the town in vans, cycles, mopeds and autos. They would scurry across backyards and over walls constantly changing their directions. Sometimes 3 to 4 columns would move in parallel in opposite directions, lashing out LTTE hideouts and also being able to provide covering fire. He made good use of the BMPs to keep the Eastern Coastal route clear.

The Vadarmachi town was held by Brigadier Samay Ram. He was a very calm man totally unperturbed. He was a hard thinker and was able to simulate the same in his subordinates. When his men were attacked from the Nallur Kandsawamy temple he refused to attack it back because of 30000 civilian refugees in the temple premises. The standoff was resolved when the LTTE keeping in mind civilian casualties choose to withdraw. A huge cache of arms and ammunition was found in the temple courtesy the son of the head priest an LTTE member. His excellent rapport with the locals, led to a lot of cooperation from the local heads. North of Jaffna extending into Kankesanthurai and Kayts island was the domain of Brig JK Ralli. Shrugging of the criticism of his units in the early battles he used innovative tactics and constantly evolving battle drills to keep the LTTE on its toes. He was the first to build an intelligence network from the ground up. A couple of units rehabilitated themselves into efficient outfits.

In the jungles of the South, around the Killinochi farmlands, rimmed by the thick jungles of Vanni were the forces of Brigadier Jaspal Singh. The IPKF devised tactics to suit the terrain. In order to sustain operations for a longer time, without having to rely on air supplies, he established road axes for essential vehicles to penetrate the jungles for as far as possible. He planned artillery & mortar cover for all his vehicles ensuring immediate fire support. The Chetaks and Cheetahs were employed to guide artillery and Mi 25s towards the targets. Instead of indiscriminate jungle bashing, attacks were made on well identified targets. Wherever the opportunity arose for operations in flat farmlands BMPs were used aggressively. The area left of Pachchilaippali, the south eastern strip of land between Jaffna & Elephant Pass on the lagoon in the south were LTTE strongholds.

As all the routes to Jaffna and Vadamarachi passed through this the IPKF tried to make inroads here. But the LTTE wisely preferred to keep low and bypass the IPKF rather than confront them. But soon under the charge of Brigadier Panag, a veteran of the Naga campaign things began to change. LTTE trails were picked up and ambushes set constantly. While the coasts were being hit, Panag kept the pressure on land with a series of deceptive mobile posts. In the lagoons a number of frail assault boats manned by Colonel Dahiya's engineers kept engaging the superior LTTE water borne forces. South across the Killinochi belt in Mulaivithu was the largest concentration of LTTE camps and cadres. In charge of this area was Brigadier Palsokar. His men were involved in the maximum number of battles. Major action was observed in Alampil (May 88), Nittukaikulam (Sept 88) and Nayuru April May 89. These places were interconnected and heavily defended indicating the presence of the LTTE leadership.

Jungle Bashing: Operation Trishul and Viraat

About this time, the IPKF's doctrine of counter-insurgency against the LTTE was evolved. The answer was not to maintain strongholds in the Jaffna peninsula, but to actively conduct search and destroy missions against LTTE camps and bases in the dense tropical forests of the North. This 'Jungle Bashing' would involve aggressive patrolling by the individual infantry units. This also resulted in the casualties mounting steadily. but the professional pride and esteem of the Indian Army served to steel its morale.

The first phase of IPKF operations in the area was codenamed Trishul and Viraat. It spread out over the Northern provinces from Mannar to Mullaitivu and Elephant Pass to Vavuniya. As the heat turned up the LTTE started operating more from the Nittaikulam areas close to the lagoons and rivulets it new so well. This was where its supplies continued to be delivered. The LTTE was hit hard losing area commanders and leaders every day. In one instance an IPKF assault in Mullaitivu in Feb 88 almost trapped the IPKF's top leadership. A gallant rearguard action by Prabhakaran's guards ensured his escape.12 LTTE men were found dead after the fight.

Operation Trishul was launched in April 1988. Its result were modest, hundreds of weapons seized and few killed but it kept the pressure up. Operation Viraat was launched in May/ June 1988. A force of 15,000 armoured personnel, infantrymen and paratroopers were used. During the operation the IPKF stumbled across well prepared defenses. It consisted of concrete bunkers with electric generators. A few guerillas were captured or killed but most melted away. But sometimes, the LTTE struck back. When they did do so, it was at the time and place of their own choosing. So vulnerable convoys and lone vehicles became the targets for ambushes. The LTTE were masters at the use of landmines and improvised explosive devices. For a while, these IED attacks were neutralised by the cutting off power to the Jaffna Peninsula. but it was not a permanent solution. Thus the Army suffered a number of causalities to these ambushes. Ambushes by gunfire were rare, and when carried out by the LTTE, they found that the army bounced back with great fervour. The army rose to the occasion in these small actions. Young officers and soldiers displayed extraordinary courage and bravery in the face of death.

Of particular mention would be two soldiers of 1/11 Gorkha Rifles. 1/11GR was one of the original battalions that was inducted for the fighting in Operation Pawan. After the Capture of Jaffna, its mission was primarily sending patrols on 'Search & Destroy' missions. One Patrol on such a mission on 16 March 1988 in the Vallankulam Pannai area ran into an ambush when enfilade gunfire rained down on them from the dense jungle growths. The Gorkhas hit the ground and returned fire. Slowly they organised themselves and extricated themselves out of the site. In the Melee, two Jawans got separated from the main column, Havildar Devinder Singh Gurung and Rifleman Rajender Bahadur Thapa were both pinned down by heavy fire. By the time they could extricate themselves, the main column has disappeared, as both were presumed to be missing in action. As both the jawans were making their way through the undergrowth, they came under fire from LTTE Snipers. In the exchange of fire, Havildar Gurung was hit in the thigh and was not able to move. Rifleman Thapa then picked up Havildar Gurung and carried him on his shoulders to a hut nearby, returning the odd burst that came his way with fire from his Ishapore rifle.

Once in the hut, Rifleman Thapa administered first aid to Havildar Gurung and surveyed the situation around him. The LTTE had identified the two soldiers hideout and slowly have started encircling the Hut from a distance. Even as the LTTE Militants slowly made their way to the hut, Rifleman Thapa picked them off with single shots from his Ishapore. His main concern was to save ammunition, and use it efficiently. Resisting the temptation to waste the ammunition in general direction of the militants, Rifleman Thapa used it only when he could clearly identify his target. The exchange of fire went on and on well into the next day. Early morning on March 17th, a patrol sent by 1/11GR in search of the two missing soldiers was drawn to the hut by the sound of gunfire. The LTTE Militants decided to call it a day on the sight of the approaching patrol and fled. Rifleman Thapa and Havildar Gurung were thus recovered safely. Rifleman Thapa kept a cool mind and as a result he was able to keep the LTTE Militants at bay for more than 17 Hours.

During the time, he fired only 22 rounds, and was well a target for hundreds of rounds fired by the AK-47 Rifles of the LTTE. Two dead militants were recovered as well as another wounded LTTE man. It wasn't always the Jawan or the NCO that displayed such bravery and courage, young officers barely out of the Indian Military Academy (IMA) thrust into the sweltering Jungles of Jaffna too showed that they could give a fitting reply to the LTTE.

On 19 July 1988, a convoy of a two vehicles of the 7th Battalion of the Assam Regiment was making its way from Madurengkenikulam to Mangani to collect dry rations. In charge of the detail was a young subaltern, 2nd Lt. Rajeev Sandhu, who was barely six months out of the IMA. 2nd Lt. Sandhu was traveling in the Mahindra Jeep, leading the way to the 1 Ton Nissan truck which was trailing 50 meters behind the jeep. Driving the jeep was Sepoy NKKS Rajkumar, 2nd Lt. Sandhu was in the next seat. Sitting in the rear was L/ Nk Nandeshwar Das and Sepoy Lalbuanga. As the vehicles reached a track junction, a rocket fired from the undergrowth hit the jeep, lifting it into the air and overturning it to the side. Immediately a fusillade of fire from the AK-47s straddled the overturned Jeep. When the volley of fire ended, and silence descended on the ambush site, the LTTE militants knew that this was one convoy that never made it to the Army base. They came out of their ambush positions to pick up the weapons and equipment of the fallen soldiers.

But one Indian Soldier still had his wits around with him. Out of the view of the militants, 2nd Lt. Sandhu, was dragging himself with his 9mm SMC Carbine out of the wreck. Both his legs were smashed when the rocket hit the jeep, the subsequent volley of fire had wounded him and he was bleeding profusely. He checked the other occupants of the jeep. None of them were conscious. In fact the initial blast of the rocket was borne by 2nd Lt. Sandhu. The machine gun fire that followed killed both Lance Naik Das and Sep Lalbuanga in the rear. Driver Rajkumar was wounded and unconscious. Sandhu tumbled out of the Jeep and crawled to a fire position. As one of the LTTE militants by the name of Kumaran approached the Jeep. Despite his legs being totally smashed and his body ridden with bullets, 2nd Lt. Sandhu lifted his carbine with blood soaked hands and sprayed Kumaran with bullets, killing him instantly.

However, the bleeding had already taken its toll. 2nd Lt. Sandhu succumbed to his wounds and injuries. A grateful nation recognised his bravery with the award of a Maha Vir Chakra in 1990. 2nd Lt. Sandhu was just 22 years old when he died in Sri Lanka. Incidents like these were what kept the LTTE from underestimating the fighting prowess of the Army. They knew that they could not compare the fighting calibre of the Indian Soldier to that of the Sri Lankan Army. The Indian Soldier was coming from a background of operational exposure in areas like the Jungles of North east and the Mountains of the North. Death and Hardship were not a stranger to him, thus He was more ready and more experienced in fighting back to the hit and run tactics of the LTTE.

As a prelude to the elections to the newly created North Eastern provincial council the IPKF launched Operation Checkmate. Operation Checkmate did bring some results, inflicting causalities on the LTTE. On one occasion, the IPKF almost caught the top LTTE Leadership consisting of Prabhakaran, Mahataya and others. But in the fluid situation, the LTTE leaders managed to slip out. Many camps and carefully sited positions of the LTTE were rooted out and destroyed. These measures ensured that the LTTE was in no position to disrupt the coming elections. The Jungle Bashing soon came to a halt, as the IPKF concentrated on the upcoming Provincial Council elections. Operation Checkmate ended by the middle of October 1988.

Consolidation, Elections, Victory and Withdrawal

With the LTTE in the jungles the ding dong battles continued. The LTTE underestimated the strength required to tie down the IPKF in Jaffna. So in August-September 88 an influx of LTTE cadres and junior leaders into the peninsula again started. Encounters and shootouts increased and many of these cadres and area leaders were wiped out. All this was achieved through aggressive patrolling rather than specific intel. The mounting pressure on the LTTE caused concerns among the religious leaders, erudite professionals and Senior Citizen groups. Upto now these groups had been mouthing LTTE drafted propaganda on IPKF massacres, destructions of civilian properties, infrastructure etc. The aim was to coerce the IPKF to restore the infrastructure so that the LTTE could use it to fight more vigorously.

The IPKF authorities continued to reason with various citizen groups about the need for a political understanding. The LTTE's stubbornness was highlighted at every opportunity. Little by little the IPKF made inroads into the civilians. The first talk of trying to reason with the LTTE emerged under the cover of a cautious ceasefire. Meanwhile the decimation of the LTTE's local leaders in the towns continued. Citizens of Kankesanthurai, Point Pedro, Killinochi and others indicated their willingness to reason with the LTTE. The turning point was the agreement of Chavakacheri to agree that too in writing. As a sign of easing tension the IPKF withdrew hundreds of checkpoints, road blocks and bunkers from the towns. But the LTTE did not budge and shooed away many of the citizenry, scolding them for their lack of understanding about the implications. The disappointed citizenry returned and subsequently could not question the IPKF on why it was destroying the LTTE.

Meanwhile Colombo issued the 13th Amendment to its constitution binging to life the North Eastern Provincial Council. Most normal life had been restored including posts, banking, trade etc. But the LTTE imposed mental barrier remained. The armed fight was not the answer as for every LTTE militant killed another would take his place as long as the idea of

'Eelam' remained. The answer was to hold take a chance and hold the political elections for the NEPC with hopeful LTTE participation. Once the IPKF suggested this idea the Indian Administrative service and Foreign Service under J. N Dixit took charge. The various Tamil groups were asked to register as political parties. The EROS and LTTE refused. Even the moderate TULF, PLOTE and TELO opted out. Only the ERPLF agreed followed by the ENDLF. Jaffnaites were upset as they expected only the LTTE to represent them. A town meeting was arranged and an open invitation issued to the LTTE.

Nut all this was to no avail and the ERPLF and ENDLF candidates were elected unopposed. Although not accepted by the Jaffnaites and other Tamils the exercise allowed the holding of the Presidential elections as well as the Parliamentary elections. This time the EROS was persuaded to stand for the elections. This however did not please RAW. There was the threat of LTTE violence and electoral officers had the protected as well as pick up other employees for duty before they could become "absent". Barring a few cases of firing on IPKF patrols the elections went peacefully although he voter turnout was low. The whole thing was monitored by Commonwealth observers. The IPKF had done its duty sacrificing a few lives to bring democracy to this embittered land.

Now that some sort of political structure was restored the next step was to set up a body to monitor law and order. It would take some of the pressure of the IPKF but also enhance the feeling of self rule amongst the Tamils as well as create job opportunities. Mooted by General V.N. Sharma, Chief of Army Staff, its idea originated from British and French examples. Also with the Sri Lankan Police virtually moribund there was no other option. Colombo baulked at this while New Delhi backed the plan.

Unfortunately due to LTTE threats against traitors, Colombo's apathy the quality of the people attracted to the force was poor. This meant that the majority were recruited from the NEPC's ruling party. And once in the CVF they tried to enforce the interests of their party. It was a long ordeal to get the CVF going.

There were now three schools of thought in the IPKF:

1. Let the NEPC and CVF handle and reduce the IPKF progressively
2. Maintain the IPKF as long as it requires to implement the ISLA (internal estimates put it at 10 years)
3. Leave the problem to the NEPC and Sri Lankan Govt.

Meanwhile the pressure on the LTTE was to be continued.

Operation Baaz-Extension of Operations: With the success of the Provincial Council Elections and Sri Lankan Parliamentary elections the IPKF resumed operations. It now faced some hard choices. There needed to be a purpose to avoid drop in troop morale due to sense of aimlessness and lack of clarity in purpose. But while it figured out the best course of actions normal Operation Checkmate was resumed.

The aim was to continue to hound the LTTE forcing it to come to the peace talks. While parleys were going on in India the IPKF focused on the strongholds in the Nittikulam district north east of Vavuniya. This led to some fierce fighting including hand to hand. One such action took place on the shores of the Nayuru lagoon, south of Alampil. The shores of the lagoon are densely forested. One of the Battalions freshly inducted after the Operation Viraat was the 6th Battalion of the 8th Gorkha rifles regiment. 6/8GR was vested with the task of being the scout unit in the Jungle Bashing mission of Operation Baaz, and they started their operations in the last week of February. On 02 March 1989, two Companies of 6/8 GR set out on a 'reconnaissance mission'. This was a mission to search and weed out any LTTE elements, the details had 48 hours worth of rations with them while on the move. The Unit was not expecting much action. Till then, their activities in Sri Lanka involved only manning of road blocks and conducting searches at these road blocks. Their only hour of excitement was when they nabbed a hidden Dinghy and an outboard motor being carried in a Tractor-Trailer.

As the Lead platoons made their way through the thick and dense jungle, One of the sections in the front ran into an ambush. The LTTE men opened fire with their LMGs and AK Rifles, killing or wounded five of the Gorkhas. Though the Gorkhas returned fire, the LTTE casualties could not be ascertained. Even as the fighting was going on, the Gorkhas realised that they had stumbled upon the outer defences of a major base.

In such a case there would be a couple of tiers of defensive positions before the main camp a good 10-12 km behind. This was the reason the LTTE outer defences were holding their ground. This spurred on the Gorkhas to renew their assault with more fervour. By nightfall the fighting became confused. The Commanding Officer of the Gorkha's Colonel V.K. Bakshi sent back calls for more reinforcements.

As the Gorkhas ran out of ammo they drew their kukhris and waded into the LTTE. Somewhere along the line Colonel Bakshi was fatally wounded. By morning the fighting was all over a 4 km front. Helicopters flew in reinforcements. An infantry company dropped from the other side of the lagoon to help the Gorkhas ran into heavily booby trapped trails. By afternoon 5 battalions of the Army were in the area moving towards the lagoon. By March 7 when the operations were over 70 LTTE personnel were killed. The main group including the leadership melted away. Colonel Bakshi was awarded the MVC posthumously.

The Mi 8s continued to fly in reinforcements. After 2 days of build up the IPKF again resumed operations. By March 15 almost a full Division of IPKF troops were involved. The IAF intensified its operations. No 109 HU ferried in troops, ammo, equipment and food. MI 25 gunships operating out of China Bay flew large number of attack sorties guided in by Chetak helicopters. CASEVAC duties were shared by Chetaks and Mi-8s.

These operations had a telling effect on the LTTE. The IPKF meant business. It will not sit by in camps. It had the will and the ability to seek the Tigers in their lair even if it meant booby traps, mines and casualties. It was this mounting pressure, while no means a defeat but a steady decimation of its units which caused the LTTE to seek peace talks with the Sri Lankan Govt on April 25 1989. The IPKF had finally brought the parties to the table for a political solution which was the only long term solution in this type of ethnic conflict.

The LTTE Agrees for Peace Talks

The LTTE while not defeated was slowly being decimated. It had to confront the inexhaustible resources of the IPKF which was prepared to stay on for years. Its cadres and junior leaders were being wiped out regularly in the urban areas. It was primarily a jungle force albeit one with the support of the majority of Tamils. Still it was worried at the increasing influence of the moderate parties, the NEPC and the CVF. Little by little people were accepting the way of life. On the other side Colombo continued to hem and haw over the NEPC. Opposition to the accord led by the new President Premadasa.

Consumed by his hatred for the Indians he even opened up secret channels to the LTTE to arm them against the Indians. Premadasa demanded that the IPKF leave the Island and asked the Sri Lankan Armed forces to throw them out. Any movement of the Sri Lankan forces outside their barracks would kill the still alive ISLA. Lt Gen AS Kalkat warned that the IPKF would retaliate if fired upon by the Sri Lankans. IAF squadrons moved to the South while naval units moved of the Sri Lankan coast. Thanks to the professionalism of the Indian and Sri Lankan armed forces a conflict was avoided. Sri Lankan commanders must get major credit for a cool and tactful behaviour.

The NEPC was further losing support by forcefully trying to increase the size of the CVF. A new Govt also took power in India. The UF Govt of V.P. Singh was committed to the withdrawal of Indian troops. Events took a rapid turn when Colombo and LTTE under pressure from the Indians agreed to peace talks in June 1989. The LTTE finally had to come to the peace table. The Tamils were now paradoxically unhappy at the IPKFs departure but had to bear the start of a new ordeal. The IPKF started reducing its units progressively. On 23 March 1990 the last of the ships left Sri Lanka with men of the paras.

EPILOGUE

The last units of the IPKF came back in March 1990. They were received by representatives of the Union Govt although the local Govt of Tamil Nadu Chief Minister Karunanidhi stayed way. To their credit the IPKF did not scramble to get out like the Americans in Vietnam. Still it was a sense of dejection, tiredness and disappointment. The IPKF had sacrificed so many of its officers and jawans to set a professional and secular example to the Sri Lankan Armed Forces and a sense of democracy to the Tamils. All this to no avail. The palm fringed towns, farms, placid lakes, beaches and lagoons soon descended into chaos. Within months the NEPC and CVF were in disarray.

The LTTE marched back in. And soon the peace between Colombo and the LTTE collapsed and bitter fighting resumed. The Tamils in Sri Lanka are being put through the meat grinder again. Many prominent Tamils who had so vociferously protested against the IPKF on the LTTE's behalf were gunned down at the first hint straying from the path. The supreme irony is that man who led the LTTE's brilliant fight against the IPKF Mahathayya was branded a RAW spy and tortured to a state of near death. He has not been seen since. It is believed that Mahathayya was done to death on Prabharkaran's orders. Voices now ask for the return of the IPKF but there is no one to listen to them.

The Sri Lankan Armed Forces were in retreat for the first half of the 90s. But since then they have regrouped and driven the war into the LTTE's camp. Jaffna is now back again in Colombo's hands and the LTTE back to the jungles. As this is being written at the end of this century the war is in a stalemate, for a brief period in early 2000, the LTTE hit back with spectacular gains in the Island. Erstwhile strong bastions like Elephant Pass and Chavakacheri in the Sri Lankan army's hands fell in quick succession to the LTTE. For a period, the fate of 22,000 soldiers of the Sri Lankan army seemed to hand in balance. This situation renewed the calls for India to intervene. Wisely, the Indian government stayed out of the conflict.

The Sri Lankan forces have since then, consolidated their positions. The stalemate continues. For the families of the 1,157 Indian Soldiers who died in Sri Lanka, it has been a life of bitter memories. Though the government has done its best to rehabilitate those affected by the conflict, It is pretty clear that unlike the Kargil conflict, where the entire country's population rallied behind the armed forces and the families of those who died defending Indian territory, there has been little or no awareness among the Indian public about the sacrifices made by these families. In short as one correspondent wrote "They died fighting someone else's war, remembered only by their families."

Unlike the Kargil war where the bodies of the dead soldiers were shipped back to their homes and the funeral rites were carried out with full military honours, the families of the martyrs in Sri Lanka received only the ashes. The practice then was to ship the bodies of the officers home, but the bodies of the other soldiers were cremated on the Sri Lankan soil itself. Amongst the Indian Army their is a marked reluctance to talk of the Sri Lanka episode. Only a couple of books have been written by officers who served there. The College of Combat did study the conflict and accordingly rewrite many of the tactics. But what is needed is an effort understand and highlight the political, military and intelligence bungling to the general public so that the sacrifice of the many men would not go in vain. This website is hopefully a small part of that process.

THE IPKF PERFORMANCE

The Indian Army had been accustomed to wars of 2 to 3 weeks. The COIN operations in the North East were not even close in comparison to what it had to handle in Sri Lanka. The 2½ year operations against the LTTE proved tough and many were found wanting. It was brutal toughening process for the Army as an institution.

Infantry

The war in Sri Lanka was primarily an infantryman's war and sadly the infantryman was found wanting in the initial stages of the war. There are a number of valid reasons for this, from organisational neglect to operational mistakes to inadequate equipment.

Organisationally, the Army and its senior leadership had been caught up in the process of fighting the next war with Pakistan in a NATO/Warsaw Pact type clash. The emphasis in the preceding years was big exercises with mechanised forces and division and Corps level manoeuvres. The basic principles of infantry combat were neglected due to lack of time & resources committed to the above mentioned exercises. Furthermore periodic tinkering with the rank structure at the unit level, caused units & sub units to stall at the death or wounding of its commander. No matter how many JCOs and NCOs are present, true responsibility & ability rest with the officers and it is unfair of JCOs and NCOs to be expected to fill the breach without any long term training.

Operationally almost all the units in the initial phases were not to full strength. Brigades were without 1 or 2 battalions and battalions without 1 to 3 companies. Many were away in course, at firing ranges and on leave. Self imposed restrictions meant hardly any supporting fire. A brigade had six 105mm guns for fire support. Maps were in short supply and antiquated. The Battle of Jaffna was fought by units with maps of 1937! Till Tamil language courses were set up, there was a shortage of translators. The LTTE had fought and built up this environment since 1983. In contrast the Indian Army had fought its last war in 1971.

The cumulative effect of all this was a tendency to crowd in numbers. The basic tactics of fire and movement was absent. Patrols would go out in large numbers making it easy for the LTTE to keep track of them. In fact it was possible to monitor the position of IPKF patrols from LTTE intercepts. The IPKF patrols failed to use this to lure enemy ambushes into traps. Add to this the impatience of the Generals caused more troops to be thrown into this furnace. Fire discipline was poor resulting in a tendency to fire off all the ammo at the enemy. patrols would advance in single file and would leave and return by the same way. More worrying was the tendency to allow weapons to be snatched from the dead and wounded. Add to this the IPKF equipment at the unit level was poorer than the LTTEs. The Indian soldiers' semi-automatic SLRs were no match in close quarter combat to the LTTE's AK-47s. The LTTE also had better webbing, lightweight machine guns and superior radios. The standard issue DMS boot, rotted in the jungle. The VM series of radio sets were too weak in built up areas. The non availability of nickel cadmium batteries meant the ANPRC-25 radio sets could not be used as standard sets.

The other problem was the aging officer corps. There were commanding officers and company commander who were in the 40 to 45 age bracket. While the younger Majors and Lt Cols performed well, these older men were found wanting. One such commander would go into operations riding the BMP open hatch. A veteran of the 1971 war, he brushed aside his men's warnings. One day a burst a heavy machine gun fire ripped him up.

The IPKF slowly learnt to cope the hard way, in the field. Training bases were provided to train the newly inducted men the techniques of urban combat and COIN operations. Camouflaged canvas was used to create an LTTE like webbing. While some men converted their 7.62mm SLRs into full auto, the army equipped a few men in every section with the 7.62 IC with burst fire. However there were two opinions about the success of this version. While some felt its barrel would drop after a burst of fire, others felt it was fine. The Army also imported 70,000 AK-47s from Eastern Europe and flew them straight to Sri Lanka. Using the principle of infrared beam shooting, torches with extremely focused light was strapped to the rifles and the circuit connected to the trigger guard, for point & shoot. Metal sheets and thick wooden planks, help deflect bullets from sift vehicles. Sandbags were used in the beds of trucks to soften the impact of mines.

In the end whatever the shortcomings there was an abundance of courage and heroism. Even in situations with more than half the men dead or wounded there was no panic and positions were held tenaciously.

Special Forces

This was an ideal war to utilize special forces. Initially however the special forces were part of the division HQ. Later a separate Special Forces HQ, was created to better utilize them. Initially the Special forces were used like normal infantry and suffered from many of the same problems. The only difference was superior battle craft skills and better fire discipline saved the day. Later as they were used in small groups, using speed & deception, they performed exceptionally well. However there was a paramount need for better & lighter equipment, more long life rations for lengthier missions and their own helicopters and supporting fire.

The other special force in Sri Lanka was the Indian Special Marine Force (ISMF) now called the Marine Commando Force (MCF) or MARCOS. This unit made its debut in the IPKF operations and came through with flying colors. Being a small startup force it did not get caught in the infantry mode, the Paras got in to.

Mechanised Forces

The terrain is not suitable mechanised operations.. It had built up areas, lagoon, and water-logged fields. Tanks were used in direct fire mode to blast opposition in built up areas. They were used to get units surrounded by the enemy to safety. eg. Paras in Jaffna Univ raid. Initial deployment was poor with no supporting infantry on the flanks, but once the infantry battalions were to full strength they were well flanked with infantry. The T-72s managed to cope with the narrow lanes, an indication of its size and manouevrability. It was exposed to severe RPG-7 fire that helped determine its weak points. About three T-72s were lost due to drums packed with 200 kg of explosives. These had been inserted before the road was tarred.

A number of BMPs were also deployed. While some commanders complained about lack of terrain to use it effectively, others did adapt and make good use of it wherever possible. Mostly it had to be used in the dismounted role as fire support platform. In the initial stages, some BMPs were lost to LTTE drum mines. Both, T-72s and BMPs, were used to run over anti personnel mines and IEDs. Overall losses of both T-72s and BMPs were less than 10.

Artillery

Deployment of artillery was restricted, because of political orders to not use heavy weapons. Although as an area weapon it was not always the weapon of choice to flush a couple of houses full of LTTE militants, it was useful in speeding up advances when troops were held up especially outside of the built up area. The artillery observers operating with infantry units performed well. Observers lying in Cheetahs were not only useful to help being down fire, but also in forcing the LTTE to not fire its mortars lest they give away their positions.

However the paucity of guns resulted in their deployment in troops and many a times fire support to patrols were limited. The lack of night vision devices limited AOP flights.

Engineers

The Engineers were in action from the time they set foot in Sri Lanka. Even before the conflict started they were involved in defusing booby traps and mines. In fact the first casualty was an engineer and two sappers in August 1987. The engineers were involved in a number of tasks, many of them civil reconstruction projects. On the military side they provided;

1. Support to infantry troops by laying mines and booby traps and defusing those of the LTTE.
2. Building helipads and roads to maintain axes of supply as far as possible.
3. Their assault boats (BAUTs) were used for patrolling and raiding the various lagoons.
4. Improvise and extend the airfields at Palaly, make the jetty at KKS functional.

On the civil side: they were involved in repairing accommodations, electric and water supplies to the towns and hospitals as well as repairing roads. The sheer variety and ingenuity of the Tiger's use of explosives came as a rude shock in the beginning. The use of plastic jerry cans and coconut shells to negate mine sweeping devices was a novelty. Still most of the casualties were due to carelessness on the part of individual or groups.

Signals

This was one of the more secretive units of the IPKF. Led by Chief Signals Officer, Southern Command, Major General Yashwant Deva, the first task was to set up a communication hub. After scouting the locations, Mandapan in Tamil Nadu was selected. It would extend broad band microwave communication to the island, interface it with the mainland troposcatter and other field communications. The relevant info about the defunct Indo-Sri Lanka microwave system (1979) was dug up and with the help of the Sri Lankan Army reactivated. With a considerable amount of innovation all Sri Lankan cities and towns were linked into our own.

Once the IPKF was inducted C3I nodes were created in Plalay, Trincomalee, Vavuniya and Batticaloa. They provided;

1. HF radio with Burst Error Control System for Teleprinter
2. Troposcatter links and satellite channels
3. Hot lines from HQ OFC down to Divisional and Brigade HQ

But it was in SIGINT (Signals Intelligence) that the Signals were hard pressed. The Tiger's ran an extremely efficient communications network based on Japanese ICON sets utilizing (148-150 MHz). The receiver could lock on to one of 10 preset frequencies which posed problems for intercepting. These were overcome with the capture of a few sets. These captured sets were later used for jamming the LTTE network. The captured set would be utilised for generating the required frequency and then amplify it. LTTE messages were short and used a number of codes. Intercepts were quickly recorded before passed on for transalation and analysis.

In order to locate LTTE transmissions, Hungarian Direction Finding equipment was flown in. The success of this is mixed. LTTE transmitters in Tamil Nadu continued to be active for a long time. VHF sets were weak for built up areas. In the future the trend should be HF sets., Radio procedures were outdated and tended to be verbose. Many a time the communications were irrelevant. Better use should have been made of other Indian languages to delay deciphering. Ground-to-air communication was poor. Many a times, the solution was to have the army officer sit in the helicopter with an PRC 25 set, to provide communications between the pilot and ground troops.

Logistics-Army Service Corps

If there was one are where the IPKF performed magnificently it was in logistics. Originally an Army Maintenance Area was created in Madras. Even then supplies came through Supply Depot, Madras it meant to cater to 10,000 troops. But the number of troops increased rapidly forcing a rethink in strategy. Although the best process would be to obtain most of the requirements in the island itself, the resultant price increase would have caused a furor. So everything had to be brought in from India.

To store petrol and aviation fuel, more tankers were brought in. Till adequate storage facilities were developed, surplus fuel from transport aircraft were offloaded in Palaly. The aircraft then flew to Colombo for refueling before flying back to India. The logistics also required coordination between all three services. Everyday late at night men from the three wings would hash out plans to ensure an uninterrupted flow of materials the next day. The men of the ASC also organised their own security while transporting goods to various units. This was the first time such composite operations were carried out and everything had to be learnt.

RAID ON JAFFNA UNIVERSITY, 12 OCTOBER 1987

The Indo-Sri Lanka accord, to establish peace and normalcy in Sri Lanka was signed on 29 July 1987. The first phase involved the supervision of the surrender of arms by the various militant groups. This was to be followed by the formation of the Interim Administrative Council with proportionate representation from various groups. The LTTE however wanted to dominate it. This led to attacks by the LTTE on IPKF personnel.

A political decision was taken to disarm the LTTE if necessary by force. Meanwhile on October 8th the LTTE carried out mortar and machine gun attacks on IPKF patrols. Following a high level Defence Ministry meeting on October 10th, the IPKF commenced its operation code-named Pawan on the night of 11/12 October.

THE BATTLE

Jaffna University (JU) was the tactical headquarters of the LTTE. The Indian military leadership planned a quick commando raid to round up the leadership and thus cut short the Battle for Jaffna. The JU area was extremely built up. From the air the city was packed with the red & green of tiled roofs and palm trees. There were just two open patches, a football field and a smaller playground.

The plan was to land a company of 70 men from 10 Para Cdo. to secure the football field. A second wave was to follow with a company of the 13th Sikh LI. If all went to plan the heliborne troops would be linked with troops coming by land. But unknown to the IPKF, the LTTE had intercepted IPKF radio communications and knew the plans. It had sighted the landing zone and was waiting. The first wave of Mi-8 flew in and began disgorging the Para Cdos. They immediately came under heavy fire especially from 0.50 machine guns. The LTTE had the range and position right.

Sepoy Lok Ram recounted, "We thought everything was fine but as we were sliding out of the helicopter we came under heavy fire from all sides. It was an impossible situation, as people would come out of the houses fire at us and disappear right back. There were gunmen on tree tops including coconut trees. Since we were ordered not to use heavy weapons it was impossible to advance. We were fighting an enemy we could not even see."

What followed is the most painful story of the Battle of Jaffna. In the dark with heavy machine gun fire the second wave of choppers brought in a platoon of Sikh LI and landed on the other smaller playground. This was a few yards from the Jaffna University but is separated by several lanes of booby trapped buildings. The Sikhs soon realized something was wrong as they landed smack on the LTTE's battlements. Bullets rained on them.

The three helicopters were hit and pilots barely managed to nurse them back to Palaly. Their grim assessment: The platoon was likely to be wiped out as would any reinforcements. The commanders made the devil's choice: leave the platoon to its fate.

Fate was hopelessly cruel to the young commander of the platoon, Major Birendra Singh. The first man to get hit on landing was the radioman. This severed contact from Palaly. They could reach the commandos on short range walkie talkies. The commandos asked him to join them. But like a good infantryman he waited for the rest of his company. Little did he know that it was not coming. And by the time he knew he was encircled.

The first assault came at dawn. The troops fought valiantly and repelled it. As more assaults were launched the situation became grim. Each assault left them with less men and ammunition. Finally at 11:30 a.m. on October 12th, with the last bullet fired the troops led a bayonet charge. They were cut down to the last man but one. That man, Sepoy Gora Singh, was taken POW and later released. Sepoy Singh helped to reconstruct one of the most poignant battles in the history of the Indian Army.

For the LTTE this was a morale booster. The Sikhs were stripped of their weapons, uniform and equipment. Their bare bodies were displayed at the nearby Nagaraja Vihar temple and then burnt with a barrel of oil. The battle field was littered with pieces of Sikh LI's uniforms and equipment along with thousands of.50 MG shells. Meanwhile the commandos were still holding out. Their commander, Lt. Col. Dalbir Singh, led a rescue mission with three T-72 tanks. The roads were hopelessly booby trapped. The commander of the tank group, Major Anil Kaul, improvised brilliantly. Knowing the rail tracks passed behind Jaffna University, he drove his tanks on the Palaly-Jaffna rail line. Passing through the narrow lanes, an RPG-7 fired on him, hitting the turret. The explosion severed his wedding ring finger. Splinters hit him in the eye and arm. His men put him on morphine and they fought their way to the Para Cdos. A little later the 4/5 Gorkhas and remainder of the 13 Sikh LI linked up.

The Para Cdos superior training saved the day. They conserved ammo and even picked up all their dead and weapons. For 18 hours they prayed and fought. The LTTE leadership came perilously close to getting wiped out. It's Chief, Prabhakaran, was injured in the foot. The 13 Sikh LI now holds a special Ardas & Akhand Panth on October 12th every year to honour their 30 lonely and gusty comrades on the brutal killing fields of Jaffna University.

Fallen members of the Jaffna Raid

13 Sikh Light Infantry	10 Para Cdo
Major Birendra Singh	Naik Babu Lal
Subedar Sampuran Singh, VrC	Naik Ganga Ram, VrC
Havildar Ajit Singh	Naik Lakhmi Singh
Havildar Swaran Singh, SM	Naik Umesh Pandey
Havildar Kashmir Singh, SM	Naik Manohar Singh Rathore
Lance Havildar Sher Singh, SM	Paratrooper Manuwa Kujur
Naik Surjit Singh	-
Naik Gurmail Singh	-
Naik Mukhtiar Singh	-
Naik Satwinder Singh	-
Lance Naik Hira Singh	-
Lance Naik Manjit Singh	-
Lance Naik Darshan Singh, SM	-

Sepoy Lal Singh -

Sepoy Ranjit Singh -

Sepoy Kuldip Singh, VrC -

Sepoy Jarnail Singh -

Sepoy Sohan Singh -

Sepoy Gurdial Singh -

Sepoy Gurbax Singh -

Sepoy Gurnam Singh -

Sepoy Satnam Singh -

Sepoy Joginder Singh -

Sepoy Sakinder Singh -

Sepoy Bakshish Singh -

Sepoy Somnath Singh -

Sepoy Harjinder Singh -

Sepoy Sukhwant Singh, VrC -

Sepoy Sukhwinder Singh -

-SPECIAL FORCES IN SRI LANKA

At the signing of the Indo-Sri Lanka accord, an Indian Peace Keeping Force was sent to help in the disarming of the Tamil militants and oversee a ceasefire. Amongst the first troops to land as part of the IPKF, was the 10 Para Commando. This was the beginning of the long involvement of Special Forces in the Sri Lankan conflict. The Para Commandos were also the last unit to withdraw from the island.

10 Para Commando is attached to the Western Command, and was optimised for Desert Operations in Rajasthan. It has been also referred to as Desert Scorpions. However like all elite troops, they would soon adapt to the rigours of urban combat and jungle warfare thrust upon by the LTTE. The first incident for 10 Para Commando would be a sign of the problems ahead. As the accord was souring, a five-man, unarmed Para Commando unit, out to pick up rations was surrounded by the LTTE in the market place. The men were lynched publicly, by neck

lacing (have burning tires placed around their necks).When the inevitable fighting started, 10 Para Commando spearheaded many of the thrusts. A company of Para Commandos were involved in a heli-borne assault to capture the LTTE leadership in Jaffna University. Unaware that their radio communications were monitored, the commandos flew in Mi-8s and landed on a soccer field. They were immediately pinned down by a hail of gunfire. 6 commandos were killed instantly.

The commandos knew that further helicopter sorties were impossible. They collected their dead and fanned out towards the objective. But in the booby trapped alleys of Jaffna University it proved to be a difficult task. As daylight approached, they came under observed fire and broke of contact. Observing excellent fire discipline and battle craft they kept the LTTE at bay till a column of tanks with their CO, Lt. Col. Dalbir Singh, broke through to rescue them.

As the Indian Army realised it was overstretched, it paused to build up. Among the units flown in were the 5th Para Btn. However its deployment was marked by confusion. It was initially assigned to the 18th Brigade, then shifted to 72nd Brigade before being reassigned a week later to 18th Brigade. Consequently both brigades could not use the resources properly. After the Jaffna operations, 5th Para shifted to the East while 10th Para Commando was in the Jaffna area.

Slowly the nature of operations shifted from elite infantry to true special forces operations. The advantage of using Special Forces in quick raids sunk in and subsequently a Special Forces HQ was formed to control all special forces in the theatre. 10 Para Commando made a heli-borne assault in the town of Moolai in November. 25 LTTE men were killed and a large quantity of arms seized.

The Para battalions continued to rotate to give the other units combat experience. A 12-man unit was also stationed in Colombo to provide security to the Indian mission. 9 Para Commando replaced 10 Para Commando in early 1988. It conducted a series of air assaults in the coastal swamps around Mullaittivu.

While the Paras did participate in the grand operations, involving multiple battalions, it was in small strike units when they provided spectacular successes. However various deficiencies were thrown up, some which could be addressed while others had to be addressed in the future. Initially the Paras were used as infantry and tended to make the same mistake of seeking security in large numbers. Once the small unit value was realised, there was a dramatic improvement in operations.

Small units would go out to set ambushes. In order to go native, they would be barefoot or wear slippers like the LTTE personnel. But in spite of all this their ability to operate for prolonged periods was limited. One of the main problems was water. The few fresh water resources in the deep forests was either booby trapped or poisoned by the LTTE. This meant carrying your own water.

Perhaps this necessitates the need for a elite jungle warfare unit, capable of sending five-man sections in the jungle to live of the land for prolonged period of times. Another need was for them to have their own helicopters. In addition the individual weapons and ancillary equipment were bulky and needed to lightened considerably.

On the midnight of 21 October 1987, an Indian Navy destroyer moored 5 miles outside Jaffna Harbour. 18 men slipped over the sides into two Gemini motorised assault craft. Clad in black wet suits with light sub machine guns, underwater explosives and daggers strapped to their sides they were a deadly lot. Each Gemini craft towed a wooden raft strapped with more explosives. The target: the narrow & heavily mined channel leading to the Guru Nagar jetty, the hub of LTTE supplies to Jaffna city. In addition to the booby traps, LTTE snipers and machine guns overlooked the channel from high rise building around it.

The journey took three painstaking hours as they had to pause to unhook the mines, every few, now & then. Once in sight they switched to the wooden rafts and paddled so that noise of the Gemini craft would not give them away. One team attached explosives to the jetty while the other sorted the LTTE's Yamaha motor equipped 35 knot speed boats. While placing explosives on the boats they were spotted and came under a hail of machine gun fire. They fired back at the tell tale flashes. Within five minutes the 2 Gemini craft roared back into the harbour and opened up covering fire.

By dawn, the 18 men were back on their mother ship with no casualties. This was the second mission of the newest special force of the Indian Armed Forces, the Navy's Indian Special Marine Force. Patterned & initially trained after the US Navy Seals, they soon proved capable of taking any mission on land, air or sea. Their debut occurred a few days before, when they were air dropped in the beleaguered Jaffna Fort. With the help of 10 Para Commando, they broke out and cleared the heavily-mined Navanturai Coastal Road, all the time under constant fire from roof tops and sniper positions. This allowed the crucial link up between 1 Maratha Light Infantry in the fort and the advancing elements of 41st Brigade.

Three days after the Jaffna lagoon raid they were back to destroy the remaining boats. This time they swam for more than a mile under water to reach their targets. Under fire they suffered a few wounds but managed to destroy the remaining boats. Lt. Arvind Singh in charge of all three raids was awarded the MVC (Maha Vir Chakra) for his outstanding performance. Throughout the IPKF operations, the IMSF was used to launch raids in the areas bordering the lagoons.

The IPKF operations gave the first opportunity to use special forces to their full potential. The war against the LTTE required a combination of stealth, surprise, speed and innovation which the special forces could offer. However a combination of factors from lack of good intelligence, paucity of equipment for independent operations, poor personal equipment and initially the fear of failure, prevented them from being very successful. The last is especially pertinent.

Initially there was a tendency not to operate in small units because of the possibility of getting wiped out by a rebel unit and the disgrace that it would bring to the regiment. But as the going got tough, small unit raids were launched on specific intelligence and paid rich dividends. More importantly the experience would come in handy in the future, when low intensity war in Kashmir, escalated to dramatic proportions in the mid-90s.

GENERAL B.C. JOSHI, PVSM, AVSM, ADC
COAS, 30 June 1993-19 November 1994
Armoured Corps, 64 CAV and 2 Lancers

General Bipin Chandra Joshi assumed charge of the Indian Army, as the 17th Chief of Army Staff, on 30 June 1993. Commissioned in the Indian Army in December 1954, into the Armoured Corps, he has held important command and staff appointments which include staff officer with the UN Force in Gaza, Brigadier General Staff at a Corps Headquarters and as a Military Advisor in Australia from May 1973 to October 1976. He is credited with raising the Rashtriya Rifles in 1990 to fight an insurgency in Kashmir.

He commanded an Armoured Regiment in the Western Sector during the 1971 Indo-Pak War. He has also commanded an Independent Armoured Brigade and an Infantry Division. He commanded a Corps in the Eastern Sector and was also the General Officer Commanding-in-Chief, Southern Command. He has also held the appointment of Additional Director General of Perspective Planning (ADGPP) and Director General Military Operations (DGMO) at the Army HQ.

He had three tenures as an Instructor in the Armoured Corps Centre & School and was also a Directing Staff in the College of Combat, Mhow.

General Joshi has been a recipient of the Param Vishisht Seva Medal (PVSM) and the Ati Vishisht Seva Medal (AVSM) for distinguished service of the most exceptional order. He passed away on 19 November 1994, at a military hospital in New Delhi at the age of 59 as a result of a heart attack. He had complained of chest pain after he played a round of golf that morning and died soon afterward in the hospital. He was due to retire in December 1995.

GENERAL SHANKAR ROYCHOWDHURY, PVSM, ADC
COAS, 22 Nov 1994-30 Sept 1997
Armoured Corps, 20 Lancers

General Shankar Roychowdhury assumed charge of the Indian Army, as the 18th Chief of Army Staff, on 22 November 1994. Born in Calcutta on 06 September 1937, he was educated at St. Xavier's School, Calcutta, Allen Memorial School and St. George's College, Mussoorie. He entered the Joint Services Wing of the Armed Services in 1953 as a Cadet. He was commissioned into the 20th Lancers of the Armoured Corps from the Indian Military Academy (IMA), Dehra Dun on 09 June 1957.

He saw action at the Chamb-Jaurian sector in the 1965 Indo-Pak War and in the Jessore and Khulna during the 1971 Liberation War.

He commanded 20 Lancers from 1974-76, an Independent Armoured Brigade from December 1980 to July 1983 and an Armoured Division from May 1988 to May 1990. He subsequently commanded 16 Corps in Jammu and Kashmir from 1991-92. He is a graduate of the Defence Services Staff College (DSSC) and held several staff and instructional appointments, including that of Director General Combat Vehicles dealing with the Arjun MBT.

He was awarded the Param Vishisht Seva Medal for distinguished service and valuable contribution. He took over as General Officer Commanding–in-Chief, Army Training Command (ARTRAC) in August 1992. He became the Army Chief upon the untimely death of his predecessor, General B.C. Joshi, on 22 November 1994. He retired from the Indian Army on September 1997, after completing 40 years of distinguished service to the nation. Post retirement, he became a member of the Rajya Sabha and has highlighted defence related issues with great passion & vigour in Parliament.

Investing in the armed forces is like paying premium for insurance. It pinches while paying, but the insurance is what saves you when the disaster strikes-General Shankar Roychowdhury

GENERAL V.P. MALIK, PVSM, AVSM, ADC

COAS, 30 Sept 1997-30 Sept 2000

Infantry, Sikh Light Infantry

General Ved Prakash Malik assumed charge of the Indian Army, as the 19th Chief of Army Staff, on 30 September 1997. Born on 01 November 1939 at Dera Ismail Khan (present-day Pakistan), he was commissioned into the Sikh Light Infantry on 07 June 1959. He saw action in the 1962 Indo-China border conflict in the Ladakh sector. He commanded the 10th Sikh LI on the Indo-China border and played an active role in counter-insurgency operations in Nagaland from 1974 to 1977.

His other assignments include Instructor in the Senior Command Wing at the College of Combat from 1977-78, Joint Planning Staff in the Military Wing of the Cabinet Secretariat from 1979-80, Deputy Brigade Commander of an Infantry Brigade from 1980-82, Colonel of an Infantry Division from 1982-83 and Commander of the 162nd Infantry Brigade in Jammu & Kashmir from April 1983 to December 1985, where he earned the Ati Vishist Seva Medal (AVSM).

In 1986 he attended the National Defence College (NDC) in New Delhi. He served as Deputy Director General of Military Operations from 1987 to 1990 during which he dealt with operational plans for the defence of northern borders as also two international operations-IPKF (Indian Peace Keeping Force) operations in Sri Lanka and Operation Cactus in Maldives. In mid-1989, he was appointed GOC-in-C of the 8th Mountain Division which was initially deployed in counter-insurgency operations in NEFA (North East Frontier Agency). He saw service in J&K again to conduct COIN operations in the Kashmir Valley from December 1989 till May 1991.

He also held the office of Additional Director General of Operational Logistics, at Army HQ from 1991 to mid-1992. Along with operational responsibility of the Indo-Pak border, he commanded XI Corps in Punjab from August 1992 till March 1994 during which he over saw anti-militant operations. A graduate of DSSC, General Malik was posted to Military Ops. Directorate at Army HQ in the section dealing with COIN operations. He attended the Higher Command Course at the College of Combat, Mhow and was posted as an instructor in the Tactical Wing at the Infantry School, also in Mhow. As Commandant of the Defence Services Staff College (DSSC) in Wellington, from April 1994 to July 1995, he was instrumental in updating the syllabus and computerisation of staff work. In July 1995, he was appointed GOC-in-C Southern Command before being shifted to Army HQ in New Delhi as the Vice-Chief of Army Staff (VCOAS) in August 1996. He was decorated with the Param Vishist Seva Medal (PVSM) by the President of India, in the 1996 Republic Day Parade.

General Malik assumed the charge of Indian Army on 30 September 1997 and concurrently with the appointment, he took over as Chairman of the Chiefs of Staff Committee with effect from 01 January 1999. He coordinated and oversaw the planning & execution of Operation Vijay to successfully defeat Pakistan's attempted intrusion in the Kargil sector during May to July 1999.

He was felicitated with the *Excellence in Leadership* award by the Atur Foundation of Pune and also the *Distinguished Fellowship* of the Institute of Directors, New Delhi in 1999. The Doon Citizens' Council gave him the *Pride of the Nation* award in July 2000. He was Colonel of the Sikh LI from 1990 to 1998 and continues to be Honorary Colonel of the regiment for life. He retired on 30 September 2000, after completing more than 41 years of distinguished military service. During his tenure he was the Colonel of the Sikh Light Infantry.

General has settled in Panchkula, near Chandigarh and since retirement, keeps himself engaged spreading awareness and sharing his views on India's national security challenges and international relations, in India and abroad. He was a member of the National Security Advisory Board (NSAB) for two years. Currently, he is an independent director on the board of some well-known private sector companies and advisor to various foundations and trusts. He has authored and edited various defence related books and has written chapters and articles for several other security-related books.

GENERAL S. PADMANABHAN, PVSM, AVSM, ADC
COAS, 30 Sept 2000-31 Dec 2002
Regiment of Artillery

General Sundararajan Padmanabhan assumed charge of the Indian Army, as the 20th Chief of Army Staff, on 30 September 2000. Born in Trivandrum, Kerala on 05 December 1940, he is an alumnus of the prestigious Rashtriya Indian Military College (RIMC), Dehra Dun and the National Defence Academy (NDA), Khadakwasla in Pune. He was commissioned into the Regiment of Artillery after graduating from the Indian Military Academy (IMA) on 13 December 1959.

His illustrious career included several prestigious command, staff and instructional postings, besides having participated in numerous operations. He is a graduate of the Defence Services Staff College (DSSC) at Wellington in 1973 and the National Defence College (NDC) at New Delhi. He commanded an Independent Light Battery from August 1975 to July 1976 and later on commanded the Gazala Mountain Regiment from September 1977 to March 1980. This mountain regiment is one of the oldest artillery regiments of the Indian Army and has participated in several wars.

He served as Instructor Gunnery at the School of Artillery in Deolali, been a Brigade Major of an infantry brigade on its raising and served as Colonel General Staff of a Mountain Division from January 1983 to May 1985, where he was awarded the Vishisht Seva Medal (VSM). He has also spent two tenures as Instructor at the IMA. Within army circles, he is affectionately known as Paddy. He commanded an Independent Artillery Brigade and a Mountain Brigade before attending the prestigious NDC course at Delhi.

He commanded an Infantry Brigade from December 1988 to February 1991 at Ranchi, Bihar and Punjab and was then appointed as the General Officer Commanding of an Infantry Division in Punjab from March 1991 to August 1992. He served as Chief of Staff, 3 Corps from September 1992 to June 1993. After his promotion to Lieutenant General, he was commander of the 15 Corps in the Kashmir valley from July 1993 to February

1995. It was during his tenure as the 15 Corps Commander, that the Army made big gains over the militants in Kashmir and could even scale down its operations. He was awarded the Ati Vishisht Seva Medal (AVSM) for his services as the 15 Corps Commander.

General Padmanabhan held the appointment of Director General Military Intelligence (DGMI) after the successful culmination of which, he took over as the GOC of the Northern Command at Udhampur on 01 September 1996. Before being appointed as the Chief of Army Staff, he was the GOC of Southern Command. He retired on 31 December 2002, after completing more than 43 years of distinguished military service. He is a prolific writer and has even authored two books. He presently resides in Chennai.

4

LIEUTENANT GENERAL SUNDARARAJAN PADMANABHAN-A PROFILE

Lieutenant General Sundararajan Padmanabhan has been appointed as the next Chief of Army Staff (COAS) of the Indian Army. He assumes office on 01 October 2000. We will examine his biography, and attempt to predict what we may expect from his tenure as COAS. Lt. Gen. Padmanabhan was born on 05 December 1940 in Trivandrum, Kerala. He is an alumnus of Rashtriya Indian Military College (RIMC), Dehra Dun, and National Defense Academy (NDA), Khadakwasla. He was commissioned into the Indian Army in the Regiment of Artillery after graduating from the Indian Military Academy (IMA), on 13 December 1959.

His early career included two stints at the IMA, and one as a gunnery instructor at the School of Artillery in Deolali. He also served as Major in the General Staff (GS) of a newly raised infantry brigade, and as a Colonel (GS) of a mountain division. His first command was the Gazala Artillery Regiment. He was promoted to Brigadier in 1985 and had the distinction of commanding one artillery and two infantry brigades in vastly different terrain. He was promoted to Major General in 1991 and was given command of a frontline infantry division in the western sector. He then served as Chief of Staff of a Corps in the Eastern Sector. In 1993, he was promoted to Lieutenant General. A rapid promotion in less than three years indicates how highly the Army regarded him.

His charge was the highly sensitive 15 Corps in the Kashmir valley. The newly promoted Corps Commander was to have a baptism by fire in his first months of command, when terrorists created an international furor by occupying the revered Hazrat-Bal mosque in Srinagar. It is a testament to his negotiating skills, and to his deft handling of the siege of the mosque, that the terrorists surrendered without firing a shot, and without getting any concessions from the Indian government. This period also marked the turning point in the counter-insurgency war, with the Indian security forces under a unified command led by Lt. Gen. Padmanabhan slowly gaining the upper hand over the terrorists.

Along with his able Brigadier (GS) Arjun Ray, he also initiated a more open & sophisticated media management approach, which gradually won over the hostile local media and earned plaudits from the national media. Again, he was rapidly promoted to the next level, and appointed as Director General of Military Intelligence (DGMI) at the Army Headquarters in 1994. As DGMI, and later, as the Commander of the Udhampur-based Northern Command, he broke the back of local militancy in Kashmir by persuading local militants to come over ground and join the pro-India Ikhwan organization. The retirement age for Lieutenant Generals was raised to 60 in 1998, and to prevent stagnation among serving army commanders, there was a shuffle of commands under which Lt. Gen. Padmanabhan got command of the Pune-based Southern Command. This one time occurrence makes him one of the very few Indian generals who have commanded two different commands. The added experience should be of great use, as he takes over the reins of the Indian Army from the retiring General Ved Prakash Malik.

Lt. Gen. Padmanabhan's high profile postings in the 90s make possible some predictions about his style of managing the routine work of a COAS, and the substance of the changes he is likely to bring about. The bitter experience of the capable, but abrasive, Admiral Bhagwat shows that both style and substance are equally important in the realm of higher defense management. Lt. Gen. Padmanabhan's record of accomplishment in Kashmir attests that he brings to the office formidable negotiation skills to help him champion the cause of the army. Unlike the army generals up to the 1980s who led careers secluded from the rough and tumble of Indian governance, he and Gen. Malik have earned their spurs in an environment which calls for close cooperation with politicians, bureaucrats, intelligence agencies, paramilitary forces, police, and the mass media. The school of hard knocks has taught such men to be equally adept at managing king-size egos, playing hard-ball with recalcitrant parties, and inspiring subordinates. As Gen. Malik has shown already, such a set of skills is invaluable in keeping the wheels of Ministry of Defense running smoothly and without the angst & high drama that have marked some other tenures in South Block.

All officers are products of their times and their professional experience. General Sundarji, for example, developed his vision in the broad expanses of the desert, and in leading the elite armored division (1 Armoured Division) and strike corps of the army. Leaders like him have the luxury of dreaming grand dreams of armored thrusts through the desert; dreams that turned to horrors when confronted with the messy limited conflicts such as Blue Star and IPKF. Lt. Gen. Padmanabhan, on the other hand, has thrived in the convoluted battleground of Kashmir. Dirty counter-insurgency battles produce pragmatic and politically perceptive generals who are comfortable with the constraints of limited wars and peace keeping. Modern limited wars place much greater demands on training, equipment, and motivation of small units, as opposed to mass maneuver and heavy mechanization required by total wars. This means that Lt. Gen. Padmanabhan will pay close attention to preparing the Indian soldier for the kinds of conflicts he is likely to encounter.

Lt. Gen. Padmanabhan epitomizes the growing divergence between the post-independence crop of generals and the current bunch. The British were inclined towards a deliberate, attritive mode of warfare, and their Indian pupils diligently copied them in '47, '65, and '71 (western front). Even a visionary like Gen. Sundarji went in for the brute force, frontal approach in

Operation Blue Star. To the Indian Army's credit, another breed of maneuver minded leaders slowly began to emerge-witness Lt. Gen. Arora and Lt. Gen. Jacob in '71, Lt. Gen. A. S. Kalkat with his multiple pincers in Operation Pawan, and Maj. Gen. Mohinder Puri with his superb concentration of forces in Kargil. Lt. Gen. Padmanabhan belongs squarely in the latter camp-for example, it would be hard to imagine him recommending the use of brute force in breaking a siege in a religious place!

We now move on to the likely substance of the initiatives he will undertake during his tenure. These initiatives will be dictated by the politico-economic-strategic situation prevailing in the country. Lt. Gen. Padmanabhan assumes office at a time when the political scene is stable, and the government is supportive of initiatives for restructuring defense management and military modernization.

An improving economy and a growing realization of the necessity of conventional deterrent permit generous financial allocations for all three services. The lessons from Kargil, the continuing low intensity conflict in J&K, and the North East, and from other wars such as Desert Storm and Kosovo, have opened the Indian establishment's eyes to the potential of Information Warfare. There is a growing realization that India should not be left behind in this increasingly prevalent form of warfare. The army, under Gen. Malik, has already launched a computerization and computer literacy drive.

Other means, such as reconnaissance drones and satellites, and modern Electronic Warfare (EW) equipment are likely to be inducted in the coming years. A new, dedicated defense intelligence agency may be raised in the near future, and the role of the newly formed National Security Council will evolve as experience builds in its working.

These general trends will all direct and shape the initiatives that Lt. Gen. Padmanabhan will take, and in turn, he will have an opportunity to leave his mark on them. Lt. Gen. Padmanabhan is familiar with the increasingly sophisticated covert war in Jammu & Kashmir. The situation has placed a high premium on modern Electronic Intelligence (ELINT) and EW equipment, on proactive media management, on manpower management in security forces, and on intelligence operations.

By experience and inclination, he is comfortable with the new modes of thinking that modern low intensity conflicts require. Given this composite picture of the man and times he works in, his tenure is likely to usher in a revolution in the way the Indian Army fights Information Wars (IWs), in much the same way as Gen. Sundarji revolutionized Mechanized Warfare.

There is an upbeat mood among the defense management community at the prospect of things to come. Lt. Gen. Padmanabhan will assume office at a time ripe with possibilities. He has the aptitude and the experience to seize the opportunities, and we wish him the best at his finest hour.

GENERAL N.C. VIJ, PVSM, UYSM, AVSM
COAS, 31 Dec 2002-31 Jan 2005
Infantry, Dogra Regiment

General Nirmal Chander Vij assumed charge of the Indian Army, as the 21st Chief of Army Staff, on 31 December 2002. Born in January 1943 at Jammu, he completed his studies at the SRML Higher Secondary School, also at Jammu. He joined the National Defence Academy (NDA) in 1959 and subsequently commenced his distinguished career in the Indian Army upon being commissioned into the 4th Dogra on 11 December 1962.

Within weeks of his commissioning, he saw action in the Walong sector during the 1962 Indo-China War. Since then, he has served in the eastern sector on six separate occasions, a unique achievement in the Indian Army, the last time being as the GOC 4 Corps.

During the 1971 Indo-Pak War, his company was the first one to occupy the 'Chicken Neck' and also capture the 'Chhote Chak' post of Pakistan in the Miran Sahib Sector. He commanded the 16th Dogra from June 1978 to September 1980. A specialist in military operations, he has served as the General Staff

Officer of an Infantry Division, a Director in the Military Operations Directorate as a Colonel and Deputy Director General of Perspective Planning (Strategic Planning) as a Brigadier at Army HQ in New Delhi. Among his numerous achievements in the Indian Army was the planning & execution of Operation Khukri-to extricate trapped Indian peacekeeping troops in Sierra Leone.

General Vij served as the Major General General Staff (MGGS) at the Western Command in Chandimandir, Chandigarh (Punjab) in 1996 and was decorated with the Ati Vishist Seva Medal (AVSM) for his services. He was then appointed as the Director General Military Operations (DGMO) and held that post during the 1999 Kargil Operations. For his distinguished services as the DGMO, he was awarded the Uttam Yudh Seva Medal (UYSM).

The formations he has commanded include the 44th Mountain Brigade involved in active counter-insurgency operations in the north east, the elite 18th Infantry Division (RAPID), the 21 Strike Corps based at Bhopal, Madhya Pradesh and the 4 Corps based at Tezpur, Assam. As GOC of 4 Corps, he was instrumental in ensuring large-scale surrender of United liberation Front of Assam (ULFA) insurgents.

For his exceptional performance as the GOC of 4 Corps, he was awarded Param Vishisht Seva Medal (PVSM). On 01 October 2000, he was appointed as the GOC of Southern Command at Pune and led the Indian Army's rescue efforts during the 2001 Gujarat earthquake. In October 2001, he was appointed as the Vice Chief of Army Staff (VCOAS) at New Delhi and in January 2002, he was appointed as the 10th Colonel of the Dogra Regiment and the Dogra Scouts.

On 31 December 2002, he took over as the Chief of Army Staff. As the COAS, it was through his passion and untiring efforts that the border fencing in Jammu & Kashmir was completed. The wide spectrum of activities that received an impetus due to his intimate involvement were the Married Accommodation Project (MAP), the establishment of professional colleges and the Ex-Servicemen's Health Scheme (ECHS). Also during his tenure as COAS, the Royal Bhutan Army and the Indian Army undertook a joint operation to evict the United Liberation Front of Assam (ULFA) from their bases in Bhutan in December 2003.

He was also appointed as the Chairman of the Chiefs of Staff Committee (COSC) on 31 December 2004. He is married to Mrs. Rita Vij and they have a son, Nalin, who is a software engineer in the United States. General Vij retired on 31 January 2005, after completing more than 42 years of distinguished military service. He is presently the Honorary Colonel of the Dogra Regiment & Dogra Scouts and also Deputy Chairman of the National Disaster Management Authority, Government of India.

GENERAL J.J. SINGH, PVSM, AVSM, VSM, ADC
COAS, 31 Jan 2005-30 Sept 2007
Infantry, 9 Maratha LI

General Joginder Jaswant Singh assumed charge of the Indian Army, as the 22nd Chief of Army Staff, on 31 January 2005. Born on 17 September 1945 in Bahawalpur (now in Pakistan), his family migrated to Patiala in Punjab after partition in 1947. He is an alumnus of the National Defence Academy (NDA) and was commissioned into the 9 Maratha Light Infantry (LI) on 02 August 1964. He received the colour of the Battalion from President (Late) Dr. Zakir Hussain at the Investiture Parade in 1968.

Hailing from a family of warriors, General Singh is a third generation soldier. His grandfather served in the 1/67 Punjab Regiment during the First World War in Mesopotamia and Kut-al-Amara-both in present day Iraq-along with the 103rd, 105th, 110th, 114th and 117th Mahrattas.

These five battalions subsequently joined the Maratha Light Infantry, the same regiment General Singh was commissioned into 50 years later. His father, Colonel Jaswant Singh Marwah (Retd), served in the Electrical & Mechanical Engineers (EME) from 1943 to 1973 and is also a veteran of the Second World War.

During his tenure with the 7th and 9th Maratha LI and also while on higher command & staff appointments, General Singh has served in Jammu & Kashmir, Nagaland, Arunachal Pradesh, Sikkim and Joshimath in Uttarakhand. He was awarded the Vishisht Seva Medal during his command tenure of the 9 Maratha Light Infantry in Arunachal Pradesh. He later commanded the 5th Maratha LI at Hyderabad in the rank of Colonel.

A consistent front runner, he was the youngest and one of the first in his batch to attend Staff College, Senior Command, Higher Command and National Defence College courses. He has contributed articles for regimental and other professional journals and his thesis on 'Sino-Indian Border Dispute' and 'Strategy to Boost Defence Exports' have been highly acclaimed. He has the honour of being India's first Defence Attaché to Algeria (1987-1990).

After returning from Algeria, General Singh successfully commanded the 79th (Independent) Mountain Brigade in the Baramula Sector, Jammu & Kashmir, during the peak of insurgency there in 1991-92. During this tenure, he was gravely wounded in action leading from the front, in a fierce engagement with terrorists infiltrating across the Line of Control (LoC).

For that operation, he received the War Wound Medal and was awarded the Chief of Army Staff's Commendation. He was nominated to attend the prestigious National Defence College (NDC) course in 1993. He was posted as Deputy Director General Operational Logistics in Army HQ after the NDC Course and later commanded the 9th Infantry Division from 1996 to 1998.

General Singh was then selected for a key appointment as the Additional Director General Military Operations (ADGMO) at Army HQ, Military Operations Directorate. During his tenure as ADGMO, he contributed positively towards evolving India's policy on the Sino-Indian border issue and visited Beijing as part of the Joint Working Group.

He was also part of the Ministry of Defence team for talks with Pakistan on the Siachen and Sir Creek issue in 1998. He also visited Sierra Leone with the Defence Minister, where an Indian contingent carried out successful operations as part of the UN Mission. As the ADGMO, he became the Indian Army's public face during the 1999 Kargil conflict. He was decorated with the Ati Vishisht Seva Medal in recognition of his services in the planning and execution of the war.

General Singh assumed command of the elite 1 'Strike' Corps at Mathura. He successfully coordinated the corps level exercise-Poorna Vijay-in May 2001 in the deserts of Rajasthan. He subsequently led 1 Corps during Operation Parakram-the military standoff against Pakistan-from December 2001 to December 2002.

He was then appointed as the GOC-in-C of the Army Training Command (ARTRAC) in January 2003, where he was credited with drafting a new doctrine for the Indian Army. He was instrumental in giving ARTRAC a distinctly discernable and widely appreciated thrust towards modernisation. After his stint at ARTRAC he stated, "Every assignment has its own importance, but the one at ARTRAC, the think-tank of the Army, has been quite different as it plays a crucial role in preparing the Army for future challenges in a constantly changing battlefield milieu.

The responsibility involved development of new concepts and doctrines at the strategic and operational levels for the emerging security environment, besides framing of the training policy and providing training support to the Army in all its facets." He was awarded the Param Vishisht Seva Medal on 26 January 2004 for his distinguished services.

General Singh took over as the GOC-in-C Western Command on 01 February 2004 and his tenure at this elite Command, provided an opportunity to put into practice the concepts & doctrines evolved at ARTRAC and he refined operational planning by co-opting the battle winning role of Revolution in Military Affairs (RMA) and provided focused direction based on the recently released 'Doctrine for the Indian Army' having earlier been its architect. He simultaneously gave training a visionary direction in conjunction with principles of synergetic cohesiveness at all levels. His tenure at Western Command also saw a quantum leap in the implementation of the Ex-servicemen Contributory Health Scheme (ECHS). He was also appointed as Honorary Aide-de-Camp (ADC) to the President of India on 01 February 2004.

On assuming the office of the Chief of Army Staff on 31 January 2005, General Singh stated in a message, "We stand poised at a critical juncture in the timeline of history. Having left behind us the vagaries of the past, we purposefully stride towards economic growth, social harmony, peace and prosperity.

Simultaneously and seamlessly, we are also making the transition to a highly motivated and modern Army, driven by the engines of high technology and Revolution in Military Affairs. I assure our countrymen that the Army will remain at the service of the nation, at all times, ready and eager to take on any challenge with determination and resolve to emerge victorious." He is widely considered to be a thinking soldier and is a through professional.

Affectionately known as General JJ within army circles, he was appointed Colonel of the Maratha Light Infantry on 10 October 2001. He is an ace shooter and plays basketball, squash and golf. He is also a keen mountaineer who has trained under the late Tenzing Norgay at the Himalayan Mountaineering Institute in Darjeeling.

He is married to Mrs Anupama Singh and they have a son and a daughter. He is fluent in both Arabic and French, the widely spoken languages in Algeria. He retired on 30 September 2007, after completing more than 43 years of service to the Indian Army and the nation.

GENERAL DEEPAK KAPOOR, PVSM, AVSM, SM, VSM, ADC
Chief Of the Army Staff (COAS)

General Deepak Kapoor assumed charge of the Indian Army, as the 23rd Chief of Army Staff, on 30 September 2007. Born in 1948, he was commissioned into the Regiment of Artillery on 11 June 1967. His distinguished career in the Indian Army, spanning an illustrious four decades, is a blend of professional and zealous soldiering, during which he has held varied command and as well as staff appointments.

A veteran of the 1971 Indo-Pak War in the eastern theatre (Bangladesh), he is an alumnus of the Defence Services Staff College (DSSC) in Wellington and has completed the Higher Command Course at the National Defence College (NDC) in New Delhi. He served as the Chief Operations Officer for UNOSOM II (United Nations Operation in Somalia-Phase 2) during 1994-95 and was awarded the Vishisht Seva Medal (VSM) in January 1996 for his splendid efforts.

General Kapoor commanded the 161 Infantry Brigade in Uri, Jammu & Kashmir which was actively involved in operations along the Line of Control. He led from the front and constantly guided his units in maintaining prime operational readiness and was thus awarded the Sena Medal in January 1998 for his devotion to duty.

He commanded the 22nd Mountain Division as part of a Strike Corps during Operation Parakram in 2001-02. He was thereafter deeply involved in counter insurgency operations effectively tackling insurgency in Assam, as Chief of Staff of 4 Corps in Tezpur. On promotion to Lieutenant General, he commanded 33 Corps at Siliguri, West Bengal. For his distinguished service as a Corps Commander, he was awarded the Ati Vishisht Seva Medal in January 2006. On elevation to the appointment of Army Commander, he commanded the Army Training Command (ARTRAC) in Shimla.

Thereafter he moved to spearhead the Northern Command, the largest and most sensitive operational command in the Indian Army, deployed over varied terrain and was once again actively involved in COIN operations. Due to his relentless efforts, he not only brought down the insurgency level and subsequent infiltration, but also won the hearts & minds of the local populace. For his commendable efforts, he was awarded the Param Vishisht Seva Medal in January 2007.

General Kapoor has been appointed as the Honorary Aide-De-Camp to the Supreme Commander of the Armed Forces, the President of India. He is also the senior Colonel Commandant of the Regiment of Artillery. As Vice Chief of Army Staff, he has been instrumental in taking critical decisions at the highest level with far reaching implications.

Besides conceptualizing the Indian Army's vision for the future, these issues range from man management of the second largest Army in the world, procurement of weapons & equipment to ensuring a high state of operational preparedness at all times. He is also a keen sportsman and besides being an avid golfer, he has played hockey, basketball and tennis at various levels.

He has an abiding interest in self improvement and acquisition of knowledge, in pursuance of which he acquired three Master's Degrees in Political Science, Military Science and Business Administration, the latter which he completed at the Indira Gandhi National Open University in New Delhi. He also holds a diploma in Business Management. He is married to Mrs. Kirti Kapoor and they have two children-a daughter and a son, both of whom are married.

Upon taking over as Army Chief, General Kapoor said: "It is with immense pride and humility that I take over the reins of the world's most professional and second largest Army. To begin with, I pay homage to our gallant soldiers who have made the supreme sacrifice, in the line of duty. The Indian Army has always displayed unparalleled standards of professionalism, valour and un-stinted loyalty to the tri-colour, be it while defending the territorial integrity of the country, countering internal unrest, assisting in natural disasters or overseas, during peace keeping operations.

The motto of *Service Before Self* is supreme in our ethos and is amply demonstrated in all our deeds. My illustrious predecessors have all been visionaries and astute leaders. It shall be my sincere endeavour to consolidate on the foundations laid by them, to uphold the dignity and good name of our Army and take it, along with you, to greater heights. We stand at the threshold of transformation and change, to meet the myriad threats and challenges of the foreseeable future. It shall be my priority to modernize the Army rapidly and upgrade the structures and facilities that support it. I want to assure you that your welfare and that of your families will also be my priority. I assure our citizens that we will strive to enhance the efficacy and professionalism of our Army, so that it is always prepared to meet the challenges with determination and victorious will. I also take this opportunity to extend my good wishes to all ranks and civilians of the Army and their families, as also the veterans, who remain an important source of inspiration."

Women Happy to Serving in the Indian Army

Pallu (Rajasthan), May 3: Two women officers of the Indian Army say they are very happy to be serving in uniform and acquiring financial independence and that the majority of women in service-nearly 1,500-share their views. "I fit in as well as any other officer," Captain Manul Singh, the only woman officer to have served in the Siachen Glacier, a battleground between Indian and Pakistani troops for over decades in the snow-bound Himalayas, said.

"The army has made me financially independent," Lieutenant Ramandeep, who uses only one name, maintained. The two officers were speaking here on the sidelines of a war game here after being felicitated by Indian Army Chief, General JJ Singh, for their sporting achievements. Pallu is located some 400 km from the Rajasthani capital of Jaipur. Captain Manul Singh is a national-level skier, while Lieutenant Ramandeep has performed creditably on the shooting ranges and has even represented the country abroad.

"Today, what I am is because of what the army has made me," declared Lieutenant Ramandeep, who belongs to the Army Ordnance Corps (AOC) and represented India at the World Shooting Championships in Norway in 2006. Fifty countries participated in the event.

"The army has definitely made a difference to my life. It has made me financially independent," she added. "The army has given me a lot of exposure which would not have happened had I been in any other place," said Lieutenant Ramandeep, who belongs to Jalandhar in Punjab and was inducted as a Short Service Commission (SSC) officer from Chennai's Officer's Training Academy (OTA) in 2005. Two months later, she volunteered for an army inter-command trial and was selected for further training in the 25 meters sports pistol event at the Army Marksmanship School at Mhow, Madhya Pradesh. This helped her prepare for the Norway championships. As for interacting with male colleagues, she said she had no complaints. "I receive respect in equal measure as an officer and a lady. I'm happy about that," she added.

Captain Manul Singh won a silver medal at the National Alpine Skiing Championships earlier this year. She was also the first reserve for the Asian Skiing Championships in China in January-February. "It is very satisfying to be in the army. I have got the kind of exposure I might never have otherwise got," she maintained.

Captain Singh belongs to Jabalpur in Madhya Pradesh. She was commissioned as an SSC officer from the OTA and was assigned the Army Service Corps (ASC). She volunteered for a skiing course at the High Altitude Warfare School (HAWS) at Manali in Himachal Pradesh, one of 25 women officers to do so. She was the only one to be selected after a vigorous screening test that lasted a month. "Skiing is one of the most expensive sports.

It also requires high levels of physical fitness. In both cases, the army has been a great mentor," Captain Singh maintained. Did she feel uncomfortable serving in a largely male-dominated army? "Not at all. I fit in as well as any other officer," she retorted. Both maintained that the majority of women officers in uniform shared their views.

There have been reports in the past few months about dissatisfaction among the army's women officers. These apart, the suicide of a woman officer apparently over the mundane duties assigned to her had made headlines around the country. The army is currently trying a retired woman officer for corruption. The air force dismissed a woman officer on the same charge last year. Both cases are firsts for the armed forces. Women serve in the Indian Army's support arms like the ASC, the AOC and the Corps of Signals. Women constitute the backbone of the Army Medical Corps (AMC) and the Military Nursing Service (MNS) in which they are granted permanent commissions and have risen to the rank of three-star generals. There have been demands that permanent commissions be granted to women in the other arms too-and that women also be inducted into combat arms like the infantry, the armoured corps and the artillery. The Chiefs of Staff Committee that comprises the heads of the Indian Army, the Indian Navy and the Indian Air Force had studied the demand last year and concluded that it would be a while before this happened. A total of 1,468 women, not including those in the Armed Forces Medical Services, currently serve in the military-918 in the army (out of a total of 40,000 officers), 100 in the navy (6,000 officers), and 454 in the air force (15,000 officers).

5

THE WOMAN OFFICERS OF THE INDIAN ARMY

INTRODUCTION

As India celebrates its 57th Republic Day, we look at our most profound symbol of national pride — the Indian soldier. In a time of dwindling virtues, it is in them that Indians have rested great hope and found exceptional pride.

Almost a decade after the Indian armed forces began inducting women officers into active service, more and more young women are opting to join the defence forces. They have trained alongside men, made good officers and carved a place for themselves in what was perhaps the last male bastion.

Rediff features a batch of young lady officers undergoing training at the Air Defence College. Only the second batch of women to be inducted into the regiment, this is a slice of a day in their lives.

It is 8 am in mid-January, but the training ground seems like a baked sheet of concrete under the scorching sun. If the 28 young women and men in the middle of the ground were not officers of the Indian Army, they would have preferred to laze on the tree covered beachfront close by.

But for these officers — 9 women and 20 men — between the ages of 21 and 25, this is part of a regular training day. As only the second batch of women officers inducted in the Air Defence Regiment, the women are doing the gun drill with their male colleagues, part of the YOs or Young Officers course. Dressed in fatigues and berets, their skin is tanned, and beads of perspiration cover their brow. With every crisp command of the Junior Commissioned Officer (JCO) on the microphone, they do and redo the drill many times over on guns one only sees in battle scenes in the movies or at the Republic Day parade.

The L/70 and Double Barrel

They stand in groups of six behind the L/70 gun. At the crack of the command, the group consisting of female and male officers load the gun in five seconds flat. Each officer has her/ his assigned task on the equipment, that is rotated constantly to give each officer a chance to do every task.

Costing Rs 20 million (Rs 2 crores), the L/70 can launch 300 rounds of ammunition in a minute and was used in the 1971 Indo-Pak War. Four air defence units, equipped with this gun, have won battle honours and training on this weapon takes three weeks. During wartime, and in the units, the weapons are handled by the jawans (soldiers) under the command of the officers. Drills are essential for operating the guns effectively in the battlefield and the regiment's main role is to provide air defence protection to the assets of a field army.

"These officers will lead the actions of their jawans, so they need to be trained in operating all weapon systems," says Major Amit Baveja, the instructor, gunnery. The officers are also taught about the maintenance and upkeep of the weapons. Lieutenant Anuradha Mulasi, who hails from Dehradun, and Lieutenant Iman, a native of Patna, move from the Swedish-made L/70 to the Russian-origin, double barrel 23mm ZSU-23-2 gun which needs a crew of five to operate it.

Known to be a versatile weapon, it has been used on the Siachen glacier and at the Line of Control (LoC) in Jammu & Kashmir. This gun is very accurate and can bombard an enemy aircraft with a very high volume of fire, but this morning, Lieutenants Mulasi and Iman's target is a remote controlled airplane model for which they have to calculate the estimated speed, engage and fire. During the six-month training program, the officers are trained in handling guns, radars and missiles. "The better you train in peace, the lesser you bleed in war," says Major Baveja taking us through the gun drill. With just over a month left for the course to conclude, the officers are towards the end of the tactical leg — when they learn how to employ weapon systems in different theatres of war.

After a five-minute break, Lieutenants Neha Singh and Ratna Malik along with Captain Neharika Bhardwaj take position for the Igla-19K310 surface-to-air missile that weighs around 18 kg on their shoulder. They jog with the hands clenched in a fist near the chest, prop the missile on the shoulder and take aim. A heat seeking missile, the Igla latches on to the strongest heat signals and is used by the army, navy and air force. The drill is conducted using a simulator that can indicate different parameters of engagement and also the errors of the officer who fires.

Training is also done by using an aeromodel fitted onto a vehicle. The size of the aeromodel, distance of the vehicle from the officer who fires, the speed and direction can be varied to simulate different types of targets. For an outsider, the sight of young women operating sophisticated weapons is not only novel but hugely impressive. 21-year-old Lieutenant Neha Singh, says once they return to their units, they will be troop commanders. A troop consists of 25 to 80 men.

The Power of One

The lady officers have come from army stations — where they are only the only women in their unit — across the country and say they could not have had a better career that gave them experience, others their age could never have. "Like you cannot fire a weapon outside (the armed forces). Where will you get a chance? You cannot fire the L/70. They are huge guns. You feel good," says 23-year-old Lieutenant Vidya Nair, a native of Bangalore.

Being the only lady officers in a unit of 500 to 700 men does not seem odd, they say. "More and more lady officers are joining the defence forces now. Once we are selected and commissioned we get used to it and take it up as a challenge," says Lieutenant Neha Singh, whose mother is a teacher in Agra. Lieutenant Singh wanted to join the army as soon as she finished graduation from Faridabad in Uttar Pradesh and was selected to join the Officers Training Academy (OTA) in Chennai as a 20 year old.

"Lady officers or male officers — the thought never crosses our mind because you are treated like an officer," adds another lady officer. With her unit posted in Srinagar, Lieutenant Anuradha Mulasi, 24, says: "Otherwise also when people hear she is a girl and she is an army officer, people turn and look at you." Her father served in the Air Force and she says as a child she only had one dream — to join the defence forces.

In the Order of Merit

"This is the second batch of the YOs course, where lady officers have trained and they have done a great job," says Colonel A K Sharma, Instructor, Weapon Systems Wing. "Their performance is equally good. Two, three girls are in the first five in the order of merit."

The officers spend two hours in outdoor training and move to indoor classes — which include theory, training class room variants of radars like the Reporter which in actual size can only train three officers at a time, sand model displays of war exercises, electronic labs where they learn the circuits of an actual radar, etc.

The day's training ends at 1:00 p.m. Major Baveja says the officers are summoned again for a gun drill in the evening, if they have not been up to the mark in the morning. Officers say the gun drills require a very high level of physical fitness and robustness. "It is only in the mind that one makes it a big thing that lady officers are coming, will they be able to do it or not. It is not a big issue at all. Everybody is coping well and we have almost completed the course at the same pace. It has been good," says Lieutenant Ashish Agashe, a male officer in the same course.

The Goal

This course is the first on-the-job training program the officers undergo after their training as cadets at the Officers Training Academy (OTA), Chennai. Here they are taught how to lead air defence troops independently. "We maintain a very high standard of training with discipline and implicit obedience because when you give an order it has to be obeyed. The lady officers are trained to become good officers so that her troops respect her, so that they are willing to do anything for the officer," continues Colonel Sharma.

To be a good officer is a common answer that runs through the women officers at the Air Defence College. Ask them their goals, where they see themselves five years later — and this is their one and only answer. "Actually, the answer is this only — to be a good officer," smiles Lieutenant Sujata Mandotra who is married. Her husband is undergoing another training program at the same college.

Lieutenant Mulasi reasons that serving in the defence forces is not-about just looking at it as a badge of patriotism. "You cannot just treat it like that. It is a profession and you have to be good at it. For that we have to study and that is what we are doing here." The girls are required to have a degree in science to enter the Air Defence Wing. They are selected for the Officers Training Academy (OTA) after a series of tests and interviews held in different centres in India.

The Officer and the Instructor

Almost all the senior officers we spoke to at the college say the officers never forget their Young Officers course, that they remember their instructors and batch-mates forever. "This is a very impressionable age and YOs carry memories of their instructors," says Colonel Sharma. R Prakasan, a Junior Commissioned Officer and the L/70 instructor who has been training young officers for the last 16 years, says he pulls up his students when they make mistakes but respects the entire team. Though junior to his students in military rank, Prakasan is referred to as 'Saheb' by the young officers.

The other indoor training activity is conducted by senior officers, mostly between the ranks of major and colonel. "Defending our country is our main task," says Lieutenant Ratna Malik, the daughter of a serving army officer, providing an insight to the training process at this point of their fledgling careers.

> *"But since we are not fighting a war right now, our aim is to be prepared for that eventual day. Besides that we do a lot of things — administrative jobs in the regiment, for instance. As an officer you have to take care of your jawans, there are other administrative matters which is all part of our work."*

After the Training

When the training day ends at lunchtime, the officers rush to their living quarters in Chhamb Block where two officers share a two bedroom flat. They quickly change out of their fatigues into olive green uniforms and troop into the Officers Mess for lunch. Twelve cooks and 16 to 18 bearers look after the meal arrangements.

The Officers Mess is situated on a hill and offers a beautiful view of the Bay of Bengal. After lunch the officers retire to their block and meet for games in the evening between 4:00 and 5:30 p.m. They study or spend time catching up with the rest, in the time before & after dinner. Wednesday and Saturday is their evening off, the latter usually being dedicated to a social event.

The college has a shopping complex, movie theatre, a stunning beach which is out of bounds for civilians and has an enclosure for hosting parties on the beachfront. There are days when the young officers are given the responsibility of hosting a cultural evening, which is all part of their overall grooming.

"We encourage them to participate in public speaking, debates, lectures, writing military book reviews," says Major Baveja. He also adds, "An officer cannot be an introvert because a leader has to have communicative skills to lead her/his men effectively. With more and more officers joining us from smaller towns, at this level this is the last time they get training on an organised basis. After this they don't need it."

The Memories, oh, the Memories

As the lady officers chat with us after the day's training, we discover they have known each other since their days at the Officers Training Academy (OTA) as cadets. They say after having done their basic training together, they know each other 'in and out' and feel sad that the course is getting over. "Every single day from this college is so memorable. Everything we've learnt. How four of us sat inside a radar. Once we get back to the unit, even when we have to run we will recollect how we would wait for the other to join us," recalls Lieutenant Vidya Nair.

Lieutenant Megha Chibber and Lieutenant Anuradha Mulasi who are flat-mates laugh aloud after friendly banter. The former points out it is sometimes incorrect when people think that only people from a defence background join the army. "It is a notion which is not fully true," says Lieutenant Chibber who hails from Delhi. Lieutenant Mulasi will marry this October and all the lady officers hope to make it for the wedding — with big gifts of course, at her request. Her fiancé is also in the army and the couple will get a spouse posting after their marriage which will enable them to be together.

'WE ARE SOLDIERS'

Observing their remarkable camaraderie, I ask if the experience is reminiscent of college days and Lieutenant Sujata Mandotra sums up their sentiment eloquently: "We are not students, we are soldiers. We are not teenagers — then our goals were different. Here things are totally different, we are not living in that mindset. That way it is totally different." The lady officers say the training has made them more mature, more confident. From the days of being a cadet to being an officer is totally different.

Major Baveja says training the officers costs between Rs 16,000 and 18,000 per officer, per week. Indian Army rules allow women officers to serve in the army for 14 years which includes a mandatory five year initial stint. Most lady officers at the college we spoke to said they would decide their next course of action at the end of year five.

Unlike Lieutenants Mulasi and Mandotra — the latter who comes from a family of officers in the armed forces — Lieutenant Vidya Nair is from a non-armed forces background. A 'proper civilian' family, as she put it. Her mother is a teacher, her father served in Hindustan Aeronautics Limited (HAL). The youngest in her family, she joined the army because amongst her relatives there are doctors and engineers and she wanted to be someone different.

Lieutenant Neha Singh's mother is also a teacher. Lieutenant Meghna Chibber's father served in the Ministry of Defence. Of the nine lady officers, four are from a non-defence forces background.

The women joined the army when their friends aimed for MBA degrees and other lucrative jobs. A career in the army may not be a high paying job but the lady officers say it is a good career for those who want job satisfaction. After spending a day with these impressive women officers one tends to agree. This unique band of sisters will command men into battle one day and inspire a generation of young women after them.

INDIAN ARMY WOMEN SCALE MOUNT EVEREST

Indian Army's women mountaineers created history by becoming the first women's expedition to scale the Mount Everest. Captain Shipra Mazumdar, Captain Ashwini Pawar, Cadet Tshering Ladol and Trainee Dechin Lhamo scaled the 8848-metre high peak between 0615 and 0939 hours.

The peak was also summitted by five members of the support team — Major S S Shekhawat, Subedar Surjeet Singh, Naib Subedar Jagat Singh, Havildar Topgey Bhutia and Commando Kaman Singh. The Indian Army's women mountaineering team scaled the world's tallest peak from the Chinese side through the North Col Route, the Army said in a release. With this unprecedented feat, the Indian Army has scaled four eight thou sanders in the last four years and Mt Everest has been climbed thrice by the Army in the last five years. The Army Women Everest Expedition, was flagged off by the Chief of Army Staff General J J Singh on 18 March 2006.

The Army Chief, who is a mountaineer himself, has congratulated the team on its feat. Defence Minister Pranab Mukherjee congratulated the successful women's mountaineering team of the Army, saying the success of the expedition has brought laurels to the nation in general and Indian Army in particular. "The achievement will go a long way in infusing sense of enthusiasm and spirit of teamwork in the youth of the nation. This feat will provide impetus to the growth of adventure sports in the country," he said.

A BEFITTING SALUTE

It's six in the morning and 59 women cadets are put through their paces at the Physical Training Grounds of the Officers' Training Academy (OTA) in St Thomas Mount, on the outskirts of Chennai.

The rigorously demanding exercises are spread over an hour. A short break is followed by another hour of hard marching marked by shouted orders and the stomping of heavy boots. A day full of classes in military strategy and history, swimming, games, special coaching and more exercises ends when the lights go out at 10:30 p.m.

This group is the 20th batch in an academy that is one of its kind in Asia. This year, these women cadets have qualified for the Indian Army's Short Service Commission (SSC) and have been absorbed as officers-crowning a program that has completed a successful decade. Here are the women who live-and lead-in a man's world.

The Indian Army began recruiting women officers in 1993, a move that opened the doors of an all-male bastion. Besides, a more pro-woman atmosphere, the reasons for opening up included the increasing vacancies arising out of falling recruitment, notably amongst the junior positions. The defence establishment is now also competing with other more lucrative career options available to the country's young people. Every six months, about 5,000 women graduates and postgraduates between the ages of 21 and 25 years apply to join the Army. Barely one-fifth clear the written test and only a tenth of those who do are selected.

The women officers commissioned are recruited for a period of five years, extendable up to ten. The Zozila Company becomes their new home-and office. The current batch of graduates will bring the total number of women cadets recruited to 744.

Once they complete their maximum of 10 years of service-while still in their early to mid-30s-the women are expected to retire with only their savings and provident fund accumulations. The first batch is yet to be decommissioned but high morale appears to have overcome any pangs of the looming insecurity. Explains Colonel Murlidhar, Commanding Officer of the Shivaji Battalion (under which the Zozila Company comes), "The Army effectively screens and trains the most physically fit and mentally robust.

It is expected that these women, quite like the short service gentlemen officers, will be sought after by civilian firms in administrative positions, chiefly in security-related assignments." Says Captain Geeta Gawali, Platoon Commander in the same Company, now directly supervising the course she graduated from over four years ago, "It is a degree and experience like no other.

The Army's training in man management has no parallel." She says this with no irony, the gender anomaly notwithstanding. Over the last decade, the course has continually evolved. To begin with, the fitness regimen had to be redefined in view of differing physical capabilities.

The focus for the lady cadets, as the Army's protocol requires them to be called, is on muscle-building and power exercises. The programme lasts only six months as opposed to nine months of training for male cadets.

Moreover, it was found that women were nearly ten times more prone to pelvic injuries, backaches, stress fractures and cramps during the gruelling schedule-conditions which forced medical leave, resulted in loss of training time and affected morale.

Doctors from the Sports Medicine Department of Tamil Nadu's Dr MGR Medical University, worked with the OTA team to suggest amendments. Several changes are on the anvil-the Academy is in the process of setting up its own sports medicine wing.

The thrust is now on stretching and strengthening exercises, and using boots lined with special soles imported from the United States to reduce the shock on the pelvis. The course, and its proactive nature, only goes to prove that women are equal-but different.

Says Captain Gawali, the first person in her family to join the defence services, "Most women who come here have a sports-oriented outlook or a National Cadet Corps background. A greater percentage of the men who join do so because they view the Army as a secure career option.

Most women, on the other hand, come looking for adventure, to do something different." According to Captain Gawali, discrimination is not an issue. "Even when we are posted at all-male stations, there is no difference. Only if we think and behave differently will we be treated differently. Otherwise, we are all the same."

Women officers take salutes, bark orders and pack a commanding punch into their slight frames. But the looming spectre of discrimination is barely seen behind the veil of formal correctness. Says one woman officer who does not wish to be named, "It is the gentlemen cadets who feel discriminated against. We earn the same pay but do not train for as long or as hard. There is resentment, and it is inevitable. Gender cannot be forgotten. Three hundred-odd years of male attitudes cannot change so fast, but Army ethics include respect for women, which is a help."

Women officers are also not deployed at the frontline, though recent amendments have ensured that they are posted in field areas, sometimes less than 50 metres away from actual combat. In their 10 years of service, the women officers can only hope to rise up to the level of a Major.

The glass ceiling is very visible here. Postings are across the country and usually in the Engineers, Ordnance, Signals, Army Service, Education, Intelligence, Legal Branch or EME (Electrical and Mechanical Engineering) Corps. Women officers married to Army men are often able to get transferred to the same place-but only if vacancies exist.

Otherwise, says Captain Reeta Bakshi, "It is something we have to be prepared for. Families are often separated in the Army, when the men are posted to non-family stations. All that is needed is respect for each other's profession.

The difference is only biological. In fact, you remember you are a woman only when you wear (salwar) suits and sarees." For women cadets like computer engineer Namrata Waghray of Secunderabad and MBA Renu Ratra, who left a marketing job in Bhopal, this job "gives security and is very challenging."

And then there is Riya Shrivastava, a 25-year-old postgraduate from Dehra Dun. A war widow whose husband died on the Jammu & Kashmir front just eight months after the wedding, she is here "to carry on from where he left off." The Army set-up caters to most of her needs, and also provides an environment that does not stigmatise her.

Another cadet, also bereaved, has a two-year-old son who will join her soon when she becomes an officer. Says Major R S Gill, who supervises the women's training: "Women stepping into a man's world are more motivated, dedicated and determined to prove a point. They are excellent assets, no matter where they are deployed." A fitting salute to the modern Army woman.

6

ARMS AND THE WOMEN

The fact that women are as competent as men in a wide variety of areas ranging from sports to academics to professions that require high levels of training and education has now come to be widely accepted. Armed forces are, unarguably, one of the most progressive, secular and professional organs of the state, whose contribution in making the country what it is today, is phenomenal. The induction of women in the Army occurred in 1993, when the Women's Special Entry Scheme (WSES) was introduced. India is proud to have its daughters, Rani Padmavati and Chand Bibi, who shone out as soldiers and generals in a period when women were under the suppression of the veil. Can anybody deny the administrative skills and chivalry of Rani Laxmi Bai? Young ladies who have opted for the Army have shown their grit against heavy odds, whether it is the snow-bound Siachen Glacier, or the sweltering Rajasthan desert, or the impenetrable jungles of the North-East or the coastal regions down the south and above all, in the face of invisible enemy, the militant. When the opportunity to meet some of these dynamic women officers of the Golden Arrow Division arose, it was like a dream come true.

Lieutenant Sophia Qureshi: A postgraduate in biochemistry, Lieutenant Qureshi while justifying her decision to join the Army, said: "The Army is the only career that enables you to lead a life full of adventure. If you have a sense of daredevilry coupled with the courage to withstand hardships, then the Army is the answer. The life of a service officer is a blend of varied experiences hard work, constant alertness and an opportunity to travel to various places in India and even abroad," says the proud officer who is the first Signals' lady officer to be made sparrow and given a challenging task of commanding a brigade signals company. Had she not joined the Army, she would have gone in for a job at the DRDO. She is proud of the fact that the women officers attended the same training courses as men and performed the same duties. The question of gender disparity does not arise, she feels. However, she admitted that there were some initial hiccups in getting adjusted to a hitherto male-dominated organisation. She adjusted to the set-up very soon and hesitatingly admits that she enjoys an enviable reputation for professional competence.

Captain Dinesh Bhardwaj Singh: "From a very young age, long before the Indian Army decided to allow women into the armed forces, I wanted to join the services" says Captain Singh, a smart young officer posted with the Golden Arrow Division. "I am not the kind of person who would fit into the regular nine to five job. Had it not been the Army, I would have joined the Indian Police Service," she asserted. A postgraduate in physics, she is married to a BSF officer and has a daughter. She feels that joining the Army is in no way any impediment to leading a normal family life, provided there is determination.

Lieutenant Sonali Gupta: An ordnance officer posted with the Golden Arrow Division, she feels that joining the Army is an excellent career move. The daughter of an ordnance officer in the Indian Army, she reveals that since childhood she was so fascinated by her father's uniform that she always nourished a desire of donning the same one day. Recalling her first day of service in Bombay, Lieutenant Sonali recounts that the moment she entered the ordnance complex, she saw a smartly dressed chap in front of her office and presuming him to be a senior officer, she saluted him. Later on, to her amusement, she found that the chap was working as a sahayak [security staff] in her office.

Lieutenant Parul Sharma: From the Engineers, she confides that it was Shah Rukh Khan in the television serial Fauji, who inspired her to join the Army. An honours in mathematics from Delhi University, when Lieutenant Sharma was asked why she chose Army as a career, she had only this to say, "Why not? Women officers have to work twice as hard as men to prove themselves but then the same is true for women in any other field of work. The Army offers excellent opportunities for personal development and overall growth." So, there is no question of regretting the decision to join the force.

Lieutenant Kalyani Deshpande: Another smartly turned up lady officer, believes that, "To begin a career with the Indian Army is an excellent training ground for any woman with aptitude. The Army prepares officers mentally, physically and psychologically for various levels of social interaction. We develop well-rounded personalities that enable us to adapt to any environment and emerge winners in all circumstances." claims Lieutenant Deshpande.

Asked to say a few words for the wannabe girls thinking to join Army. "Just do it!" they chorused. Do women make good soldiers, and are they ruthless enough to kill if the situation demands? "Yes"! is the unanimous reply of all these lady officers elegantly dressed in the combat gear. Their smart uniforms, neat hairdo, and a confident and firm stride places them in a different league altogether. Without losing out on their essential feminity they stand out even in civvies. Meeting a motivated lot of soldiers was a thrilling experience by itself and a reaffirmation of faith in the daring breed of women who have made their presence felt in the profession which has been conventionally associated with male dominance.

I BELIEVE...

I believe that women make better officers than men...And we have good reasons for saying so. It is now eight years since the army started inducting women into the forces. The Officers Training Academy (OTA) has seen sixteen batches and the training levels have only improved with each batch. Tangible proof of this improvement exists in the academy records confirming that women make better target shooters than their male counterparts. We believe that much of this excellence emerges from the sincerity with which women pursue their goals and their dogged determination to pass out of the academy with flying colours. Even so, the army remains a male dominated bastion. Lady officers have yet to prove themselves. We are still not allowed into active combat. But we believe that all this will change and women will move shoulder to shoulder with men during combat. It is only a matter of time...

Today we have made history...We were born into a farming family hailing from Lakhimpur Kheri which is a three-and-a-half-hour drive from Lucknow. Apart from our parents MS and Usha Chauhan, we have an elder brother, Captain MKS Chauhan who, too, is in the artillery unit of the Indian Army. We are three sisters with two years separating each of us. People often wonder how we made it to the same batch in the OTA despite our differences in age. This was essentially possible because of Roli. She had attempted the Services Selection Board (SSB) the previous year and had not scored a merit. This only increased her desperation to join the forces. She had even filled out forms for the AFMC (Armed Forces Medical College), the IAF (Indian Air Force) and what not.

The point was that it had to be the defence services or nothing else. Because the forces had been a passion with all of us, and because of the bond we shared, we along with two of our male friends decided to take up studying for the SSB together. Thus began an endless tour of libraries, burning midnight oil, playing twenty questions...We had made up our mind to get into the forces and we were going to get there. It really did not matter that Ruchi, the youngest, was just 19. It had to be the OTA and it had to be all three of us together! Sure enough we made it. We still recall the day we discovered that we had finally made it into the merit list. Our joy knew no bounds. It was as if doors had opened to an incredible future and all our dreams and those of our parents would finally see the light of day. Today we have made history. We are the only three sisters to have passed out of the OTA in the same year. Our father has already approached the Limca Book of Records as well as the Guinness Book of Records for the same.

Our parents have brought us up like sons...It was our father's desire that we join the forces and today with his three daughters and his son in the forces, our father feels that he has a *fauj* (army) of his own. For him it is a dream that he has lived four times over through us, his children. He had always wanted to be in the army and could not clear the medical tests. Thereafter he joined the Punjab National Bank and after working there for ten years gave up the job to tend the family fields. Our mother hails from Muradabad and as is the case in small towns which suffer from parochialism, was forced to give up college education because the college was in a Muslim-dominated locality. She was married off at the age of 18 and has always regretted her inability to complete her education. But we believe that modernity is really a mindset. Our parents though humble farmers had the strength of conviction, of belief and faith.

They have brought us up like sons with no restrictions as such. My mother was insistent that we complete our education however tough the going might be. In fact we started giving tuitions on our mother's suggestion. It was tough coping up with studies and teaching other people as well. It left us no time to freak out like the other kids. There were times when we really did envy our friends. They'd come to school in fancy cars and always caught the latest movie running whereas the three of us had to slog in school and then go home and slog as well. I, being the eldest, also had the additional task of handling household chores like fetching vegetables, milk, paying the electricity bills, etc. Even amongst my cousins, we are the only girls who have taken up a career...Expectations were high from all ends-even my teacher, Father John, in school whenever he saw an official vehicle would exclaim, "One day I'll see Rakhi step out of one of those cars." And sometimes it just did not seem fair at all. But today, as I see my friends Varsha who is into computers and Shalini who is doing her MBA, I feel I have fared the best of the lot. Computers and MBA might be the fad of the day, but the army is not just a fad. For people around me, I have broken into a male bastion. I am different.

Even amongst my cousins, we are the only girls who have taken up a career. Ours is a conservative Rajput family where girls are married off after the 12th standard. My relatives were obviously opposed to the idea of us joining the army. Now, I think they'd have wanted their kids to have brought them the same name and fame that we have brought to our parents. My parents always wanted us to do well, get fame. The one example that my mother always put forth was that of Kiran Bedi who too came from a middle class home and yet she worked her way up to fame and name. She wanted us to be like her and she has always been my role model and that of Ruchi's. Roli has always been the softer of the three, the more emotional one, so it is no surprise that she looked upon Mother Teresa as her role model. And really, in the academy also, if anyone needed a compassionate hearing, they'd all run to Roli!! Since ours is a middle-class, conservative Rajput family, relatives often taunted my mother saying it was high time we were married off and that we were given too much freedom. My mother bore it all saying that she had complete faith in her children and their abilities.

Our parents persistence paid off. We were always academically inclined and we invariably did well in school and college. I had an excellent academic record and did very well in my curricular activities as well. Everybody expected the same from Roli and Ruchi too. We had our goals set-we would either join the IAS or the forces. We became even more focused on the forces after our brother got inducted in 1995. He would often write to us about the academy, all the fun they had there and at his Passing Out Parade (POP), I had the opportunity of meeting lady officer, Lt Shovna Tripathi. She was inspiration personified. She looked smart and elegant, bearing her uniform with a practised pride. She told me that there was no better career than the forces and that's what did it for me-the obsession set in! For Ruchi, the youngest one among us, inspiration came by way of a sense of an inherent sibling rivalry. Everybody always thought that I would be the one to set the path for Ruchi and Roli. But Ruchi wanted to be the first, the youngest one to start earning.

At the academy, your status as female is effectively erased from your mind...The academy has been an experience for us. We have trained under the best men the country has to offer. It has undoubtedly been a gainful experience. The main aim at the academy is to toughen you up physically as well as mentally and that requires discipline and perseverance. One has to follow a tough, rigorous routine starting with PT at five in the morning and ending with classes at eight in the evening. Any slip ups and you are punished without remorse. Each day as such is an adventure and holds an unique memory. But invariably, your most memorable days at the academy are your first and last. The first because you come in feeling so uncertain, so unsure. I fumbled so much with everything, so much so that when it was time for lunch at the mess, I was confused with the perfectly laid out forks and knives and ended up spilling everything around me!

Though the focus in the academy is actually to toughen you up for any situation, in one queer sense, the academy is perhaps the most protected of all places. Despite housing men and women in contact with each other at all times, the one thing you do not encounter at the academy is eve teasing. In fact those are the six months when your status as female is effectively erased from your mind. The boys are technically 'superior' to us in the sense that as opposed to our six months of training, they are trained for a longer period of nine months. Their training begins about three months prior to our training and they are all our seniors. Their training structure is also more demanding. For instance, their cross country is longer than ours; they swim about 5 metres more than we do; they go for a 40 km route march while we go for a 25 km route march and most importantly they have the choice of getting into combat which we cannot even consider at this stage.

But despite these differences in training structure, the training procedures are the same and the girls are never discouraged by the men. If anything, they are always there to help us out. For instance, just before my swimming exam, I remember, I was totally down in the dumps-I had this sinking feeling that I'll plug. I could not sleep, eat or do anything. One of the Gentlemen Cadets (GC) Pavan Kalkal observed I was picking at my food and came up to me to ask me what the problem was. I told him I was definitely going to plug my swimming test. We had to swim about 25 metres while I could just about manage 18. My problem was that my head would go down-I could not keep my head up! GC Pavan advised me to think of my mother. "Imagine she's standing at the end of the pool and that if you don't reach her she'll drown. That is exactly what I did and that is how I passed my test," he told me encouragingly. You won't believe it, I actually visualised my mother at the end of the pool and in a desperate bid to reach her-I actually made it!

This is the first time that we will be separated...As was the case in school and college, comparison between the three of us was always there. But the difference here was that the comparison was a healthy one, encouraging the best out of each of us. For instance, the instructors would always urge Ruchi to be the best between the three of us because she is the youngest. And that I think, did a whole lot of good to Ruchi because she has always wanted to get out of the shadow of being the youngest and therefore the one to toe the line. Roli, being the middle sister has always been the peacemaker, the bond between us three. She is the cool, calm, collected one. Even at the academy she acquired the reputation of being a motherly figure-"Don't tell Roli you did this," they would say, "She'll dole out a motherly lecture!" After passing out, Ruchi and I have chosen the Electrical Mechanical Engineering (EME) branch and Roli because she has done biology instead of physics, chemistry and maths has had to opt for Ordinance. It is the first time that we will be separated-which I think is nice. I think Roli badly needs this separation to become more independent emotionally.

We are convinced that there is no better career option than the army...It is really a pity that women who opt for the Indian Army cannot go into combat, just as yet. There is no way that we are inferior to the men but perhaps this decision has been based on physical problems like the lack of all-female barracks in the insurgence areas. Also, in these areas often times, there are no barracks or shelter, in which case the officers have to lie down in the open with the jawans. I'm sure I can be comfortable doing the same but it requires more than the Lady Cadet's (LC's) comfort of mind. It involves changing a whole social mindset including that of the jawan who the lady officer will be commanding. That might take a while.

There is still no other institution that accords you the kind of discipline and respect as the army. We are yet to join our units and actually get into the real job of being in the army. Yet, we are convinced that there is no better career option than the army. For a woman, the struggle has always been to be recognised as a man's equal, to be looked upon with respect and dignity. Well, even if you as a woman officer have yet to prove a few things, there is still no other institution that accords you the kind of discipline and respect as the army. It is the magic of the uniform, the stars that adorn your shoulder and the realisation that you as an officer are responsible for the men under your command. In the civilian world as well, the uniform commands a respect that no other profession, no matter how glamourous, can ever command. I recall this incident at the railway booking station where the booking clerk was being rude to the general public. The moment he saw me approach him, his attitude changed from highhandedness to politeness. That is the kind of respect the uniform invites. So if it is a satisfying career you are looking for, there is no place quite like the defence forces. And if you are a young woman who aspires to be in the forces, the first thing for you to do is to forget that you are a woman. Think equal, think big...and just go for it!!

Sisters in Arms-Lt. General S.S. Grewal PVSM, AVSM, SM, VSM

In 1992 the first batch of women comprising 50 young girls was inducted into the Officers Training Academy (OTA) in Chennai. Since then, we have been taking in two batches per year and are finding the response from women extremely good. These girls have been commissioned into the Arms and Services. But combat is a difficult assignment with its own ruggedness and difficulties of field. Therefore we are cautious that a young lady must be given an atmosphere where she can function effectively and contribute to the service.

All young ladies taken into the OTA have to go through a rigorous selection process. The army has its own tests that determine her psychological and physical fitness and also her aptitude. We also take into account her communication skills as she has to lead and direct men. The response we get in each batch is tremendous. Girls take the same tests as boys and they not only fare well but never show any lack of enthusiasm. They might be in the service cadre but their first posting is always a field posting and they rough it out like any other soldier in the field. They have tremendous courage and their performance has been more than satisfactory. We are proud of them. They are an exceptional lot and to me, they are not just savvy, but super savvy.

I must admit that we were all a little surprised when we heard that the three Chauhan sisters were passing out of the same batch of the OTA. It is a record of sorts where a family has contributed three girls in the same course. Their performance has been good and competitive, along with the other girls. We are proud of them. They are a shining example for other young girls. Here is a family that has chosen to send all their three daughters into the Indian Army when normally, parents send in only one child or hesitate to send even one. Here, I understand, it was the parents who were really keen on seeing their daughters in the army. There must be a very good reason for the parents to send them in the Indian Army. Indeed the army offers a wonderful life. If young girls decide to join the army, let me assure them, it is the most honourable profession in the country. You will never regret it.

THE GENERAL IN A SARI

Lieutenant General Punita Arora was appointed as DG-Medical Services (Navy) on 20 June 2005 and presently holds the rank of Vice Admiral.

With a precision that comes most naturally to the armed forces, a gleaming black army Ambassador pulls into the driveway of the VIP guesthouse at the Armed Forces Medical College in Pune. Dot on time. A uniformed trooper runs to the rear door with an open umbrella to shield the officer who steps out. Dressed in the Indian Army's olive green uniform, the officer pulls the pleats of her sari and walks up. Don't know how many of you have seen an officer of the Indian Army dressed in a sari. For us, it is a first time. And when the officer is the first woman to attain the rank of Lieutenant General of the world's fourth largest army, well, what can you say? Wow! Amazing! Yes! Lieutenant General Punita Arora is a warm, friendly officer who refers to the Indian Army as "us, ours" — as if it were an extension of her personality — and is bemused with all the fuss surrounding her in the last two weeks. "If my fellow male officer picks up a rank, he also feels great isn't it? I'm sure even they feel very proud, I also felt the same way," she explains. "I never felt that I am a woman and I've reached this position, so I've done something very great."

A Refugee from Partition

Lieutenant General Arora arrived in India after Partition when she was a year old. The only possessions her family had when they reached India were a blanket and a glass. Like the one million others who left their homes for a hard and uncertain future in a land they chose to live in after Independence, her family saw tough times. They started from scratch, made many sacrifices along the way and built their lives brick by brick. "A very strong point they had was unity of the family. If one working member got some money it was shared equally. My father was the eldest. His brother who expired just a year back at the age of 95, looked up to my father till the end," she says.

Sitting across in her living room, the general gives charming, everyday examples of the beauty of Indian family from her own life. Of the time her mother accompanied her on her first posting to Fatehgarh, Uttar Pradesh in 1968. How her younger sisters, mother-in-law took turns in being with her on various postings; and that one time when her 75-year-old *Nani* came to live with her only because she did not want her grand-daughter to be alone.

"Our family system is so beautiful. If we disintegrate like nuclear families we are losing a lot. Today what I am I wouldn't be without the support of my family," says the officer whose husband retired as a Brigadier from the Army Medical Corps.

I am in the Army Now

As far back as Lieutenant General Arora can remember, her father wanted her to become a doctor. "At every step I used to think if I want to be a doctor can I get my ears pierced or not? I was conditioned that way." When she went for admission to the government college in Saharanpur, the college told her it was only for boys but she could get a seat if she found two other girls. She did and got admission. She joined the Armed Forces Medical College, Pune, as an undergraduate in 1962, did her post graduation, came back as faculty, was posted to its command hospital and has now returned for its top job as commandant.

> *"I've seen this college from every angle. I know its strengths and certain areas which I felt at that time, that it should be like this (changes to be made). Now that I am here if I can improve on those particular things I consider myself very privileged." In those early days, when she joined AFMC — one of India's premier medical colleges — it did not have the required infra-structure. "We never had a hostel, we were 23 girls in one barrack. There were so many departments that were in barracks but everything was compensated by the excellent teaching and care we got."*

The Posting in the Wild

Twenty-one year old Lieutenant Punita Arora arrived in Fatehgarh after doing an internship in Ambala. Till then she had lived in reasonably big cities and found herself in what was the bad land of that time. "In 1968, Fatehgarh was infested with dacoits. I'd never seen a place like that before. Everybody roamed with a lathi or a gun." At the hospital, people mistook her mother who was comparatively young, as the doctor sahib and thought of her as the daughter accompanying her. In hindsight, Lieutenant General Arora feels it could not have had a better beginning. The area did not have many hospitals, no specialists and the nearest big hospital was in Kanpur or Lucknow, four to six hours away. The only train in that direction left at midnight. "If the patient missed the train you'd have to look after him/her yourself. So that gave me lots of confidence. It was a good tenure."

The 1971 War: When the war with Pakistan broke out, she was still posted in Fatehgarh and had married her doctor husband who was at the base hospital in Srinagar. She had come to the scenic city to deliver her son — currently a Squadron Leader in the Indian Air Force — and left a month before the war began. Her husband who used to be on airport duty witnessed the bombardment, and Punita saw the war preparations in Jammu & Kashmir, where the situation was completely different from her base in Uttar Pradesh. "Fatehgarh never saw any war. People hardly knew what was happening. Like sitting over here, I'm sure you can't even imagine what's happening up there [in J&K]. If you go and spend even 15 days over there, you'll come back with a totally different feeling."

The Summer Tragedy

In May 2002, when terrorists entered an army camp at Kaluchak near Jammu, killing soldiers and their families, Lieutenant General Arora was the commander at the base hospital in Jammu. The crime was dastardly. Terrorists travelled to the camp in a Himachal Pradesh Roadways bus and targeted the soldiers' wives and children. They also killed seven passengers on that bus. Some who died in the tragedy were infants. The dead and wounded were brought to the army hospital where Lieutenant General Arora rallied her staff to administer prompt medical assistance. For her leadership and quick response to the mass casualty, the President of India decorated her with the Vishisht Seva Medal, an award instituted for exceptional service and leadership rendered in the armed forces. "It was very tragic. Our aim was to treat them. My driver, my staff in the casualty, my doctors, surgeons, anaesthetists, nurses. It was team work."

Did it make Her Angry?

"Do we gain anything by being angry? Yes, when you see your soldiers being killed, for a moment we thought we should go and kill everyone who is responsible. Not only me, anybody who is there would say — 'why, these innocent children, why this family?' Like you feel angry with what happened in the school in Russia. But then those three terrorists died, whom do I take out our anger on? Probably I'll be losing my temper on some innocent people. These things need to be sorted out politically which are leaders are doing so beautifully. We leave it to them. Our job is to secure our borders and treat our soldiers."

Here I Am

Lieutenant General Arora has received 15 medals and awards in her career. She also received a Sena Medal for establishing gynae-endoscopy and oncology facilities at the armed forces hospital. Joining the army just happened, she says. "I joined AFMC, then the army, and here I am today — proud of being an army officer and that too of the Indian Armed Forces." For an army that is short of officers, Lieutenant General Arora is an impressive brand ambassador. Listen to her speak, and she may just win you over.

"Guys, this is what you miss out on: First of all, the youth don't know what the armed forces is. I think they miss out on so much because they really don't know. Secondly, people think you will be posted from one place to another and will not have a comfortable life from the money point of view. After all, how much money do we spend on food? What we spend on is the quality of life — a club, squash court, a pool, good life — the army gives you better than that.

We have infrastructure — lovely messes, swimming pools, health clubs. How many can afford going to Shillong or Ladakh? They'll be paying through their nose, people take holiday packages and spend money to live in tents. While we naturally stay like this over there, isn't it?. The armed forces gives you 100% free medical treatment. So the quality of life is excellent."

The Fauji and the OG colour 3 tone

"Have you ever thought why people join the Lions and Rotary Clubs?" she asks. "Because they want to belong to an organisation. It's a big thing to belong to an organisation. Even if I'm anywhere and I see an OG [olive green] colour three tonne [truck], I feel yes, it is mine.

Our person if he falls sick and comes to our fauji hospital, he'll say ah, bas I've come to my hospital. That is the sense of belonging we have. In the army, you associate with each other. It's something great and this is what you miss out. I don't say other jobs are not good, army is equally good."

Five Doctors and a General

The gynaecologist, who is one of the seven lieutenant generals in the Army Medical Corps, has a family of doctors. Husband Brigadier P N Arora (Retd) served the army as a dermatologist. Son, Squadron Leader Sándeep Arora is also a dermatologist posted at the Air Force base hospital in New Delhi. His wife too is a doctor.

Daughter Sabina left the army after a 6½ year tenure to pursue a post graduate degree in Connecticut. "When my daughter wanted to go abroad, we didn't know how to go about it. We had nobody in America. We told her you have a good career but she was determined. She did everything herself and I'm proud of her."

Lieutenant General Arora's India

In a time when it is easiest to find fault in a system that fails us repeatedly, the general sees the brighter side. Her India does not suck. It delivers. Whether it is getting a train reservation, a car registration, or State-promised compensation. "How much we criticise," she reasons, citing the example from the passengers on the Himachal Roadways bus travelling to Kaluchak. "Believe me, by afternoon payment was made to each and every person who was injured.

People think otherwise, but the government machinery works. One patient who received Rs 25,000 was a labourer who had never seen more than 2,000 in his life. He became so insecure that he wanted t. leave with all the tubes stuck to his body. He was scared that someone would run away with his money. He even became suspicious of his wife. Think about it, do we ever get to see human nature, feelings from so closely?"

Lieutenant General Punita Arora, SM, VSM

If you are driving near the Southern Command headquarters in Pune, the board outside the gate to what will be Lieutenant General Arora's home in the city will make you stop and notice. The feminine name stands out amongst the neat row of male officers' homes.

The house behind the gate is being readied for its new occupant. Till then, Lieutenant General Arora will live at the guesthouse, where she leaves for her office at 8:15 a.m. and returns by 5 p.m. "The moment I come home, I have a cup of tea and go for a walk. That's a must. I don't like to exercise inside the room at all — where's the greenery? On a walk you see a little bird, a squirrel, in the room you see only those four walls, nothing else."

Just then the phone rings. The general takes our permission to answer the call and thanks her bhabhi who is on the line to congratulate her. A few cards neatly stand on a table. A defence staff reminds her about tomorrow's keynote address. "I know, that will not take much time," smiles India's first lady Lieutenant General, someone who has never felt out of place in a male dominated army. She is an officer of the Indian Army and that's how she'd like to be known.

LAST SALUTE: WOMEN IN MUFTI

Ten years ago, on 06 March 1993, 25 feisty women made history when they joined the Indian Army. For each one of them, it was an olive green dream come true. One they lived every day for the last 10 years. Now it's time to give it up. Come March, and it will be goodbye to the uniform and the heady salute.

No wonder Major Priya Jhingan, OIC, Judge Advocate General (JAG) branch in Chennai HQs, refuses to think about it. "I was in Class X when I shot off a letter to then Chief of Army Staff, General S.F. Rodrigues, demanding that I be recruited." Her eyes turn luminous as she talks of herself as a headstrong Shimla girl who told her police officer father in no uncertain terms that it was nothing but the Army for her. "I loved the uniform, the Jongas, the snappy salute, everything."

It was ditto for most of them. Captain Jatinder Preet Kaur, an Army Education Corps officer at the Delhi HQs, still remembers the way her heart used to thump every time she saw an Army vehicle whiz by at Bathinda.

The one-page advertisement inviting women Army officers in 1992 came as a pleasant surprise to most of them. "When I told my father, a sergeant in the Indian Air Force, he simply smiled and said 'I knew you would go for it'," remembers Captain Ushasree Kumar, an Ordinance officer at Pathankot. A few months later, she went on to become the youngest woman officer to join the Officers' Training Academy (OTA) at Chennai.

The OTA didn't know how to deal with this spirited bunch. "I got the feeling they were handling us with kid gloves," remembers Priya. But all that became history when she outran the boys in the cross-country.

"The physical training was no problem at all," says Ushasree, a national-level athlete and kabaddi player, who still sprints past her fellow male officers in the 5 km Battle Physical Endurance Test (BPET). The battle-hardened instructors were surprised when the girls took to the weekly 25 km-long marches like ducks to water.

"I loved them, especially the chocolates at the end," says Jatinder, getting all misty-eyed. Today, ten years on, they look back with fierce pride. And hearty affection. It's not been roses all the way but these ladies never let the thorns hurt. Five years ago, a sozzled jawan barged into Priya's room at a remote station in the Northeast.

"I gave him quite a thrashing," says the little spitfire. Later, he was court-martialled and booted out. But Priya insists it could have happened anywhere. "Look here," the petite dynamo is quick to rid you of any evil thoughts about the fauj.

"I am in the legal branch and I've seen the dark underbelly of the Army — the corruption, misappropriation, gang-rapes, but I can tell you it is the cleanest institution in the country."

Which is why these girls can't understand the national disinclination to join the Armed Forces. "They're fools," snorts Ushasree, who says nothing in civilian life can compare with the salute, the quality of life.

But it comes at a price. That may explain why only eleven of her course-mates have stuck on. It's the high josh quotient that makes these lady officers an object of high regard. Ask any new Lieutenant from the Indian Military Academy, Dehra Dun, about the instructors there, and chances are that he will talk in hushed tones about Captain Varsha Mohan. "She knows how to put you in your place."

Mind you, that's a compliment. The jawans, the lady officers say, put them on a pedestal. "Wherever I've gone, they've just had one grouse against me-that I swear in a fashion most unladylike," grins Captain Ushasree, who quite enjoys spouting a string of wholesome epithets. Any Commanding Officer who dares to chide her gets the standard repartee, "Sir, I'll stop the moment you do."

Now with only days to go, she sighs: "Actually, I'll miss this sirring too." And a lot more that they leave unsaid. The Army is sacred, so they will wave away any spiel about their devoting the prime of their life to it. Jatinder hints that though she is okay with retirement at a ripe young age of 30-something, an extension would be welcome.

Some officers have already sought five more years from the Chief. Pucca Armywallahs, some like Captain Vincy Thomas of ASC politely refused to parry any questions. "You'll have to seek permission from the CO," they let you know, going strictly by Army's 10 commandments, one of which warns against establishing any contact with the media. Their present may be picture perfect, but the future is a trifle tense.

Ten years have just flown by, leaving them with nothing but a clutch of fond memories, some gratuity, and an uncertain tomorrow. And the parting hurts. As Priya, her voice suddenly husky, puts it: "Whenever people ask me, 'So, you are leaving the Army?' I say no, the Army is leaving me."

THEY SERVE WITH FLYING COLOURS

"From a very young age, long before the Indian Army decided to allow women into the armed forces, I wanted to join the services," says Shobha Nair, a smart young officer at the prestigious Officers' Training Academy (OTA) in Madras. She is one of the 47 women cadets who will be commissioned into the Indian Army this year, along with 173 men.

The excitement of their forthcoming passing out parade is felt all over the OTA campus with its well maintained, sprawling parade and drill grounds. Women cadets Priya Bedekar, Neena Kanwar and Cherry Singh insist that joining the army is an excellent career move.

Their short haircuts or neat plaits make them stand out from other women their age. But even without make-up they exude a strong femininity. They are not women trying hard to be men. Do women then make good soldiers, and are they ruthless enough to kill if the situation demands? "Yes!" is the unanimous reply.

Fascinated by the Uniform

"Initially I was drawn to the army because of the 'romance of the uniform,' because my father wore one," reveals Ipsa Ratha, "but I had no idea that to earn this uniform, one had to undergo such rigorous training. Not that I have any regrets," she adds. Like many of these women cadets, Ratha comes from a family steeped in army tradition.

Reveals Major General G.H. Israni, the Commandant of the Staff, of the Officers' Training Academy (OTA) in Madras, "Women make excellent officers because they have the right temperament, especially when it comes to mental stamina and intelligence." While a lot of the physical training and group activities are common for both men and women, it is slightly less strenuous for the women cadets. "The first week is the worst," says Cherry Singh. "I felt my legs would fall off if I did any more training!"

"With all the stretching exercises, push-ups and jogging, I think we do a great job at the Indian Army in getting our women cadets into figures that are comparable with the Miss Indias and models," laughs Major General Israni. The curriculum also differs for the two sexes. Living quarters in the form of spartan dormitories are separate for men and women cadets, with women cadets having women orderlies (like men have batmen) to help them with polishing their shoes and getting their uniforms ready.

Rigorous Selection Process

The selection process involved in joining the Indian Army is rigorous and usually lasts for up to four or five days. "No amount of influence can get you past this selection committee, since we are committed to choosing the very best," says Colonel Verma, who is head of the faculty of intellectual development, that looks after much of the training, education and overall development of these cadets. He has been on many such selection committees himself, and reveals, "We essentially look for a positive personality, or someone who is capable of being a leader. At times, we screen up to 25,000 applicants, only to choose 25 candidates!"

While the Army needs to expand its training centres and increase the number of officers, the actual cost to train each runs into several lakhs. "By the time a cadet leaves the academy he/she has saved about a lakh of rupees in her bank account, because her expenditure at the OTA is minimal. The army takes care of all their needs when they are here," says Colonel Verma, and goes on to add, "but one must remember that bravery has no price. These cadets are trained to fight, to the last bullet. One single Maha Vir Chakra pays the price for all the rigorous training that these officers receive at the OTA."

Why Women?

The decision to induct women into the army was taken by the Defence Ministry in 1992 for many reasons. To begin with, there are many services in the army, such as the Corps of Engineers, Signals, Ordnance, Education, Advocates, Service and Intelligence, which do not require combat soldiers to work in them.

"The Indian Army faces a great shortage of officers and to augment the numbers, we decided to include women, especially since women have been successfully inducted into the army the world over," says Major General Israni. "I am personally very proud of our women cadets," he says with almost paternal pride. "They have proved to be as good as their male counterparts, if not better, and have refused any special gender-based concessions or privileges."

Exciting Career Option

Captain Mini John of the OTA says that the army is an exciting career option till one is ready to settle down into married life. Given the demanding work schedules and the transferable nature of job, that could even take them to the battle front, most women officers opt either to marry within the services and continue to serve the army, or leave after a period of five to 10 years.

"Women have joined many professions, so why not the army?" argues Jaya Mary James. "We work twice as hard to prove ourselves, and that is true of women in other male dominated fields as well. We have grown to love the life that the army offers us, despite the rigorous training. The army offers excellent opportunities for personal development and overall growth," adds woman cadet Navneet Khangura.

Women Officers are Vital to the Pyramid

The patriarchal structure of the Indian Army however, does not allow women to rise above a certain level in the hierarchy. Women cadets tend to be granted short service commissions for five to ten years only, depending on their performance.

Combat training options are severely limited as women are not expected, nor trained, to perform on the battlefront, although the OTA familiarises them with the basic front combat operations.

Is this initiative to induct women into the army a token gesture by the Ministry of Defence? No, avers Staff Officer for Education B.S. Parmar. "The Indian Army is a pyramid in terms of hierarchy," he explains. "It is unlike the Indian Administrative Service or the Indian Foreign Service, that are more cylindrical in terms of promotion opportunities and ranks. The middle and bottom half of the Indian Army's pyramid needs to be filled, and women officers have been taken in to do that."

Major General Israni also vehemently denies that the Indian Army's decision to include women is only a token gesture. "The decision to include women cadets in the army on an experimental basis was taken in 1992. It was meant to fill the middle level positions in the Indian Army. However, most women do continue for another five years, after the five-year short term commission, and a lot of them opt for permanent posting."

"While there are women who have risen to the level of Generals in the Indian Army, it has been restricted to the nursing and medical corps. Today, a woman can rise to the level of a major, in a tenure that spans to a maximum of 10 years during the short term commission." Although the top layer of the Indian Army pyramid remains out of reach for women, it has not dampened the cadets' determination to break through the ceiling.

Ipsa Ratha says, "I believe that to begin a career with the Indian Army is an excellent training ground for any woman with aptitude. The army prepares officers mentally, physically and psychologically for various levels of social interaction. We develop well-rounded personalities that enable us to adapt to any environment and emerge winners.

It trains us to be a valuable asset in any other job that we may later take up in the private sector." *To Serve With Honour* is the motto of the cadets at the OTA, and the young women cadets who will pass out as officers this year do just that and a whole lot more.

A decade ago, on 21 September 1992, the feisty Priya Jhingan enrolled as 001 — the first lady cadet to join the Indian Army. "It's a dream I have lived every day for the last 10 years," says Major Jhingan, formerly OIC, Judge Advocate General, at the Chennai headquarters.

That dream ended two days ago for her and 24 of her batch-mates who served out their 10-year commission. Jhingan does not want to think too much about what life's going to be like here on end. She's applying to various banks for administrative jobs.

Returning to the dream, she says it was her single-mindedness that won her an entry into the Army. Soon after she finished her graduation, she wrote a letter to the then Chief of Army Staff, General Sunith Francis Rodrigues, requesting him to open the doors of the armed services to women.

The General wrote back saying the Army was planning to induct women in a year or two. Jhingan dropped all plans of becoming a police officer — her father was one — and decided to wait till the Army called her.

"The signed letter from the General remains one of my prized possessions," says Jhingan. To bide her time, she studied law. When the full-page advertisement inviting women to join the Army appeared in 1992, she knew she would make it. "There were two seats reserved for law graduates. I was just curious to find out who the other person might be." Jhingan was right. Soon, she came down to the Officers Training Academy (OTA) in Chennai.

The batch of 25 spirited women did not know what to expect and did not have much of an introduction. So, they walked into the OTA with their trunks filled with fancy clothes they thought they would wear to all the social dos. With a shake of her head, Jhingan says, "Our commanding officer almost hit the roof when he saw our trunks and the list of requests — warm water, tube lights and a saloon."

A rigorous physical training with stringent standards that matched the male cadets wasn't a problem, says Jhingan. She is unhappy that the standards for ladies have been lowered now. "It is no longer challenging." The parallel training, however, did create some awkward moments for the shy lady cadets who never imagined they would have to get into the same swimming pool as the gentleman cadets or train under the watchful eyes of male officers.

"We wrapped the towels tightly around us and refused to let go of them. Finally, our platoon commander Captain P S Behl had to come and order us to stand in attention. The towels fell and we marched forward," says Jhingan, embarrassed by the memory. In her first posting at Ahmedabad, there was only one toilet and she had to share it with other male officers, but she didn't let that bother her.

"Often, I would go in and see someone else using the facility. So, soon I devised the system of knocking hard on the door before entering. But never once did I think that I should be allotted a separate facility," she says. When a sozzled jawan entered her room five years ago, she gave him a good thrashing. He was later court-martialed and booted out.

Jhingan waves away the initial apprehension of male officers that women were inducted just to 'add colour' to the Army. She explains their refusal to call her m'aam as just one of the "problems that every working woman faces while breaking stereotypes."

But this mother of a five-year-old son, Aryaman, is willing to admit that her priorities have changed. "I am always thinking of what will be a good move for my son," she says. Ask her whether the Army took the right decision in curtailing the lady officers' service to 10 years, she will shoot back, "No way. Why should they decide what is right for me and my family?" She did not write to Army HQ seeking an extension because, "I never want to tell the Army not to detail me in for a case because I have other personal obligations.

I can never do that." When Jhingan was commissioned on 06 March 1993, she requested that she be posted in the infantry. Her commanding officer told her may be her great-grand-daughter would get a chance to serve in the infantry. "I am waiting for that day," she says.

The Gallant 21: Param Vir Chakra winners so far

The Param Vir Chakra is the highest gallantry award for officers and other enlisted personnel of all military branches of India, for the highest degree of bravery, in the presence of the enemy. The PVC is the post-independence equivalent of the Victoria Cross-Britain's highest medal for gallantry.

The PVC was established on 26 January 1950, by the President of India, with effect from 15 August 1947, and presently it is the second highest award of the Government of India, after the Bharat Ratna (amendment in the statute on 26 January 1980, resulted in this order of wearing).

The medal was designed by Mrs. Savitri Khanolankar (born Eva Yuonne Linda Maday-de-Maros to a Hungarian father and Russian mother) who was married to an Indian Army officer. By coincidence, the first PVC was posthumously awarded to her son-in-law, Major Somnath Sharma for his bravery in the Kashmir operations in October 1947.

The medal was designed to symbolise Rishi Dadich, who donated his thigh bones to gods for making Vajra and Shivaji's sword Bhawani.

The medal is of 1-3/8" radius and is made of bronze. In the center, on a raised circle is the state emblem, surrounding which are the four replicas of Indra's Vajra.

The decoration is suspended from a straight swiveling suspension bar. On the rear, around a plain center, two legends separated by lotus flowers. The words Param Vir Chakra are written in Hindi and English.

The ribbon which holds the PVC is of 32mm length and purple in colour. The award carries a cash allowance for those under the rank of Second Lieutenant (or the appropriate service equivalent) and, in some cases, a lump-sum cash award. Subedar Major Bana Singh, 8 JAK LI, was the only serving personnel of the Indian defence establishment, with a PVC, till the Kargil operations. Lieutenant Colonel (retd.) Dhan Singh Thapa, 1/8 GR, was the other surviving PVC awardee, till the Kargil operations. He was awarded the PVC, when he was a Major.

The Param Vir Chakra winners to date:

1. IC—521, Major Somnath Sharma, 4 Kumaon, 03 November 1947, Kashmir (posthumous).
2. 27373, Naik Jadunath Singh, 4 Guards (former 1 Rajput), 06 February 1948, Kashmir (posthumous).
3. SS-14246, 2nd Lt. Rama Raghoba Rane, Corps of Engineers, 08 April 1948, Kashmir.
4. 2831592, Company Havildar Major Piru Singh, 6 Rajputana Rifles, 18 July 1948, Kashmir (posthumous).
5. IC-22356, Lance Naik Karam Singh, 1 Sikh, 13 October 1948, Kashmir.
6. IC-8497, Captain Gurbachan Singh Salaria, 3/1 Gurkha Rifles, 05 December 1961, Congo (posthumous).
7. IC-7990, Major Dhan Singh Thapa, 1/8 Gurkha Rifles, 21 October 1962, Ladakh.
8. JC-4547, Subedar Joginder Singh, 1 Sikh, 23 October 1962, North-East Frontier Agency (posthumous).
9. Major Shaitan Singh, 13 Kumaon, 18 November 1962, Rezang La (posthumous).
10. 2639885, Company Havildar Major Abdul Hamid, 4 Grenadiers, 10 September 1965, Khem-Karan (posthumous).
11. IC-5565, Lieutenant Colonel Ardeshir Burzorji Tarapore, 17 Poona Horse, 16 September 1965, Pakistan (posthumous).
12. 4239746, Lance Naik Albert Ekka, 14 Guards, 04 December 1971, Gangasagar (posthumous).
13. 10877 (P), Flying Officer Nirmal Jit Singh Sekhon, No.18 Squadron, 14 December 1971, Kashmir (posthumous).

14. IC-25067, 2nd Lt. Arun Khetarpal, 17 Poona Horse, 16 December 1971, Shakargarh, (posthumous).
15. IC-14608, Major Hoshiar Singh, 3 Grenadiers, 17 December 1971, Basantar River, Shakargarh.
16. Naib Subedar Bana Singh, 8 JAK LI, 26 June 1987, Siachen Glacier, Jammu & Kashmir.
17. Major Ramaswamy Parmeshwaran, 8 Mahar, 25 November 1987, Sri Lanka (posthumous).
18. IC-56959, Lieutenant (Acting Captain) Manoj Kumar Pandey, 1/11 Gorkha Rifles, 03 July 1999, Kargil (posthumous).
19. No.2690572, Grenadier Yogender Singh Yadav, 18 Grenadiers, 04 July 1999, Kargil.
20. IC-57556, Captain Vikram Batra, 13 JAK Rifles, 07 July 1999, Kargil (posthumous).
21. Rifleman Sanjay Kumar, 13 JAK Rifles, 04 July 1999, Flat Area Top, Kargil.

7

HOMAGE TO A HERO

Lieutenant General Jagjit Singh Arora, who passed away recently on 03 May 2005, is fondly remembered in Bangladesh for his role as the commander of the India-Bangladesh joint forces in the 1971 Liberation War.

The death of Lieutenant General Jagjit Singh Arora, on May 3rd, who as commander of the Indian Army's Eastern Command led the Bangladesh-India joint forces to their historic victory against the Pakistan Army in December 1971, rekindled memories of the events that shaped the destiny of Bangladesh. Lieutenant General Arora presided over the historic surrender of the Pakistan army in Dhaka on 16 December 1971, which finally ended the presence of the occupation forces in the former East Pakistan. This particular incident elevated him to the stature of a rescuer, as far as the people of Bangladesh are concerned. Lieutenant General Arora's death, at the age of 89, sparked off a series of spontaneous condolence meetings. These, together with the newspaper coverage of the death, gave the impression that the people, despite many ups and downs in Bangladesh politics, keep alive memories of the liberation war.

However, after 34 years of Independence, Bangladesh is not united in remembering the Indian General who commanded, in the final stage of the war, both the Mukhti Bahini (Bengali liberation fighters) and the Mitra Bahini (allied Indian forces), which forced 93,000 Pakistani troops to surrender in Dhaka along with their local collaborators. There are many reasons for the disunity. Bangladesh does not have the same philosophical mindset that it had in 1971, thanks to the military rulers who ruled the country directly or indirectly for nearly 15 years and undermined the nation's secular moorings. Following the assassination of their nationalist leader Sheikh Mujibur Rahman in 1975, the military rulers changed the country's Constitution, grossly undermined secular values and floated political parties which promoted anti-liberation and communal elements. The coalition of the Bangladesh Nationalist Party (BNP), the Jamaat-e-Islami and the Islami Oikya Jote, which is in power now, has added a new environment to the Bangladeshi polity by opposing everything that is pro-liberation. The Jamaat-e-Islami, the country's best organised fundamentalist outfit, had sided with the Pakistan Army to oppose independence.

Many commentators said that the state should have recognised and honoured Lieutenant General Arora during his lifetime for his historic role. But there are people who have tried to erase the history of the nation's war of independence by distorting it. In fact, the present generation of Bangladeshis seems to be confused about the nation's history. Nonetheless, an overwhelming majority of the nation's independent media took up the issue on Lieutenant General Arora's death. Those who participated in the war that left nearly three million people dead commemorated his accomplishments. Dozens of condolence meetings were held across the country, at which the role of the Indian people and the government led by Prime Minister Indira Gandhi, and the sacrifices of soldiers of the Indian Armed Forces, who fought side by side with the Bengali freedom fighters, were recalled. India's High Commissioner in Dhaka, Veena Sikri, and Deputy High Commissioner, Sarbajit Chakrabarti, attended many such meetings, which were organised by various freedom fighter groups and political & socio-cultural organisations.

But, ironically, the government's response was very different. There were no official condolence messages from President Professor Iajuddin Ahmed and Prime Minister Begum Khaleda Zia. While leaders of all secular opposition parties, including the Awami League, which led the war of liberation, paid tributes to Lieutenant General Arora with a deep sense of gratitude, leaders of the BNP, the Jamaat-e-Islami and other constituents of the four-party ruling alliance kept away from condolence meetings. The Bangladesh Jatiya Sangsad (Parliament) did not include the name of Lieutenant General Arora in the obituary references in its last session. However, Speaker Jamiruddin Sircar agreed to include his name when the freedom fighter-turned-parliamentarian, Kader Siddiqui, pointed out the lapse. The late General was remembered also for his unique style of operation, which minimised civilian casualty at the time of the joint forces' advance towards Dhaka in the first week of December 1971. Sidetracking the Pakistani positions in the countryside, the advancing forces swiftly encircled Dhaka, where Pakistan's Eastern Headquarters was located. Civilian casualties were at a bare minimum.

The Pakistani soldiers were destroying everything during their retreat, thanks to the combined assault by the Mukhti Bahini and the Mitra Bahini. The entire civilian population was badly exposed to the Pakistan Army's brutality. So, Lieutenant General Arora, as the man in charge of subduing the final resistance, had to proceed very carefully. He accomplished the task with remarkable precision. The 93,000 Pakistani troops, led by Lieutenant General A.A.K. Niazi, had to surrender. Lieutenant General Arora was also praised for the discipline with which he conducted the post-surrender phase. While the Geneva Convention was strictly honoured in protecting the Prisoners of War (PoWs), there was no butchery of the Pakistan Army's local collaborators, or looting of property. Although the chief of the Bangladesh liberation forces, General M.A.G. Osmany, died years ago, most of the sector commanders of the historic war fondly remember Lieutenant General Arora.

"He was a great friend of Bangladesh and played his role sincerely," said A.K. Khondoker, deputy chief of the Bangladesh liberation forces during the war. Khondoker, also a former Air Chief, represented the Mukhti Bahini at the surrender ceremony at the Race Course (now Suhrawardi Uddyan). "Since my acquaintance with him in 1971, I met him several times and was present with General Osmany at the discussions with him. I saw him always trying to help us in all possible ways," said

Khondoker, adding, "We learnt a lot from him." The retired Air Vice-Marshal, who participated in Lieutenant General Arora's funeral in Delhi, said: "All those who knew him will miss the great soldier." One of the leading sector commanders of the liberation war, Major Rafiqul Islam, who wrote the book *Tale of Millions*, said Lieutenant General Arora was deeply moved by the suffering of the Bangladeshi people. Major Islam said, "As a professional soldier, he could not imagine the genocide and brutality of Pakistani soldiers to our people. So, he decided to help us. He was sympathetic to us and committed to helping us for our cause."

Recalling the motivation that Bangladeshi forces received from Lieutenant General Arora, K.M. Shafiullah, then commander of the S-Force, said, "General Arora was a father figure for us." The former Army Chief said, "We got all sorts of help from him during the war...the role he played during the war makes us heavily indebted..." In a message to Prime Minister Manmohan Singh, Sheikh Hasina, chief of the Awami League, conveyed her deep sympathy to the members of Lieutenant General Arora's bereaved family and said the people of Bangladesh would always remember his contribution in their liberation war. She also recalled the supreme sacrifice of Indian soldiers during the war. Foreign Minister M. Morshed Khan, in a message to his Indian counterpart K. Natwar Singh, said: "I am deeply shocked and grieved to learn of the passing away of Lieutenant General Jagjit Singh Arora." He expressed his sympathy to the bereaved family. Books written by various Indian generals who took part in the war have essentially highlighted the role of the Indian Armed Forces, but ignored the heroic role of the Mukhti Bahini. Lieutenant General Arora was an exception. He told this writer in an exclusive interview in 1994, "I would like to make a special mention about the Mukhti Bahini. I think the organisation, though suffering from many handicaps, rendered valuable service."

Lieutenant General Niazi, who did not think much of them militarily, had to concede in his own words that it made him "deaf and blind." Lieutenant General Arora said, "I took personal interest in the training and launching of the Mukhti Bahini groups before the active hostilities started. I was greatly impressed with the enthusiasm and devotion of those young people. Considering that they had no previous knowledge or experience of covert and subversive activities they adapted to these roles very quickly." Distortion of history has been a part of Bangladesh politics ever since the brutal assassination of Sheikh Mujibur Rahman, the architect of independent Bangladesh, in 1975. The level of distortion has been so acute that school textbooks, re-written during the present regime of Khaleda Zia, have grossly subverted the history of the socio-political and cultural movements against the Pakistani military rulers. The BNP-Jamaat coalition has also promoted Ziaur Rahman, the founder of the BNP, as the main leader of the nation's independence. Despite the distortions, one particular photograph of the country's history cannot be erased. The historic picture shows Lieutenant General Niazi signing the instrument of surrender in front of Lieutenant General Arora at Dhaka's Ramna Race Course.

REMEMBERING SAGAT SINGH (1918-2001)

Amidst the turbulent events of September 11th and its aftermath, when the world's attention was fixed on the global war on Terrorism, the death of Lt. General Sagat Singh, Padma Bhushan, PVSM on the Sept 26th, 2001 at the Army Hospital Research and Referral in Delhi went relatively unnoticed. The total lack of news of his demise in the national media or in the press was in no way reflective of the dynamic and illustrious career that Sagat Singh had during his tenure with the Army. He was a soldier's soldier, a brilliant tactician and above all, a good performer and leader who fetched great results in the times of war. He had a fine reputation as a frontline soldier and was known to have an unorthodox and aggressive attitude to military matters, especially in times of war where most commanders tend to go strictly by the rule book.

Sagat Singh started his career in uniform when he was commissioned in the Jaipur State Forces. On the amalgamation of the State forces with the Armed Forces of the Indian Union in 1950, Sagat Singh was posted to the 3rd Gorkha Rifles

Regiment, joining the 3rd Battalion as its 2nd in Command. Sagat's association with the 3 GR Regiment was to last the rest of his career and when he retired he was holding the Colonel of the Regiment title for 3GR.

Sagat's first command came in February 1955, when on promotion to Lt. Col., he was posted as the CO of the 2nd Battalion, 3 Gorkha Rifles Regiment, then located at Ferozepur. 2/3GR was a well renowned fighting unit, with the battle honors of Pir Kanthi during the 1947-48 Kashmir War. His command lasted just over an year. He was posted as the CO of the 3/3GR in March 1956, then located at Dharamsala.

Pegasus Beckons

His career was till then was nothing out of the ordinary. But one fine day in September 1961, He was promoted to the rank of Brigadier and posted as the Brigade Commander of India's only Parachute Brigade, the 50th. This was a bolt from the blue.

The 50 (Independent) Parachute Brigade, known as the Pegasus brigade was considered an elite formation, It was a prestigious formation and had the unique distinction of being one of the very few Independent Brigades under the direct command of Army HQ. Considering the fact that the Indian Army had only Six Infantry Divisions, 50th Brigade enjoyed a special status and privilege under the Army's Orbat. What was amazing was not that Sagat Singh was selected to command it, but the fact that Sagat was an infantry man, a non-paratrooper.

The Brigade till then had as its commanders only officers who were paratroopers and served with the para forces at one time or the other. And here was a hardcore infantry man from a rifle regiment who never had para experience being asked to command India's most prestigious and only airborne formation. On taking over command of the Para Brigade, what struck Sagat Singh the most was the outstanding comradeship, zeal and *espirit-de-corps* prevailing among all ranks of the Brigade. Not wanting to waste time in being accepted by the members of the Brigade, Sagat Singh went about earning his "Para Wings" in record time, even making four Para jumps in a span of two days to reach the requisite number of jumps required to earn the wings.

Liberator of Goa

Immediately afterwards earning his maroon beret and para wings, Sagat was called to the DMO's office in Delhi sometime in November 1961. There he was briefed on his first operational assignment of his career, To be part of the advance of the Indian Army to liberate the territory of Goa from the Portuguese. His Para Brigade was to form the northern prong, while 17th infantry Division was to advance from the west and south in two prongs. Though a planned parachute landing by a battalion of the formation was given up, the tasks given to Sagat was to assist the main effort of 17th Division under Maj. Gen. K P Candeth. Since there were atleast four major riverine obstacles in the Para Brigade's path to Panjim, not much was expected out of Sagat Singh's effort. The Army's whole attention focussed on the main force under Candeth.

Sagat Singh surprised everyone by making a lightning advance against the Portuguese forces, when the operations began on Dec 18th, 1961. Even though his main task was only a supportive role and the capture of the Goan capital of Panjim was never tasked as its objective, his troops overwhelmed the Portugese forces and achoieved objectives that were beyond his initial purview. Using improvised resources wherever possible, the troops of his Brigade crossed its riverine obstacles by rafts and local boats and were the first troops to enter Panjim by Dec 19th, 1961. On Sagat Singh's orders, the troops entering the capital removed their steel helmets and wore the Parachute Regiment's maroon berets. This was Sagat Singh's way of making a statement. The people of Goa welcomed Sagat Singh and his para brigade as liberators. When the army started redeploying the Para Brigade to Agra, numerous telegrams and petitions were sent to the Prime Minister Nehru to reinstate what they called as the "Maroon Beret Friends" back in Goa. Under popular pressure, Nehru ordered the Para Brigade back to Goa.

The rapid capitulation of the Portuguese saw that there were a large number of POWs with the Indian Army. Sagat Singh's Brigade was tasked with the job of looking after them till the time of repatriation. Sagat Singh's fame as the liberator of Goa was carried all the way to Portugal. Soon after his brigade moved back to Agra, one day Sagat was visiting the Clarkes Shiraz Hotel in Agra. He was in civilian clothing when four American tourists approached him and enquired if he was "Brigadier Singh". When a surprised Sagat asked them how they recognised him, they told him that they had just come in from Portugal. Apparently they saw posters with his photograph in many café's and restaurants announcing an award of Ten Thousand US Dollars for anyone who captures and delivers Sagat Singh to the government of Portugal! Sagat Singh made a good natured offer to surrender to the tourists and asked them to take him and hand him over to the Portuguese. The offer was declined.

The Para Brigade moved back to Agra in Mid 1962. Sagat Singh was still in command when the Indo-China Border war erupted. However the Brigade was not called upon for action even though a couple of its sub units were requisitioned away to NEFA.

Counter insurgency in Mizo Hills

Sagat Singh left command of the Para Brigade in 1964 and went on to XI Corps HQ as its Brigadier General Staff. He was with XI Corps during Operation Ablaze, when the Kutch incursions took place in April 1965. Soon afterwards, he was promoted to major General and posted to the North-East as the GOC of 17th Mountain Division. As the GOC of the Division in the troubled Mizo Hills, most of his time was taken up in Counter Insurgency operations. It was here that Sagat renewed his close relationship with the Indian Air Force and began to understand the application of Air Power and logistics in a ground campaign. Sagat fully appreciated the use of Helicopters in movement of ground troops, and support of ground operations and he was to apply his learnings to effect when his next big assignment came up.

From the command of the Mountain Division, Sagat Singh was posted briefly to command the static formation of 101 Communication Zone located in Mizoram. Though he had a change of formation, it was no change in terms of operational requirements. He was involved in counterinsurgency operations in the Mizo Hills throughout the period. For his distinguished services and pivotal role in quelling the insurgency in Mizoram, he was awarded the Param Vishist Seva Medal.

In December 1970 he was promoted to Lt. General and took over the command of IV Corps HQ1[i]. IV Corps was at that time located at Tezpur. With the looming of warclouds in 1971, The area of operations earmarked for Sagat Singh was the entire East Pakistani territory west of the River Meghna. IV Corps HQ was split into two. The Advance HQ under Sagat Singh moving down to near Agartala. Sagat Singh had under him, three Mountain Divisions. 8 Mtn Div in the Sylhet Sector. 57 Mtn Div in the Agartala Sector and 23 Mtn Div in the Comilla Sector. Once again the task given to him was the occupation of East Pakistani territory west of the River Meghna. Dacca was never mentioned as an objective when allocating the tasks for Sagat Singh and his IV Corps.

Op Cactus Lily: the liberation of Bangladesh

Maj. Gen. Sukhwant Singh, who was the DDMO during the 1974 War, recollects the meeting when they were discussing the plans for IV Corps. Sagat Singh was insisting that the primary task of his Corps be the reduction of the fortress at Comilla while the DMOs office was insisting that it should be the capture of the Ashuganj Bridge over the Meghna River. Ashuganj Bridge was the only bridge that spanned the huge Meghna River which at its narrowest point was more than 4000 yards wide. Sagat Singh saw no point in its capture when Dacca was never given as an objective for him. But when someone mentioned that its capture would enable "*IV Corps win the race to Dacca*", It bought a "*glint into his eyes. One could safely assume that once the battle was joined, Sagat would join the race to Dacca himself even though this was never been specifically assigned as his task*"

Dacca as it happened was the objective of II Corps2[ii] which was to advance from the east in the Jessore Sector. Besides II Corps, no other formation was tasked with the objective of capturing Dacca. As it happened, when hostilities broke out in December, II Corps failed to reach its objective. Even though the battle in its sector was going on fine, a reversal at Kushtia saw an overreaction from the Corps and Divisional Commander which diverted the attention of the corps from its major push towards Dacca.

The Flying General

In the northernmost subsector of his area of command, the Sylhet Sector, the objective was to take command of the maximum Enemy territory as possible. With tasks laid out on capture of important towns and cities. 8 Mtn Div under Maj. Gen. K V Krishna Rao carried out the tasks in due course of time. It was here for the first time that the corps employed heliborne troops for the first time. When at one point the advance bogged down, Acting on some information that Sylhet town was being lightly held, Sagat wanted to airlift a battalion to just outside Sylhet to throw the Pakistanis regrouping there offbalance and possibly capture the town. After a drop zone was identified by Gp Capt Chandan Singh, who commanded all the aviation resources allocated to the corps, 8 Div helidropped an two infantry companies in the outskirts of Sylhet between Dec 7th and 9th. A Force of just Nine Mi-74 Helicopters airdropped 584 Troops in some 60 sorties by Dec 9th, when the heli-effort was diverted to Meghna., However the helidropped troops found themselves countered by Pak troops in the vicinity and with due reinforcements and supplies they were able to settle down and keep the pocket which were holding secure for the rest of the war.

The Southernmost subsector of Comilla, the rapid advance of the 23 Div saw that all Pakistani troops in the area withdrew to the fortress town of Comilla where it was contained successfully till the end of the war. Major objectives like Chandpur and Daudkondi were captured virtually without a fight, as the enemy was in total confusion regarding the location of Indian troops and preferred evacuation rather than battle. Lt. Gen. Sagat Singh was continuously monitoring by helicopter the operations along his wide front.

While on a visit by helicopter to Daudkandi, Sagat Singh wanted to take a look at Chandpur to see how our troops were faring. Arriving over Chandpur, flying at low level, they could see no ground activity in Chandpur. Lots of civilians were waving flags. Observing this, Sagat instructed the pilot to land the helicopter at a field nearby, and getting down from the helicopter walked down to some locals standing nearby to get information. The locals managed to communicate to him that the Pakistanis have already vacated Chandpur. Immediately Sagat got back to the helicopter and made to the nearest Indian army post at Laksham. There he instructed the ground troops to go to Chandpur and take up positions. By the evening of 7th December Chandpur was in Indian Hands and Sagat Singh was credited with having captured Chandpur single-handed!3[iii]

The fact that Sagat Singh was pushing himself and taking chances by his low level Helicopter sorties became apparent one day, when on another one of his recce sorties over Bhiarab Bazar, the Alloutte in which Sagat Singh was flying was straddled with ground fire. The pilot Flt Lt. Sodhi of No.115 HU was severely wounded and the helicopter was flown back to base by the co-pilot. Sagat Singh himself had a bullet graze his hand and forehead, becoming the only corps commander to be wounded4[iv] during the war. This however did not deter him from carrying on with his campaign.

Psychological Warfare

One of Sagat Singh's innovative ideas was to harrass the Pakistani troops round the clock. He knew that there were two Caribou STOL Transport aircraft stationed at Agartala during the time. These aircraft were primarily tasked with Casualty evacuation. Sagat suggested to Group Captain Chandan Singh that the Caribous be used as nuisance bombers. They were to load up with 500lb bombs and fly over where Pakistani forces were concentrated in fortresses, like Maulvi Bazar, Bairab

Bazar, Lalmai, Comilla. The Caribous flew at high altitudes, out of range of small arms fire. They circled their targets and randomly dropped one bomb at a time, thereby keeping the Pakistanis on their toes all the time. When one Caribou had exhausted all its bombs, the second aircraft would come and take over the station. The airforce had only conceptualized the usage of An-12s as bombers. But Sagat Singh takes the credit for taking this concept to the Caribous.

Sagat's Flying Army

It was in the central sector of Agartala that Sagat Singh's formation undertook the most brilliant move that very rapidly hastened the outcome of the war. The task in this sector for 57 Mtn Div (under Maj. Gen. B F Gonsalves) was to occupy the territory leading upto the wide Meghna river. The only way across the river was over the Ashuganj Bridge which very soon became a fortress where an enemy division had consolidated itself. Though the objectives in the sector were achieved, Sagat had a bigger prize in mind. He wanted Dhaka. Accordingly he convinced Gonsalves to airlift troops across the 4000 yard Meghna River and drop troops on the other side.

Once a significant force had been built up, there was no recognisable enemy force between the helidropped force and Dhaka. Brilliant in its conception, the idea was fraught with risks and dangers. First the Pakistani troops north of the identified dropzone at Raipura should not interfere with the buildup. Second the Airforce could hardly muster 14 Mi-4 Helicopters for the task. The troops that were helidropped will not have artillery or armoured support. Even then, Sagat Singh went ahead with the decision and starting December 9th, Troops began to be airlifted to Raipura which was just south of the Ashuganj Bridge, and once the position was consolidated, the troops were helilifted straight to Narsingdi. From Narsingdi the road to Dacca lay bare for IV Corps to take. To provide support for the heliborne troops, PT-76 Tanks were told to ford the Meghna River. The tanks broke down after overheating in the water midstream and were towed to the other side using mechanised boats.

By December 14th, Sagat Singh had accumulated a force of over 2000 troops, airlifted by the Mi-4s after carrying out more than 200 sorties. He planned to add another brigade before mounting the assault on Dacca itself. However by that time the Pakistani High command in East Pakistan had lost its nerve. Faced with troops at its doorstep in the east, and also from the north (By the paradrop at Tangail), Niazi sued for peace and had to surrender by the evening of December 16th. Sagat Singh had the honour of witnessing the surrender ceremony as Lt. Gen. A A K Niazi signed the Surrender deed.

Honors and Accolades

For his leadership and command for the race to Dacca, the Indian Government honored Sagat Singh through an award of Padma Bhushan, Sagat Singh being the only other corps commander besides T N Raina and Sartaj Singh to be so awarded in 1971. Sagat Singh attributed his successes to the close working relationship with the Air Force during his counterinsurgency and para days and he remained the favourite of the Air Force Brass during the war.

After the war, Sagat resumed the peacetime operational duties of combating insurgency and taking care of the Chinese threat. Sagat Singh retired from the army on 30th November 1976. Not before enduring the tragic demise of his son Captain Digvijay Singh in May 1976. Digvijay traced his father's footsteps and was commissioned into the 3 Gorkha Rifles regiment in 1971. During a frontline posting with his regiment at Poonch, Digvijay had a Jeep accident and died of injuries soon after. This was the only personal setback faced by this soldier in his career with the Indian Army.

Many books that appeared after 1971 are all praise for Sagat Singh and his push to Dacca by IV Corps. Lack of space here prevents us from reproducing the praise heaped on Sagat's planning and execution by many military writers post 1971. There was no doubt that in 1971, If Gen Niazi had decided to make his stand in Dhaka instead of prematurely surrendering, It was Sagat Singh who was posed to strike first. His formation was the only formation with the means and the leadership to do so. After retirement Sagat led a quiet life, apart from penning his experiences for authors who approached him for information on his role in Goa and in 1971. Lt. Gen. Sagat Singh, Padma Bhushan, PVSM breathed his last at the Research and Referral Hospital, New Delhi on 26 September 2001. Bharat Rakshak takes this moment to salute one of India's greatest soldiers and a legend of his times.

THE HERO OF SKARDU

Since Independence, India has witnessed three wars with Pakistan in Kashmir. The stories of gallant deeds and valour of our soldiers continue to haunt our minds. One such heroic tale is of late Brigadier Sher Jung Thapa, MVC. But for his siege of Skardu in the Ladakh region of Kashmir for over six months, Ladakh might have been wiped out from the Indian map. Brigadier Sher Jung Thapa died in Dharamsala a couple of months ago at the age of 90 years. He is remembered and revered as the Hero of Skardu. Though he is no more, his heroic deeds are today part of the glorious history of the Indian Army. Sher Jung Thapa was born in Abbottabad on 18 June 1908. His grandfather and father were distinguished soldiers. Thapa had his college education at Dharamsala. He was an excellent hockey player and frequently played with stalwarts of 1 Gorkha Rifles, Regimental Centre, Dharamsala. In the hockey field, he became a close friend of Captain Douglas Gracy, Adjutant of 1 GR RC, who encouraged Thapa to join the forces of Jammu & Kashmir state as an officer. Thapa took his advice and was commissioned on 01 September 1932. Thapa met Gracy again after a lapse of 25 years under different circumstances.

Lieutenant Colonel Thapa was a Prisoner of War (PoW) in Pakistan and General Sir Douglas Gracy was the Commander-in-Chief of the Pakistan Army. Lieutenant Colonel Thapa's friendship with General Gracy came to his rescue otherwise he would have met the fate of other prisoners of war who were killed by the Pakistani Army. A small and narrow valley at a height of 7500 feet above sea level, Skardu is divided into two parts by the Indus river. Before the arrival of Lieutenant Colonel Sher Jung Thapa at Skardu, the Wazir Amar Nath

Mahajan saw the signs of a gathering storm. Skardu tehsil had a greater area under it than a normal tehsil. There were five jagirdars called Rajas, who exercised considerable influence over the population in their respective areas. They were Raja of Rondu; Raja of Khapalu; Raja of Shigar; Raja of Skardu and Raja of Kharmang. On 11 February 1948, Skardu was surrounded by an enemy of about 600 troops, while the strength of soldiers under Lieutenant Colonel Thapa of 6 JAK Rifles was only 130. He had to face many odds during the war against the Pakistani forces as scores of Muslims in the Skardu area had secretly joined the enemy. Not only this, many of the Muslim soldiers in Indian platoons deserted the army and joined the enemy. So much so that three Muslim wireless operators operating from the Bungalow of Lieutenant Colonel Thapa also deserted, thus jeopardising the signals. Once having worked as Brigade Signal Officer, Lieutenant Colonel Thapa himself operated the wireless set.

Lieutenant Colonel M.L. Chhiber (Retd.) in his book Pakistan's Criminal Folly in Kashmir has quoted Brigadier Thapa on the indifferent attitude of Muslim community in Skardu area towards Indian troops. He said, "Every Muslim civil officer, schoolboys, servants of local shopkeepers and all who were employed to secure information about the enemy did not do so. They knew that the enemy was coming. They took all precautions to see that we were kept in the dark and then were attacked by surprise. This attitude of the Muslims there goes to prove how determined, united and eager they were. They wanted the Pakistan flag to fly. The Pakistan agents here did a thorough job." Gradually, the ration position started worsening. The Dogra soldiers who were addicted to smoking, used tree leaves and rice husk for smoking. They even went to the extent of rolling up tea leaves in mulberry leaves to make cigarettes.

Recounting those days later, Sher Jung Thapa said: "I vividly remembered 17 June 1948. We saw Sepoy Amarnath of 5 Kashmir Infantry being captured by the enemy at Parkutta. He was sent by the enemy to persuade us to surrender. The man was tutored to demoralise our men. He carried a letter from Colonel Shahazada-Mata-Ul-Malek, commanding the enemy forces. The offer was outrightly rejected by me." The night falling between 13 and 14 August 1948, saw a fierce battle at Skardu between Pakistani and Indian troops. Thapa said, "We used our last box of ammunition. Everyone knew our plight and there was panic and chaos all over. The women started committing suicide by jumping into the Indus and poisoning themselves in order to save their honour. There was an instance where a girl jumped thrice into the Indus to kill herself but each time the waves carried her back to the shore. My troops fought under very adverse conditions and held Skardu for six months and three days. Then was left with no alternative but to surrender. The surrender was followed by mass murder. All the Sikhs were shot dead. Captain Ganga Singh, my Adjutant was tied, laid on the ground and shot. The only Sikh who escaped was Kalyan Singh, my orderly who was staying with me."

In 1949, Prime Minister Jawaharlal Nehru visited Srinagar soon after the ceasefire to see the troops in the frontline. General Thimayya, Commander of 19 Infantry Division, also addressed the officers. In his address, General Thimayya said: "My strategy to save Ladakh was to hold on to Skardu at all costs so that Pakistani forces may be prevented from reaching Kargil and Leh. Fortunately, I had the right man in Skardu to fulfil this mission. No words can describe the gallantry and leadership of Lieutenant Colonel Sher Jung Thapa who held on to Skardu with hardly 250 men for six long months. It is one of the longest sieges in the annals of war. While ordering him to defend Skardu to the last man and last round, I had promised to send him reinforcements and supplies. Unfortunately neither could reach Skardu. I also tried to air drop more rations and ammunition but these were merely helping the enemy. At the end of six months, when he completely ran out of ration and ammunition, I asked him to surrender. My General Staff Officer, Colonel Shri Ram Oberoi, gave this order to the gallant officer on radio in August 1948. Thapa's response is etched on my mind and I can never forget it. He said, 'I know that I cannot hold out without rations and ammunitions. General Thimayya has failed me. I know the fate my troops will meet after surrendering to the enemy. I cannot do anything now against the enemy but I will certainly take revenge in my next life.' It is officers of this stamp who make great armies and great nations." Lieutenant Colonel Thapa was conferred with Maha Vir Chakra and he retired as a Brigadier in 1960. The extracts from the citation for MVC are worth quoting, "Throughout the period of siege, Lieutenant Colonel Sher Jung Thapa showed outstanding leadership and great determination in holding out...in spite of the enemy offering him liberal surrender terms and knowing that there was no hope of ever being relieved. By his personal example and indomitable spirit he kept the morale of both his troops and civilian refugees at a high level...his conduct has been in the best traditions of the Indian Army."

THE VALIANT DOGRA WHO SAVED PARADISE ON EARTH

Dogras have been counted among the most ferocious warriors all over the world. One such quiet, unassuming, and dedicated Dogra soldier was Brigadier Rajinder Singh, who by his personal example, leadership of high order, indomitable courage and unflinching loyalty to his ruler laid down his life in the wee hours of October 27, 1947, and saved paradise on earth from being grabbed by Pakistan. On 30 December 1949, Brigadier Rajinder Singh was posthumously decorated as the first recipient of independent India's gallantry award Maha Vir Chakra.

Brigadier Rajinder Singh was born on 14 June 1899, in Bagoona village, 35 km east of Jammu city in Samba Tehsil. Almost a century ago, his ancestor General Baj Singh, who served under Maharaja Gulab Singh, made the supreme sacrifice of fighting the enemy to his last breath in defence of Chitral. His grandfather, Hamir Singh, was a war veteran who had seven battle scars on his body. His father Subedar Lakha Singh had also served the motherland as a loyal soldier. Due to the untimely death of his father, Rajinder Singh was brought up under the care of his uncle, Lt. Colonel Govind Singh, since he was just six months old.

Rajinder Singh grew up to be a sober, studious, and a withdrawn young man. On completing his graduation from Prince of Wales College (Now GGM Science College), Jammu, he was commissioned on 14 June 1921, in the J&K Armed Forces. Devoting all his energies to his work, he developed into a towering personality and cultivated all the qualities of a trusted and capable army officer. Rajinder Singh rose to the rank of Brigadier in May 1942. He had been approved for the rank of Major General when he became the Chief of Army Staff (COAS) of the J&K Forces on 25 September 1947. He had taken charge from Major General H.L. Scott. It was a time when the state was in a deep military and political crisis.

The Indian subcontinent had been partitioned into India and Pakistan. The ruler of J&K, Maharaja Hari Singh, was finding it difficult to arrive at a decision-whether to join one of the two dominions or to stay as an independent country. Finding himself in a fix, the Maharaja offered to sign a stand still agreement with India and Pakistan. The latter agreed but India did not. Behind this feigned friendship, Pakistan sneakingly began to prepare a military adventure to occupy the Kashmir valley by force.

On 03 September 1947, under Operation Gulmarg, Pakistan initiated its raids across the state borders. This was a forerunner to the major operation to capture Srinagar, the seat of the ruler at that time. The state administration was in a shambles and the unending streams of refugees from Pakistan created many problems for the ruler. The state army had been rocked by the mutiny against it by a large section of Poonchhie and Punjabi Muslim officers & soldiers.

The then British C-in-C of the Pakistan Army himself signed and cleared Operation Gulmarg to take control of Kashmir. The invading force consisted of nearly 6000 tribals, who were mostly Afridis, Mashuds, Wazirs and Swatis. Besides these tribals, there were regular Pakistani troops. The 6000-strong force was divided into six *lashkars* of 1000 raiders each. The Pakistani regulars joined the invaders as stiffners. Each *lashkar* headed by a Malik was provided with one Major, one Captain and 10 JCOs.

The entire force was commanded by Major-General Akbar Khan, who was assisted by Brigadier Sher Khan. Akbar Khan, who was a native of J&K, was very familiar with the terrain of the state. The main force of the tribals was led by Khurshid Anwar, who was earlier an emergency commissioned officer of the Indian Army. Now he was Chief of Pakistan's Muslim League National Guards. The main thrust of the operation was to capture Srinagar and declare the formation of the 'People's Government' from the state capital. While six *lashkars* proceeded on the Rawalpindi-Srinagar road via Muzaffarabad, Domel, Uri and Baramulla, two *lashkars* each had to subsequently move via Hajipur to Gulmarg and to Bandipore. At the same time the 7th Division of the Pakistan Army was ordered to be ready to move via Murree-Abbotabad to provide support to the *lashkars* to consolidate hold over the entire valley.

On the intervening night of October 21st and 22nd, the main thrust force stationed itself on the other side of the then international border near Muzzafarabad. Akbar Khan along with his trusted lieutenants, including Khurshid Anwar, established contact with the two companies of the 4 JAK Regiment, consisting of Poonchhie Muslims. In the name of *jehad,* they succeeded in instigating the Muslim men in uniform against their fellow soldiers. These Muslims betrayed the confidence of their Commanding Officer, Lt. Colonel Narain Singh, who had vouched for the loyalty and devotion of these persons, setting aside all intelligence reports and rebuking the reporting agency by stating that he trusted his Muslim men more than the Dogra soldiers. These soldiers in the wee hours of October 22nd (Dasehra day that year), drawing arms from the armoury, killed all Dogra men and officers who were asleep in their barracks, including Lt. Col. Narain Singh and his Adjutant, Captain Ram Singh. The rebels joined the invaders and guided them at every step. The Pak force entered the strategic town of Muzaffarabad and wreaked havoc on the settlement. Besides looting and raping women, they brutally killed civilians, including children. These marauders had to be persuaded to move forward, where they were told they would get more booty and far more beautiful Kashmiri damsels. This force was equipped with arms that were more sophisticated than the ones possessed by the state forces.

This news reached the capital late in the afternoon. The Maharaja got worried and decided to cede to India. He dressed up in uniform and decided to lead his force at the border. Before proceeding, he summoned his COAS to brief him. Brigadier Rajinder Singh reached the palace, dissuaded the Maharaja from leading the forces and offered to lead instead. He was ordered to halt the march of the enemy till the Indian troops reached there, for which the Maharaja's emissary had already been sent to Delhi. He was asked to collect as many men and officers from the Badamibagh cantonment and proceed immediately towards Uri. He could collect only about 150 men with their obsolete weapons. Since there was shortage of petrol (Pakistan had blocked all supplies to Kashmir) and no vehicle was readily available, the COAS and his men used private transport (buses and trucks) and left Srinagar at 6:30 p.m. The rain, slippery roads and old vehicles slowed their movement. The group reached Uri at 2 a.m. on 23 October 1947. Leaving a platoon at Uri *nullah,* he proceeded to Garhi.

At Garhi a fierce battle was fought. In the first phase, heavy casualties were inflicted on the enemy. By virtue of their numbers and far superior weapons, the enemy ultimately had the upper hand. The Brigadier realised that to halt the invading raiders, it would be better to withdraw to Uri and hold a defensive position. The raiders, however, entered the settlement to repeat the sordid drama they had enacted in Muzaffarabad. As Ashok Jairath observes, "Those who assisted these tribals, considering the ethnic similarity were subjected to humiliation as they, the tribals, not only stayed at their dwellings at nightfall but also raped their womenfolk and while leaving their dwellings, they plundered what could have been their assets and the dwellings were set on fire roasting their womenfolk and children on the spot. It is the history that who betrayed and invited these rustics were subjected to mental agony and perished in due course of time as their kith and kin boycotted them on all fronts." The small defensive force could hardly come to the rescue of the helpless people. The Brigadier went to Baramulla to communicate the happenings to his HQ and asked for supplementary support in terms of men and material. Brigadier Faquir Singh at the HQ promised to send 70-80 men.

In the capital, the ruler finding the situation getting out of hand took over command of the Army HQ at Srinagar. He sent a written army order to Brigadier Rajinder Singh through Captain Jwala Singh on 23 October 1947.

> *"Brigadier Rajinder Singh is commanded to hold the enemy at Uri at all costs and to the last man. Reinforcement is sent with Captain Jwala Singh. If Brigadier Rajinder Singh is not contacted, Captain Jwala Singh is commanded to hold the enemy at all costs and to the last man. He will do his best to contact Brigadier Rajinder Singh."*

Captain Jwala Singh reached Uri at 3:00 am on October 24th with a small contingent of reinforcement and handed over the Maharaja's army order to Brigadier Rajinder Singh. Finding the situation quite precarious and the defending force quite small in comparison to the swarming tribals, the Brigadier ordered Captain Nasib Singh to blow up the steep girder bridge over the Uri stream. This act led to a wide yawning gap on the far side of the bridge, sufficient to halt the march of the enemy for quite some time. Firing ensued from both banks. The enemy suffered heavy casualties and fell back. After about a couple of hours, the enemy launched another massive attack and the tribal raiders seemed to be everywhere. The defensive force fell back to Mahura for another defensive position. The Brigadier and his men reached Mahura at 10 p.m. He had, no doubt, in the literal sense, disobeyed the order of the ruler to halt the onward march of raiders to Srinagar, but it was a prudent decision.

The enemy resumed attack at 7:00 a.m. on October 25th. The defence was so effective that the raiders sent some columns to cross the Jhelum upstream on footbridges to attack the defense from the rear. Brigadier Rajinder Singh, sensing the move, asked Captain Jwala Singh to move upstream and blow up the bridges. The task was completed by 4:30 p.m. but by then some enemy troops had already crossed over to this side. Again the Brigadier moved to Rampur to put up a defence near the Pathar ruins. Trenches were hastily dug and the troops could not rest throughout the night as they had to dig waist deep bunkers. On 26th morning the enemy firing started from all sides. The defence was, once again, so effective that throughout the day raiders could not launch an assault. Then they planned to put up road blocks to block even the tactical retreat. The Brigadier, at dusk, ordered a withdrawal to Seri bridge just west of Baramulla to put another halt to the enemy move. Retreating vehicles moved at 1:00 a.m. on October 27 and enemy fire again started from all sides. The first roadblock was cleared without any loss but at the second one near Dewan Mandir (Buniyar), the leading driver was hit and killed. The convoy halted.

When Captain Jwala Singh got down to clear the block, he found that the drivers of the first three vehicles had been killed. Somehow he managed to get these three vehicles pushed aside and made four vehicles move on but the Brigadier was in none of them and Captain decided to retreat to Baramulla. In fact at the second road block the Brigadiers' driver had been killed and then Brigadier Rajinder Singh himself took control of the steering of his vehicle which was number two in the small convoy. In no time he was also mortally wounded in the right leg from the MMG fire, thus impeding the plan. He forcefully ordered his men to put him under the culvert with a revolver since he had promised his ruler that the enemy would advance only over his dead body and ordered them to swiftly and safely move to the planned defensive position to check the movement of the enemy towards Srinagar.

Thereafter nothing more was heard of this brave and fearless soldier who always placed duty and country before self. It was at about 2:00 am on 27 October 1947, that he lay down his life, so that the coming generations could enjoy the fruits of freedom. The Maharaja's plea for acceding to India was accepted and endorsed on the evening of October 26th. It was within a couple of hours of the supreme sacrifice of this noble and brave Dogra soldier that Indian troops landed in the state saved it from the tribal hordes, abetted and assisted by the Pakistani troops. Brigadier Rajinder Singh was posthumously awarded the Maha Vir Chakra (MVC). The first Indian COAS of the Indian Army, General (later Field Marshal) K.M. Cariappa, presented the award at Srinagar to Ram Dei, widow of Late Brigadier Rajinder Singh, on 30 December 1949.

With an active participation in the operation, Brigadier Rajinder Singh inspired his men to follow the Maharaja's order to keep the invaders away from the capital. His quick decisions to dismantle bridges and put up effective defenses, not only hampered the march of the enemy but delayed the thrust for full four days. In fact, his decision to blow up the bridges, particularly the one across the Uri stream, has been hailed as a masterstroke that immediately halted the march of the raiding hordes. During these crucial four days not only were the formalities with regard to the state's accession to India completed and Indian troops airlifted to reach the spot, but Sheikh Mohammad Abdullah also got sufficient time to raise a force of Kashmiris to fight and repulse the invaders. Although the settlements of Muzaffarabad, Garhi, Uri and Baramulla suffered heavy losses, the capital city and the rest of the areas were saved. Brigadier Rajinder Singh's action prepared the grounds for Colonel Ranjit Rai and others to drive away the encroachers from many of the occupied areas and put an end to their onward march. On 27 October 2001, Jammu & Kashmir became an integral part of the Indian Union. Not only the state of Jammu & Kashmir, but the whole of India, must observe the martyrdom day of Brigadier Rajinder Singh in a befitting manner every year.

COLONEL NARENDRA KUMAR

Colonel Narendra Kumar (Retd), PVSM, KC, AVSM, FRGS is an internationally known mountaineer. He was born on 08 December 1933 in Rawalpindi (now in Pakistan). He has successfully led mountaineering expeditions to the highest peaks of Bhutan, Sikkim, Nepal, Garhwal, Kashmir and Eastern Karakorams. Out of 13 the highest peaks above 24,000 feet climbed by Indians, nine have been climbed under his leadership.

In 1960, he was amongst the first eight in the world who had crossed the high altitude barrier of 28,000 feet. In 1965, he was the Deputy Leader of the Indian Mount Everest Expedition which put nine people on the top-a world record.

Colonel Kumar's unique contribution towards the world of mountaineering was the ascent of Kanchenjunga from the North East spur. For 45 years, several expeditions tried to climb the Kanchenjunga peak from the dangerous Sikkim route and were unsuccessful. The 1931 German Expedition almost tasted success, when it had to return from 3000 feet below the summit. This achievement was considered so great that it was awarded the Gold Medal at the Los Angles Olympics. He conceived and successfully led an expedition to this mountain in 1977.

Lord Hunt described this achievement as being "...far greater than the Conquest of Everest as it involved technical climbing and objective hazards of a much higher order than those found on Everest." Colonel Kumar is the only Indian to have commanded three premier mountaineering institutes of the country. He has been the Principal of the Himalayan Mountaineering Institute at Darjeeling, the Principal of the National Ski School at Gulmarg from 1971 to 1977, the head of the Indian Institute of Skiing & Mountaineering at Gulmarg and Commandant of the High Altitude Warfare School (HAWS) also at Gulmarg. He is presently the President of Ski Federation of India and Vice President of the Indian Olympic Association. He is better known as Bull amongst his friends and has over the years gained the reputation of a mountaineering legend.

Colonel Kumar was the first man in the world to cross the Siachen Glacier from the snout to its source. He also skied down all the passes on the Glacier such as the Bila-Fondla, Saltoro Pass, Sia-La, Turkistan-La, Indira-Col and Pass Italia and led successful expeditions to Saltoro Kangri (25,400 feet) the highest in Eastern Karakoram. Since the start of his career, he has successfully led mountaineering expeditions to the highest peaks of Bhutan, Sikkim, Nepal, Garhwal, Kashmir and Eastern Karakoram. In his true to heart pioneering spirit, he introduced much of the World to 'The Himalayas'. He is today the most highly decorated mountaineer in Indian history.

Colonel Kumar has set also numerous world records and led expeditions to the following peaks;

- Toshe Maidan
- Siachen Glacier
- Mount Blanc European Alps
- Kanchenjunga-8598 Meters
- Kamet-7756 Meters
- Teram Kangri-7464 Meters
- Nanda Devi-7434 Meters
- Indira Col-7422 Meters
- Abi Gamin-7355 Meters
- Chomolhari-7327 Meters
- Saltoro Kangri-7312 Meters
- NunKun-7135 Meters
- Neelkantha-6597 Meters
- Brahma-6416 Meters
- Harmukh-5784 Meters
- Sia Kangri-5776 Meters

Being a mountaineer, trekking naturally was one of Bull's many loves. Over the years he has successfully explored and charted many new trekking routes all over the Indian Himalayas. His hands on knowledge of the Himalayas and its culture adds an enviable flavour to all his treks. He was responsible for the training of the first batch of Indian ski teachers. He later led the Indian Ski Team down the Trishul Expedition and has skied down from 23,360 feet to the Base Camp at 15,500 feet.

The ascent took the team 10 days while the descent only an hour and a half. Colonel Kumar is the privileged and proud father of Shailaja, who represented India in the Winter Olympics at Calgary, Canada, in 1988. He was awarded the United Nation's fellowship for Ski Teaching and was trained in

Switzerland and Austria for 4 months. In his efforts to launch river rafting in India, he made the first descent of River Indus in Ladakh and the Teesta in Sikkim.

THE SOLDIER WHO WON INDIA'S FIRST PARAM VIR CHAKRA

Lately many pleas have been made that Mohammed Afzal Guru's execution should be stayed because his death could fuel separatism in Jammu & Kashmir. The state chief minister himself has been an ardent advocate for clemency for the terrorist who attacked the Indian Parliament in December 2001 (and nearly provoked a war between India and Pakistan). The secular protagonists claim that his execution will make a martyr of Afzal. I will not enter into these fallacious arguments, but the time has perhaps come to remember a true martyr: Major Somnath Sharma who on 03 November 1947 saved Srinagar Airport (and Kashmir) at the supreme cost of his life. Had he not sacrificed his life, Afzal's defenders would not today make front page news in the Indian press, for the simple reason that they would be Pakistani citizens living under a military dictatorship.

Our story starts during in the early days of October 1947 when Prime Minister Jawaharlal Nehru received a message from a former deputy commissioner of Dera Ismail Khan [one of the province's main districts] in the North West Frontier Province. The bureaucrat warned of a scheme to send armed tribals from Pakistan to the Pakistan-Kashmir border; some of them had already moved towards the area in transport provided by the Pakistan government. Arms confiscated from non-Muslims had been supplied to these tribals. As Maharaja Hari Singh of Kashmir was reluctant to sign the Instrument of Accession to India, Prime Minister Nehru refused to take any action. Two weeks later a large contingent of Afridis, Mahsuds, Wazirs, Swathis and regular soldiers of the Pakistan army 'in mufti' began to enter Kashmir.

During the night of October 22nd, the 'raiders' burnt the town of Muzaffarabad. They then overran Uri and captured

Mahura, the electric power station, fifty miles from Srinagar. The city of Srinagar was plunged in darkness. In these dramatic circumstances, V P Menon, Sardar Patel's faithful collaborator, went to Jammu and got Maharaja Hari Singh's signature on the printed Accession Form. He rushed back for the historic meeting in Delhi with India's Governor General, Lord Mountbatten in the chair. A young army colonel named Sam Manekshaw, who attended the meeting, recalled: 'As usual Nehru talked about the United Nations, Russia, Africa, God Almighty, everybody, until Sardar Patel lost his temper. He said, "Jawaharlal, do you want Kashmir, or do you want to give it away?" He [Nehru] said, "Of course, I want Kashmir." Then he [Patel] said: "Please give your orders."

Everything then moved very fast. Early the next morning, the first troops and equipment were airlifted from Palam airport [in Delhi] to Srinagar. A young major was sent on his first assignment to Kashmir. He was responsible for the logistic. His name was S K Sinha (today the governor of Jammu & Kashmir). He later wrote about the first Indian jawans reaching Srinagar: 'It was indeed inspiring to see grim determination writ large on their faces. They were all determined to do their best, no matter what handicap they had to contend with. I had never before seen such enthusiasm and fervour for duty.' They knew that all eyes in India were focused on them. At Srinagar airfield, just before returning to Delhi, Sinha met an old friend, Major Somnath Sharma of 4 Kumaon. He had come a day earlier from Delhi with a broken arm. Sinha found him rather disgusted with life. With his wretched hand in plaster, no one would give him an active assignment in Delhi.

His company had now been posted to Kashmir, but he was looking to be relieved soon from his present job and given something really active. His company's duty was only to protect the airport. Sinha tried to impress on Somnath the vital importance of the airfield to us and in that context the importance of the task assigned to him,' but says the governor, this sermonising could do little to fulfill his desire for being sent further forward. After spending an hour discussing and sipping a mug of tea reclining on his kitbag, Sinha left for Delhi. 'Little did I then know that within the next forty-eight hours, he was to die a hero's death and earn great renown, fighting most gallantly in very close proximity to where we then lay talking so leisurely.' But let us spend a moment on Somnath Sharma's life.

He was born as the eldest son of an army family. His father General A N Sharma, who retired as the first director general of the Armed Medical Services after Independence, was often in non-family postings. Som, as his friends and family called him, used to spend time with his maternal grandfather Pandit Daulat Ram in Srinagar. His favourite pastime was listening to his grandfather's on the Bhagavad Gita. This influence of Krishna's teachings to Arjun were to remain with Somnath till his last breath. At the age of 10, Som enrolled at the Prince of Wales Royal Military College in Dehra Dun and later joined the Royal Indian Military Academy. As a young Lieutenant, he chose to join the 8/19 Hyderabad Infantry Regiment. His maternal uncle Captain Krishna Dutt Vasudeva-who belonged to this regiment-had died defending a bridge on the River Slim in Malaya against the Japanese. His bravery had made it possible for hundreds of his jawans to cross over to safety. The example of his uncle greatly influenced him during his career.

Somnath fought in World War II under Colonel K S Thimmayya (later the army chief) in Burma with the British Army. An anecdote speaks tellingly about the character of the young officer. One day, Sharma's orderly Bahadur was badly wounded in action and was unable to return to the camp. Sharma lifted Bahadur on his shoulders and began walking. When Thimmayya found his officer lagging behind under the weight of his orderly, he ordered him — "Leave this man, Som and rush back to the camp."

Somnath retorted, "Sir, it is my own orderly that I am carrying; he is badly wounded and bleeding, I will not leave him behind." He eventually managed to carry Bahadur back, saving his life. He was awarded a *Mention-in-Dispatch* for this act of bravery. After the Japanese surrender in Kuala Lumpur in September 1945, Somnath returned from Malaya via Calcutta.

Before landing, a small incident occurred when the British Military Police came aboard to check for contraband. Som had an unauthorised pistol unofficially presented to him by some Japanese officer in addition to a Samurai sword (officially allotted to each officer). Somnath refused to lie or invent a story to bluff the British officer, he immediately threw the pistol into the sea through a porthole. Such was his straightforwardness! Two years later, India became independent, but fell prey to mad communal fighting. With his Kumaonis, Somnath was dispatched to aid the civil administration. From his headquarters at Parliament Street police station, he spent his time extinguishing fires between the two communities — both well armed. To complicate the matter, streams of refugees were pouring in wave after wave to the capital. The Kumaon Regiment rose to the occasion, doing their duty honestly and impartially towards both communities. At that time, Somnath was moving around with his broken arm and a plaster from the wrist to the elbow.

When his company was ordered to move to Srinagar, Somnath, though technically 'unfit for active duty in war' insisted that he had to lead his company. Before leaving for Srinagar, he spent his last night in Delhi with Major K K Tewari, his best friend and Burma companion, at the Queen Victoria Road bachelor Officers' Mess in Delhi. They chatted late into the night. Somnath remarked at one point that he was going to war again but alone this time (without his friend). Having probably some premonition, he asked for a memento from Tewari who told him that he could take whatever he wanted from the room. Somnath went straight to the cupboard and took his automatic pistol, a German Luger. Quite upset, Tewari had no choice but to honour his promise.

The next morning Somnath Sharma landed in Srinagar (where he met S K Sinha). The situation was fast deteriorating. Two days later on November 3, the 'raiders' reached Badgam a few miles away from the Srinagar airfield. Brigadier L P 'Bogey' Sen (later Lt Gen and GOC-in-C Eastern Command), the commander in Srinagar, immediately dispatched Sharma and his company to Badgam.

At 2:30 p.m., supported by 3-inch and 2-inch mortars, a 700-strong tribal force attacked the Indian jawans. Being outnumbered by 7 to 1, Sharma immediately sent a request to Brigadier Sen for reinforcements.

He knew that if the enemy advanced any further, the airport would be lost and Kashmir would become a province of Pakistan; the airfield was the only lifeline between the Valley and the rest of India. His last wireless message to the headquarters stated: 'The enemy are only 50 yards from us. We are heavily outnumbered. We are under devastating fire. I shall not withdraw an inch but will fight to the last man and the last round.' Soon after, Somnath Sharma was killed by a mortar.

Does India respect its Fallen Heroes?

By the evening, when reinforcement reached Badgam; it was too late. The Kumaonis had suffered over 50 per cent casualties though they had inflicted much heavier losses to the 'raiders' who lost 200 men and the airport and Kashmir. Major Somnath Sharma was awarded the first Param Vir Chakra, the highest Indian gallantry award (the Indian equivalent of Param Veer Chakra medalthe Victoria Cross).

The citation read: 'Keeping his nerve, he skillfully directed the fire of his section into the ever-advancing enemy. He repeatedly exposed himself to the full fury of enemy fire and laid out cloth airstrips to guide our aircraft onto their targets in full view of the enemy. His leadership, gallantry and tenacious defence were such that his men were inspired to fight the enemy outnumbering them. Major Sharma set an example of courage and qualities seldom equaled in the history of the Indian Army.'

Three days later, Sharma's body was recovered. Though mutilated beyond recognition, a few pages of the Gita that he always kept in his breast pocket and the empty leather holster of Tewari's pistol helped to identify the body. The pistol was gone. During the last chat with his friend before flying to Kashmir, Somnath had joked that either he would die and win the Victoria Cross or become the army chief. It is his younger brother V N Sharma who in 1988 became chief of army staff. Today, the world has gone topsy-turvy: true heroes are forgotten and terrorists become martyrs.

TREKKING TO TRIUMPH

The Sikh Pioneers are the forefathers of the present Sikh Light Infantry Regiment. The 23rd Sikh Pioneers, also called Punjab Pioneers or the Bengal Native Army, actively participated in the Abyssinian Campaign as an integral part of the British Expeditionary Force. Abyssinia, the present-day Ethiopia, is the place for which the Expeditionary Force was raised in 1868 in Bombay under Lieutenant General Sir Robert Napier for the release of the British hostages held on the orders of Emperor Theodore II. The Sikh Pioneers acquitted themselves creditably during the campaign.

Living up to the high standards set by its forefathers, the proud descendents of the Sikh Pioneers gave a sterling performance in operation Rhino which saw the unit bagging a total of 53 awards including the Chief of Army Staff's unit citation and the GOC-in-C's Eastern Command unit citation, three Shaurya Chakra Medals and eight Sena Medals. It was selected to represent the country abroad on a United Nations mission in Ethiopia. The officers and jawans of the 15 Sikh LI availed this opportunity to revisit the historical route taken by the Sikh Pioneers in the Abyssinian Campaign. Captain Anuj Lal Maini and Havildar Swaran Singh had the opportunity to retrace the route which their forefathers had followed and to visit the same spots where their predecessors had fought. Emperor Theodore II, also known as Negusa Negast (King of Kings), was the ruler of Abyssinia. His aim was the liberation of Jerusalem. Muslims had for centuries surrounded Abyssinia from the west, north and east. Emperor Theodore II expected to be helped by other Christian powers, especially Britain. However, the British did not want any to offer any help as it would annoy the Turks who had been the allies of Britain.

To embarrass the British monarchy and to use them as a bargaining chip, Emperor Theodore II took the British envoy

Wormuzd Rassam and 60 other British citizens as hostages and moved them to the fortress of Magdala. In spite of repeated conciliatory gestures by the British Prime Minister, the prisoners were not released. An ultimatum was given in April 1867, to the Emperor, to liberate the prisoners within three months. When the ultimatum expired and the Prime Minister received no reply, the British cabinet met and raised $2 million to mount a force and free the hostages. With the proximity of Abyssinia to India, it was decided that the force would comprise units of the Indian Army. The Commander-in-Chief of the Bombay Army, Lieutenant General Sir Robert Napier was placed in command of the force. The mixed force comprised the British and Indian Cavalry and infantry regiments including the 23rd Sikh Pioneers. It was a logistic nightmare to organise the move of about 20,000 troops, food, firewood, 35,000 pack animals and 44 Indian elephants from Bombay to the port of Massawa.

Magdala was about 720 km off south of the Red Sea at Zula. The march for Magdala began in January 1868. By March end, the Expeditionary Force reached the base of Magdala Fort. Emperor Theodore's army attacked the British army and a bloody battle was fought, in which the 23rd Sikh Pioneers played a major role. The Abyssinians were easily subdued due to superior firepower of the British, but more to the superiority of the men handling the bayonets. The total casualties suffered by the Napier's Army were 20 of which 12 were from the 23rd Sikh Pioneers. The Magdala Fort, after the clash, was captured without any resistance as the Abyssinians had deserted the place and fled. For their exceptional fighting during the campaign, the 23rd Sikh Pioneers was awarded the battle honour Abyssinia carried till date by Sikh Light Infantry Regiment.

In a bid to relive the history and glory of their illustrious ancestors, a joint Indo-British expedition to Magdala was undertaken by the 15 Sikh LI from Jan 31st to Feb 5th, 2004. The team, comprising Captain A.L. Maini and Havildar Swaran Singh, was flagged off from Adigrat, location of Central Sector Headquarters in Ethiopia by Colonel A.S. Rawat, Sector Commander, Central Sector. The team started the trek on the same route, which about 136 years ago, was taken by Lieutenant General Sir Robert Napier to reach Magdala. The trek involved scaling heights up to 2900 meters. It is impossible even to imagine today how Napier's Army would have moved their guns, motors and supplies on this inhospitable terrain.

After a trek of three days, the team finally reached the location. A sense of nostalgia dawned on the team as it was the same spot where Lieutenant General Napier stood and planed out the battle of Magdala. Continuing its trek, the team reached Aroje Plateaux and Aroje ravines the areas wherein the 23rd Sikh Pioneers had valiantly fought. The team, on reaching Selamge (Selaisse), could also feast its eyes on Sebastopol, a seven ton giant canon. The legend behind this canon, when fired, was that it would cause an abortion to all pregnant women and the old people would turn deaf and hence it was never fired. The Tomb of King Theodore, graves of the Theodore's soldiers, remains of a gate known as Kote Bir and the ruins of the once magnificent Magdala Fort interested the team. The team returned to Adigrat with a sense of pride as they have walked the path once their forefathers had taken.

8

LIEUTENANT GENERAL HARBAKHSH SINGH

Lieutenant General Harbakhsh Singh passed away on November 14th. Many don't know who the General was. Being out of sight for 30 years put him out of mind as well, and a few words is all that he warranted in sketchy obituaries and those too in local Punjab papers. Born in 1913 in Badrukhan in Sangrur and having graduated from Government College at Lahore, he was commissioned into the 5th Sikh in 1935. He was a graduate of the 1st course at IMA (Indian Military Academy) after a year's attachment with a British battalion, The Argyl & Sutherland Highlanders, wherein he saw active service on the north-west frontier. He commanded a Company of 5th Sikh in 1942 in Malaya against the Japanese.

Severely wounded in the head, a steel plate, which he carried to his last day, was a constant reminder. He was in a MH (Military Hospital) when General A.E. Percival, Allied Field Commander, surrendered all Allied forces in Malaya and Singapore to the Japanese in 1942. Then followed three years of a miserable existence and near starvation as a Japanese POW (Prisoner of War). Released at the end of the war in 1945, he remained in MH for some months with beri-beri and other problems, brought on by malnutrition and inhuman conditions in Japanese POW camps.

Posted as second-in-command of 4th Sikh on release from MH, he was perhaps the only deputy ever to ride a horse on parade in an infantry battalion, as he was too weak to march.

We now come to three episodes in his brilliant military career which makes him stand out as one of the outstanding commanders in modern Indian history.

India became independent on 15 August 1947, and Pakistani-backed regulars, irregulars and tribesmen crossed into the state of Jammu & Kashmir on October 22nd. In spite of a determined effort by the J&K state forces and by the initially inducted Indian troops, the enemy reached the outskirts of Srinagar on November 20th and the fall of the capital city was imminent.

On November 21st, reports came in of a concentration of around 3,000 enemy troops on the outskirts of Srinagar at Shalateng, just 4 miles from the city centre, preparing to attack the city. Colonel Harbakhsh Singh, then second-in-command of the newly inducted 161 Brigade was given the task of conducting the battle.

He attacked Shalateng on November 22nd with two infantry battalions, 1 Sikh and 1 (Para) Kumaon with a troop of armoured cars of 7 Cavalry and, in a brilliantly planned and executed operation, routed the enemy leaving 472 enemy dead on the field. The threat to Srinagar was now over. If the capital city had fallen, it would have been one of the greatest disasters in Indian history.

Promoted to command 163 Brigade, his was one of the two brigades launched by General Thimmaya, then in command of Sri Division (later 19 Division), on 17 May 1948, to clear the enemy out of the Jhelum Valley, up to Muzaffarabad and Domel. The first by 161 Brigade under Brigadier L.P. Sen on the Jhelum axis, and the second in a flanking move by his 163 Brigade over the Nasta Chun Pass to Tithwal and beyond. While 161 Brigade was held up near Uri, Brigadier Harbakhsh Singh's offensive, as discussed by General Birdwood in his book, *A Continent Decides,* was a triumph.

"Pakistan's situation was now grim, and had India only used air supply more aggressively to maintain the impetus of this outflanking success, her forces would so severely have threatened Muzaffarabad as to force a Pakistani withdrawal from the whole of the northern sector. Luckily for Pakistan, they paused." Tithwal fell on May 23rd. In six days, Brigadier Harbakhsh Singh had in a lightning move secured all territory starting from Handwara to the Kishanganga over the Nasta Chun Pass and Tithwal after fighting aggressive battles.

Finally after commanding 5 Division and 4 Corps for a while, during the Chinese Operations of 1962, where many soldiers believe that had he been allowed to command the Corps during the second phase of the battle by the Chinese which started on November 20, the situation would have been quite different in NEFA. Sadly for the Corps, their old GOC, Lt. General B.M. Kaul, was sent back to command, from a sick bed in Delhi, by Krishna Menon, the then Defence Minister. Lt. General Harbakhsh Singh was then given command of 33 Corps at Siliguri and he finally took over as the Western Army Commander in November 1964.

War clouds gathered once again in 1965. Pakistan took the offensive in April in Kutch and was successfully repulsed. In August, Kashmir became the target and on September 6th, India went to war. The Western Army offensive across the Punjab border which started at 4:30 a.m. on September 6 went well till Pakistan counter attacked 4 Division on the 11 Corps left flank at Khem-Karan. The 4 Division comprising 62 and 7 Brigades, a strength of 6 infantry battalions, had not quite recovered from the drubbing it received in 1962 at the hands of the Chinese, lost two-and-a-half battalions in a matter of hours, less through enemy action more by desertion, and was virtually overrun. The situation on the 7th afternoon was grim, while the Division fell back to the village of Asal Uttar and hurriedly prepared a defended sector based on the surviving three-and-a-half battalions and the 2nd (Indp) Armoured Brigade.

On the 9th, Pakistan's 1st Armoured Division, whose existence was not known to us, attacked the Division. Their operational order was captured by us. The plan was to attack and overrun the weak 4 Division, while a strong combat group was to cut the lines of communication of both 4 Division, 7 Division on the Barki Axis and finally to cut the GT Road at the Beas Bridge, effectively sealing off 11 Corps HQs and Corps troops at Raya, and the LOFC of 15 Division in one sweep. The situation was extremely grim and as a consequence Delhi panicked. Having returned to HQ Western Army at Ambala from 4 Division at midnight on the 9th and after a visit to the operations room, the Army Commander retired for three hours rest before leaving at four o'clock the next morning. The instructions to me, his ADC, was not to awaken him unless it was urgent.

At 2:30 a.m. the Army Chief, General J.N. Chaudhury, called and spoke to the General and after a heated discussion centered around the major threat that had developed, the Chief ordered the Army Commander to withdraw 11 Corps to hold a line on the Beas river. Lt. General Harbakhsh Singh refused to carry out this order.

The next morning, 4 Division stabilised the position and when the Chief visited command headquarters at Ambala that afternoon, the 10th, the crisis was over and the subject was not discussed. Had the General carried out these orders, not only would have half of Punjab been under Pakistani occupation but the morale of the Indian Army would have been rock bottom, affecting operations in other theatres as well.

His funeral was on November 15th. Very few knew about it, therefore apart from his friends and contemporaries, former officers of the Sikh Regiment of which he had been colonel for over a decade, and others such as I, who had been on his staff, gathered at the Delhi cantonment to say our final farewell.

The Army did him proud by giving him a send off befitting a great soldier. And while the ceremonies were on, and six Lieutenant Generals removed the National Flag from the body which was to be cremated, I couldn't help wondering how fortunate it was for the country to have had the right man at the right place at the right time.

The words once used to describe Field Marshal Lord Wavell, seen apt for describing Lt. General Harbakhsh Singh, "He was essentially a soldier's soldier, and takes an assured place as one of the great commanders in military history." The Last Post was sounded and the pyre lit, and as the smoke curled its way into the heavens and the bugle sounded reveille, transporting the General to Valhalla, to join the ranks of the many great soldiers who once trod this earth, there were moist eyes all around. As the mourners said their silent farewells, the words of Sir Walter-Scott from *The Lady of the Lake* came to mind:

"Soldier, rest thy warfare is o'er,

Dream of fighting fields no more;

Sleep the sleep that knows no breaking,

Morn of toil, nor night of waking."

I said my final farewell, "Goodbye my General, till we meet again."

BIBLIOGRAPHY

Ali, A.: *Mandal Commission Controversy*, Delhi, Ajanta Publications, 1991.

Anthony, J. Parel : *Gandhi, Freedom, and Self-Rule*, New Delhi, Vistaar, 2002.

Arend, A.: *International Law and the Use of Force*, London, Routledge, 1993.

Ashton, S.R.: *British Policy Towards the Indian States, 1905-1939*, London, Curzon, 1982.

Azad, Maulana Abul Kalam: *India Wins Freedom*, New Delhi, Orient Longman, 1959.

Bellamy, C.: *Knights in White Armour: The New Art of War and Peace,* London, Random House, 1997.

Bose, S. C., *The Indian Struggle, 1920-1942,* Bombay, Asia Publishing House, 1964.

Brierly, L.: *The Law of Nations,* New York, Oxford University Press, 1955.

Chandra, R.: *Judicial System in India*, Lucknow, Print House (India), 1992.

Damrosch, L.F.: *Law and Force in the New International Order,* Boulder, Westview Press, 1991.

Davies .A.: *Telecommunications and Politics. The Secentralised Alternative,* London, Pinter, 1994.

Dixit, Prabla: *Communalism: A Struggle for Power*, New Delhi, Orient Longman, 1981.

Friedman, G.: *The Future of War: Power, Technology and American World Dominance in the 21st Century,* N.Y., Random House, 1996.

Greer P.: *Transforming Central Government: the Next Steps Initiative*, Buckingham, Open University Press, 1994.

Habberton, William: *Anglo-Russian Relations Concerning Afghanistan 1837-1907*, Urbana, University of Illinois, 1937.

Heimanson, Rudolph: *Dictionary of Political Science and Law*, N.Y.: Oceana Publications, 1967.

Holsti, K.: *The State, War, and the State of War,* Cambridge, Cambridge Univ. Press, 1996.

Huntington, S.P.: *The Soldier and the State,* N.Y., Vintage Books, 1964.

Janowitz, M.: *The Professional Soldier: A Social and Political Portrait,* N.Y., The Free Press, 1960.

Jones, W.H.: *The Government and Politics of India*, London, Hutchinson, 1971.

Keane J.: *Democracy and Civil Liberty*, London, Verso, 1988.

Kelly, John B.: *Britain and the Persian Gulf 1795-1880*, Oxford, Clarendon Press, 1968.

Mackenzie, D.: *Knowing Machines: Essays on Technical Change*, London, Mit Press, 1996.

Majumdar, R. C.: *An Advanced History of India*, New York, St. Martin's Press, 1967.

Mary, W.: *Asian Power and Politics: the Cultural Dimensions of Authority*, Cambridge, Belknap Press, 1985.

Morris, W.H.: *The Government and Politics of India*, London, Hutchinson, 1971.

Nair, A. M.: *An Indian Freedom Fighter in Japan*, Bombay, Orient Longman, 1983.

Noorani, A.G. : *Indian Political Trials : 1775-1947*, New Delhi, Oxford University Press, 2005.

Posen, B.R.: *The Sources of Military Doctrine,* Ithaca, 1984, Cornell Univ. Press.

Prahlad, K.: *Governance and Public Administration for Poverty Reduction*, Salvador, Brazil, 1997.

Rosen, P.: *Societies and Military Power: India and its Armies*, Ithaca, Cornell University Press, 1996.

Rosen, P.: *Societies and Military Power: India and its Armies*, Ithaca, Cornell University Press, 1996.

Simon, D. : *Public Administration,* New York, Knopf, 1950.

Sullivan, N.: *Bureaucrats and Policy Making*, New York, Holmes & Meier, 1984.

Victor G. : *Law as a Political Instrument,* New York, Random House, 1955.

Ziring, L.: *An Introduction to Asian Politics*, N.J., Prentice-Hall, 1977.

INDEX